LIVES ON THE LINE

LIVES ON THE LINE

AMERICAN FAMILIES AND THE STRUGGLE TO MAKE ENDS MEET

MARTHA SHIRK

NEIL G. BENNET

AND J. LAWRENCE ABER

Foreword by Bill Bradley

Westview Press

A Member of the Perseus Books Group

Copyright © 1999 by Westview Press, A Member of the Perseus Books Group

Published in 1999 in the United States of America by Westview Press, 5500 Central Avenue, Boulder, Colorado 80301-2877, and in the United Kingdom by Westview Press, 12 Hid's Copse Road, Cumnor Hill, Oxford OX2 9JJ

Library of Congress Cataloging-in-Publication Data
Shirk, Martha.
  Lives on the line: American families and the struggle to make
ends meet / Martha Shirk, Neil G. Bennett, J. Lawrence Aber.
    p. cm.
  Includes bibliographical references and index.
  ISBN 0-8133-6653-4 (hc)—ISBN 0-8133-3820-4 (pb)
  1. Poor children—United States Case studies.   2. Poor—United
States Case studies.   3. Family—United States Case studies.
I. Aber, Larry.   II. Bennett, Neil G.   III. Title.
HQ792.U5S534   1999
306.85'0973—dc21   99-23948
                                                                CIP

The paper used in this publication meets the requirements of the American National Standard for Permanence of Paper for Printed Library Materials Z39.48-1984.

10   9   8   7   6   5   4   3   2   1

CONTENTS

PART 1
THE STORIES

PART 2
THE STORIES IN CONTEXT

TABLES AND ILLUSTRATIONS

Tables

Figures

FOREWORD

When I was in New Hampshire in January 2000 campaigning for the Democratic nomination for president, I met a woman named Cathy Perry. Cathy and her husband work three jobs between the two of them, raise four children, and struggle to get by. Her husband runs a household appliance repair business, where Cathy helps him part time while also working at a school helping out in the cafeteria. Despite the fact that both parents work, the Perry's annual income falls below the poverty line. No one in the family has health insurance.

When we met, Cathy told me that the oldest of her four sons got sick last year, and she took him to the doctor. The doctor diagnosed the sixteen year old with strep throat and prescribed medication. While Cathy was paying for the medicine, her son tapped her arm and said, "Mom, I'm sorry I got sick." He knew the visit to the doctor and the cost of his medicine would strain the family budget and that something else–a few days worth of groceries? the electricity payment?–would have to give.

What kind of place do we live in that a child has to apologize to his mother because he is sick? The paradoxical answer is that we live in the world's wealthiest country and one in which more than thirteen million children live in poverty, or almost one of every five children. But statistics like "thirteen million" and "19 percent of all children" do not always register. If we are lucky enough not to live in poverty ourselves, we read such facts in the paper or hear them in conversation, and they may cause us to pause for a moment and then they roll right off. But we cannot help tasting and feeling the angst of a boy who worries that getting sick will mean financial hardship and pain for his family.

So when I talk about poverty, I often share the Perry's story. If we want to do something to reduce child poverty in America–and I desperately do–then we need to build broader and deeper public support for it. That means more Americans need to understand what poverty means in real terms. More Americans need to understand who the poor are, beyond stereotypes. More Americans need to understand what child poverty is costing them. And more Americans need to understand what can be done to reduce poverty. Sharing stories is a key step in cultivating that understanding.

Lives on the Line is written in this spirit. It profiles ten American families who live in or near poverty, helping to fill out the face of American poverty and describe the struggles the poor confront every day. It also accomplishes something most books do not. A good book entertains, informs, or perhaps challenges us. An outstanding book changes how we think. *Lives on the Line* has the power to do that.

First, *Lives on the Line* dispels stereotypes about who the poor are. It is easy to assume that the poor are unemployed, inner-city loafers who are content to coast through life on welfare. On the contrary, most poor children—seven out of ten—have parents who work. But the work they find is often low wage, part time, or without benefits. And even parents who work full time, year round cannot be assured of escaping poverty; a full-time minimum wage worker earns $10,712, well below the poverty line of $13,133 for a family of three. Also contrary to popular belief, most poor families do not receive welfare (only roughly a third do), and those who do are not coasting. Indeed, the typical state welfare payment is less than half of the poverty level for a family of three. Finally, the majority of poor children (60 percent) live in suburban or rural areas, not in the inner-cities. Over the past two decades, poverty rates have increased more rapidly in the suburbs than anywhere else. Child poverty is a particularly serious problem for African Americans and Latinos, but it cuts across America's racial, ethnic, and geographic boundaries. What is certainly news to some is that the typical poor American child is white, has a parent who works, and lives in a suburban or rural area.

Second, *Lives on the Line* puts human faces on poverty. For most Americans, poverty is an abstract concept. This book helps readers feel what poverty means in dawn-to-dusk terms. Living below the poverty line does not mean simply that a family cannot buy the latest sneakers for its teenager, go to Disneyland for a family vacation, or eat in a nice restaurant to celebrate a birthday. It means lack of health insurance and unsafe child care. It means one parent works the night shift while the other works the day shift so one of them is always with the children but they are never with each other. In the Peterson family profiled here, poverty means a husband lives with his sister an hour from his wife and children because that is the only place he can find work. In the Keebler family, poverty means a daughter is molested twice before age seven because her working mother could not afford quality day care and had to leave her daughter with unreliable caregivers. In the Saylor family, poverty means that son Orlando suffered permanent brain damage at birth possibly because as a Medicaid delivery, he got substandard care.

Sometimes, poverty means tragedy, as for the Keebler daughter and the Saylor son. But always, poverty means struggle—a daily struggle to get to work, find food, and care for children. In some ways, then, these stories show that the challenges low-income families face are no different from those other Americans face. Indeed, many middle-class Americans are working several jobs, struggling to find and afford good child care, worrying about medical or prescription drug costs, and despairing of ever buying a home as nice as the one they grew up in. We see there is no clear line separating the problems of low-income families from middle-income families; the difference is one of degree, not of kind. Low-income Americans are one illness, one car breakdown, or a couple of days of missed work away from financial disaster, while middle-class Americans may be two or three bad breaks away. What this means, in part, is that "them"-versus-"us" distinctions between the poor and the middle class are myths. It also means that steps we take to reduce poverty–for example, by providing better child care, expanding affordable housing, or extending health coverage to all–help middle-class Americans too.

Third, *Lives on the Line* helps us understand that child poverty affects us all. The fact that there are thirteen million poor children in America comes at a price. The handful of children described here will probably not reach their full potential, and thus represent lost opportunities to contribute to our economy and communities. They also represent a direct financial drain when they get sick and require emergency room care that they cannot pay for, or when they get pregnant in high school, or when they turn to crime out of desperation and then fill our jails. Child poverty imposes financial costs on our society; it also diminishes the future pool of healthy, educated workers necessary to keep our economy number one in the world. If we can reduce child poverty, we will see gains in other areas. When fewer children are poor, it means more children entering school who are ready to learn, more successful schools, and fewer school dropouts. It means better child health, less child hunger and malnutrition, and less strain on hospitals and public health systems. Fewer children raised in poverty means less stress on the juvenile justice system and lower crime rates. In fact, studies suggest that for every dollar spent on programs to get low-income children off to a healthy start in life, our country saves about $7.00.

And this is a final lesson from this book: child poverty can be reduced. It takes individual effort, community support, and government policies that remove disincentives to work and create incentives. People who live in poverty are usually fighting hard to escape it, as are the families profiled here. No one wants to be poor. Most Americans in poverty will do all they can to earn at least a minimally decent standard of living for their families. Given modest assistance in the form of child care, subsidized housing, or tax relief, they can do it.

But will we as a country make use of these lessons? The epilogue that is new to this paperback edition demonstrates that two years after we first met them, the families in *Lives on the Line* continue to strive for a better life for their children against difficult odds. At the same time, they also continue to be plagued by persistent health problems, lack of health insurance, poor housing, unreliable transportation, unavailability of affordable and reliable child care, and severely constrained access to educational and career opportunities. As a nation, we can do better for these families.

In the 1990s, we have seen some progress in fighting child poverty, but not enough. Our child poverty rate in 1998 was 19 percent. That it dropped from a high of 23 percent in 1993 confirms that progress against child poverty is possible. But 19 percent is still well above the child poverty rates of the 1970s, which hovered around 15 percent, and it is well above the rates in other developed countries. And it is far higher than what is morally acceptable or economically wise, especially in this time of unprecedented prosperity and budgetary surplus.

Indeed, I believe we should make it a national goal to eliminate child poverty as we know it. We know how to do it. We can help parents to increase their earnings through such proven strategies as expanding the earned income tax credit, raising the minimum wage, and promoting public/private partnerships to encourage the development of marketable job skills. We need to improve the quality of child care and provide more of it so parents can work; currently only one in seven children who qualify for federal child care subsidies receives them. We need to provide better access to health care for the 44 million Americans–11 million of whom are children–who do not have health insurance. We need to offer safe places for children to go after school and build more roofs to shelter them at night. We need to invest more in teen pregnancy prevention programs and get rid of tax provisions that discourage marriage. We need to change our child support laws so when a nonresident parent pays child support, it goes to the family, not the state. We know what we need to do.

The question is whether we will summon the will and leadership to take these steps.

Lives on the Line is an important book, written to help build support for that will and leadership. I commend Martha Shirk, Neil Bennett, and Larry Aber for their vision and dedication in developing the book and the ten families profiled in it for their courage and candor in opening their lives to public scrutiny. I also thank the National Center for Children in Poverty, which helped make this book possible, for its excellent work in the fight against child poverty. The Center performs an invaluable service in bringing together policy analysis, demographic research, and innovative communication strategies to increase public awareness about child poverty and the commitment to reducing it.

Change comes when many people decide to make their voices heard. So I ask you: if you are moved by this book, seek to change some minds and raise voices in support of fighting poverty. Share this book with your friends and family. Send a copy to your elected officials. Ideally, every elected official could live with a low-income constituent for a week or even a day to understand the complexities of life in poverty and how government policies exacerbate or alleviate those complexities. Barring that, reading this book is the next best thing. We need action, and action follows understanding.

There are more children living in poverty today than the total of people living in the six New England states. Each of those children has a face, a story, and a future. Whether that future is one that is meaningful for the child and productive for our country is a question that is in our hands.

Bill Bradley

ACKNOWLEDGMENTS

We thank Westview Press for encouraging the National Center for Children in Poverty (NCCP) to combine its research creatively with a series of family profiles that would put real faces on the troubling statistics of child poverty in America. We'd like to thank Marcus Boggs, its publisher, and two of its editors, Adina Popescu and Andrew Day, for providing their vision and encouragement that made this possibility a reality.

Julian Palmer of NCCP deserves special thanks for his many thoughtful and substantive, as well as editorial, contributions.

Others at NCCP to whom we are most grateful are Jamie Hickner, Jiali Li, Keming Yang, Telly Valdellon, Martha Garvey, Carole Oshinsky, and Carmela Smith. They provided much support with analytical, editorial, and production aspects of this book.

We are especially grateful to Cathy Trost, executive director of the Casey Journalism Center for Children and Families at the University of Maryland, who helped bring the coauthors together.

Support from the Mott Foundation, the Ford Foundation, and Carnegie Corporation enabled NCCP to carry out the demographic and policy research contained in this volume.

We couldn't have produced these profiles without the assistance we received in finding families willing to open their lives to scrutiny. Thanks go to Sarah White of United Food and Commercial Workers Union in Indianola, Mississippi; Betty Robinson and Doug Vineyard of the YWCA's Head Start program in St. Louis County, Missouri; Haaheo Mansfield and Diana Buckley of Parents and Children Together in Honolulu, Hawaii; Mary McGovern of St. Bernard's Head Start in White Plains, New York; Sharon Newton-Caldwell and Deanna Rolffs-Elzinga of Profit FIT at the YWCA Women's Resource Center in Grand Rapids, Michigan; Danielle White, a community activist in Louisville, Kentucky; Sal Bustamante of Local

ACKNOWLEDGMENTS

1877 of the Service Workers' International Union in northern California; Cheryl Burke of Hilltop Day-Care Center in Slatington, Pennsylvania; Dorothy Ivanuck of the Western Egyptian Economic Opportunity Council in Steelville, Illinois; Denise Hayes of Columbine Kids Day-Care Center in Basalt, Colorado; and Thelma Zabel of the Roaring Fork School District in Glenwood Springs, Colorado.

In addition, we'd like to express our gratitude for the hospitality provided to Martha Shirk while she was visiting the profiled families: Jody Gaylin and Andrew Heyward in Westchester County, New York; Paula Landesman and Jerry Berger in Manhattan; John, Wendy, and Amanda Shirk in Slatington, Pennsylvania; and Margie and Bill Freivogel in Kirkwood, Missouri. John and Carol Galgani, a pediatric endocrinologist and registered nurse, respectively, provided valuable medical advice about the illnesses from which the children and parents in the profiled families suffer.

Most of all, we want to thank the ten families who let us pry into every nook and cranny of their lives, without any guarantees about how they'd look in print. Their resourcefulness and optimism give us hope.

Martha Shirk
Neil G. Bennett
J. Lawrence Aber

INTRODUCTION

You may already be familiar with the statistics. Nearly one in four of our nation's youngest children, those below age six, is growing up in poverty, along with one in five of those between six and eighteen. If you add to them the number of children growing up in "near poverty"—in households with incomes under 185 percent of the federal poverty threshold—almost half of America's children are growing up in poverty or near poverty. That is more, proportionately, than in any other Western nation.

If we are not poor, it is still virtually inevitable that our lives are interconnected with families that are poor. These families and their children are all around us, yet they're largely invisible to us as we go about our day-to-day business. Chances are they sit side by side with our own children in their classrooms or child-care centers. They play on our daughters' high school volleyball teams, if their parents have managed to come up with the fees this year, and they stand in line behind our preschoolers at the local mall as they wait to share their most fervent wishes with Santa Claus. Their mothers clean our offices, take care of our elderly aunts, or make those annoying telemarketing calls just as we're sitting down to a family dinner. Their fathers pick up our trash or mow our lawns or change the oil in our cars or cook our dinners when we go out for a night on the town.

What is it like to be growing up poor in one of the richest countries on earth? What is it like for parents in the land of plenty to be engaged in a constant struggle to make ends meet? And how can America help poor children and their families? Those are among the questions we try to answer in this book by putting human faces on the cold statistics and describing strategies that could make a difference.

The first ten chapters of *Lives on the Line* tell the stories of ten different low-income American families and their efforts to make ends meet. These chapters give a detailed sense of the barriers that are created by poverty and how individual families struggle to overcome them. In Chapter 11, we put the family profiles in a broader context and illustrate how they reflect larger economic and demographic trends. By doing so, we hope to tell the story of how the fates of families are tied in part to the fates of populations. In Chapter 12, we identify common risk factors facing low-income families and present compelling evidence that there are effective public- and private-sector strategies available that can make a major difference in preventing and/or reducing child poverty.

There are poor children all around us, and yet too rarely do we stop to think about the special burdens that their family's economic status places on them as they're growing up, much less about how we can help as individuals or how changes in public policy might affect their prospects. Nor do we often stop to think about how the well-being of our entire nation is affected—our health-care systems, our schools, our overall prospects for economic growth—by the fact that more than 13 million American children are growing up below the poverty line.

The fact that such a large number of children are poor poses great hardships for those families, but it also affects their communities, states, and the entire nation. Indeed, one of the smartest investments that our nation—including the federal government, state and local governments, businesses, philanthropies, community organizations, and individuals—could make is to support strategies to prevent or reduce child poverty. Research shows that lower poverty rates are associated with better outcomes for children, stronger families, and a more productive workforce, all of which contribute to a better quality of life for us all.

We had help from many people in finding the ten families that are profiled in this book—from social workers in Head Start programs to union organizers, community activists, and caseworkers in programs that provide all kinds of assistance to the poor. We told them what we hoped to accomplish in the book, and they looked around for willing participants.

All that we asked was that the families have household incomes below the poverty line, or, in a few cases, no more than 85 percent above it, and that they be willing to share their stories. We didn't pre-screen the families for the presence or absence of particular problems. We wanted to get as random a sample of poor families as we could—neither the poorest of the poor nor those most adept at coping, just ordinary families, struggling to make ends meet. We didn't promise anonymity, though in the end we decided to use pseudonyms, largely to protect the privacy of the children, who bear enough burdens as it is.

None of the families received compensation for their cooperation, nor did any ask for it. Their motivations for opening their lives to scrutiny were altruistic, each says. "I want policymakers and legislators and ordinary people to understand what it means to our children that they are growing up poor," says Jeanette Likio, a mother of five in Honolulu. "I want things to get better for families, especially for those who are poorer than we are, who don't even have as little as we have."

As a group, these families are fairly representative of all families living in poverty in the United States. Four are white, two Hispanic, three black, and one Pacific Islander. Four live in urban areas, three in rural areas, and three in suburbs. Most of the families are headed by single or divorced mothers, as is true of most poor families nationally, though some of our single mothers benefit from the presence in their family's life of an active, income-contributing father, a factor uncaptured by statistics on household structure. Most of our mothers gave birth to their first child while they were still in their teens, another common characteristic of persistently poor families nationally. And in almost all of our profiled families, one or both parents work, as does at least one parent in two-thirds of families with poor young children in the United States.

To learn about life below the poverty line, Martha Shirk, a journalist, spent up to a week with each of these families during the first eight months of 1998. In a few cases, she followed the family over a period of months. (This edition includes an epilogue in which families are re-visited two years later.) She rose with them, often well before dawn, followed the parents around in their jobs, visited the children in their classrooms, accompanied the families to church and to the grocery store, and spent hours with them around their kitchen table, just talking about their lives. The result is a verbal snapshot of each family's life at a particular point in time. By now, their lives could be either better or worse.

The stories of the ten families are all different, yet in many ways they are the same.

Although some of the parents grew up in middle-class families, most grew up poor. Many struggled in school, feeling marginalized by their economic status, as do some of their children. Some were abused as children, and some have been abused by their spouses or boyfriends as adults. Most have been on welfare at some point in their lives.

Another experience most of them share is the difficulty of understanding the government's eligibility rules for programs ranging from WIC (The Special Supplemental Food Program for Women, Infants, and Children) to Medicaid, food stamps, and subsidized child care. Several of the families seem to be eligible for benefits they're not receiving, either because they're unaware of the programs or because caseworkers have provided faulty information about eligibility rules. A few lost out for years on what many experts argue is the nation's single most important antipoverty program—the Earned Income Tax Credit—simply because they didn't know about it.

The ways in which their children experience poverty vary, too, depending on their ages, the resourcefulness of their parents, the supportiveness of their relatives and communities, and their own innate strengths.

Some are sailing through childhood seemingly oblivious to their parents' struggles to make ends meet, except as lack of money interferes with their ability to dress like their friends, play with the toys they see advertised on TV, or participate in school activities (almost all of which require special fees these days). But getting timely and good-quality medical and dental care is a frequent—and sometimes life-threatening—problem for almost all of the families, except for the few who have either Medicaid coverage or health insurance through a parent's job. Many of the disorders that plague them would be preventable with regular medical care. Trivial ailments sometimes turn into major illnesses when their parents delay getting them care for financial reasons.

Some of these children sometimes go to bed hungry, particularly at the end of the month when the food stamps or WIC vouchers run out or the money their parents have set aside for food has had to be diverted to keep the electricity from being turned off. "I can still remember the time when all we had to eat was saimin noodles," thirteen-year-old Keola Likio in Honolulu recalls with obvious distaste.

The homes these children live in range from a one-room apartment in Oakland, California, to a trailer in Basalt, Colorado, a homeless shelter in White Plains, New York, and a three-bedroom, lace-curtained house in southern Illinois. Conditions in their homes range from disorganized to neat as a pin. "My mom taught me even if you're poor, you can keep your house clean," said Maria Gonzalez, a mother of three in Basalt, Colorado.

Some of the children fall asleep at night to the soothing sound of their mothers or fathers reading *Goodnight Moon;* others put themselves to bed on the floor, counting the minutes until their mother returns home from her night-shift job. "Sometimes I get scared," admits nine-year-old Manuel Rodriguez of Oakland, California, who puts himself and his seven-year-old brother to bed because their mother doesn't get home from work until 11:00 P.M.

The cost and quality of child care are major problems for the families with preschool-aged children or school-aged children who require before- or after-school care. "I really hate that place," says Megan Jones, a mother in Palmerton, Pennsylvania, of the foul-smelling center that her first-grade son attends before and after school.

And the cost, availability, and reliability of transportation are constant worries. Public transportation simply isn't available in many of the areas where poor families live, particularly rural areas and suburbs. Many poor families are forced to rely instead on unreliable fifteen-year-old gas-guzzlers. The cost of an unexpected auto repair can throw a family's budget completely out of kilter.

Some of the children in the families we profile are doing well in school; others have failed several grades. "It seems like they just don't want me here," says Orlando Saylor, fourteen, a special education student in Louisville, Kentucky, who is on the verge of failing ninth grade.

Some children have great plans for their futures. "I want to be a neurosurgeon," says Letisha Washington, sixteen, of Grand Rapids, Michigan. But others have no plans at all. "I've never been able to get him interested in anything besides TV and food," says Carlotta

Saylor, a mother in Louisville, about her oldest son, struggling to graduate from high school before he turns twenty-two.

The children in the families we've profiled range in age from newborn to young adult. Although children under six can rarely articulate how it feels to grow up poor, a growing body of research demonstrates that both poverty and near poverty early in life negatively affect the health and development of children.[1] Poor young children are more likely to:

be born at a low birthweight;
be hospitalized during childhood;
die in infancy or early childhood;
receive lower-quality medical care;
experience hunger and malnutrition;
experience high levels of interpersonal conflict in their home;
be exposed to violence and environmental toxins in their neigh-
    borhood; and
experience delays in their physical, cognitive, language, and
    emotional development—delays that, in turn, affect their
    readiness for school.[2]

But many of the effects of early-in-life poverty aren't seen until children are older. As poor children become adolescents and then young adults, they are more likely to drop out of school, give birth to or father children out of wedlock, and be unemployed.[3] Some of the older adolescents and young adults in our profiled families struggle with these problems.

In the last decade, scientists have compiled evidence that extreme poverty (an income of less than 50 percent of the poverty line) early in life has a greater effect on a child's future life chances than less extreme poverty later in childhood.[4] The more we learn about brain development in early childhood, the more ominous the prospects seem for children who are spending the first few years of their lives without adequate food, with intermittent medical care, and in childcare or home environments that are unstimulating at best, and squalid at worst.

As you read about the lives of these families, we hope you'll try to put yourselves in their places. Think about what you would do if you had to choose between buying a birthday cake for your child and paying your electricity bill. Would you sleep on the floor after a long day at work so that your children could sleep in a bed? Would you postpone marriage to a man you loved because marriage would mean an end to the subsidies that enable your children to attend a good, safe child-care center while you work? Would you quit a night-shift job and go on welfare so that you wouldn't have to leave your teenage daughters alone at night in your dangerous neighborhood? The choices these parents often face are between two bad options, not between a good one and a bad one.

In the following pages, you'll encounter parents who make bad choices, decisions you yourself wouldn't have made; sometimes their priorities may seem misplaced. A few of these parents are probably going to spend the rest of their lives fighting drug addiction. Another gambles. Several suffer from disabling depression. One or two are, quite frankly, hard to like.

But whatever their shortcomings, we hope you'll be impressed by their obvious love for their children and by their bravery and perseverance in the face of challenges that would defeat many of us. For the most part, they're trying their best. And they're all their children have.

Remember that, ultimately, helping low-income children get a better start in life will help us all by creating stronger families, better schools, healthier communities, and a brighter future for our country.

The question we want to leave you with as you begin to share these families' life stories is this: what can we, both as individuals and as a nation, do to help them, and in so doing, help ourselves?

Part One

The Stories

1

PALMERTON, PENNSYLVANIA

Andrew, Justin, and Brian are growing up in a single-parent household. But it's not because their parents want it that way.

Megan Jones, their mother, and Ron Morgan, the father of the youngest two, would like to get married. In fact, they've been engaged for three years. But Megan and Ron can't afford to get married, or even to live together. They're caught in a catch-22 of the most ironic sort.

Although marriage to Ron would elevate Megan and the three children above the poverty line because he earns a good income, the fact is that the family would actually be *worse* off financially than it is now. With a combined income of $36,509, Megan and Ron would be making too much to qualify for the child-care subsidies that Megan now receives on the basis of her income alone. The catch is that the couple wouldn't be earning enough to be able to afford child care for three children. The annual cost of child care would consume more than Megan grosses—or, viewed another way, more than Ron nets.

The Jones-Morgan family's story provides some insights into a problem that few politicians mention as they extol marriage as the solution to many of society's woes: the indirect marriage penalty built into the eligibility rules for many programs designed to help the working poor. Although it's true that marriage is often the surest ticket out of official poverty for many single-parent families, for some couples, such as Megan Jones and Ron Morgan, it could actually lead to financial ruin.

Megan: Pregnant as a Teen

Megan, a large young woman with dark circles under her eyes and long, dark curly hair, grew up in Slatington, Pennsylvania, an economically depressed town at the base of Pennsylvania's Blue Mountain, which the Appalachian Trail crosses on its route from Georgia to Maine. Megan's father abandoned her mother when she was three months old. "I think of him more as a sperm donor than a father," Megan says. Her mother remarried when she was two, and Megan grew up regarding her mother's second husband as her real father.

Megan was a good student through middle school and the first two years of high school. "But I started getting in trouble in eleventh grade," she says. "I was hanging with the wrong crowd."

Early in her senior year, she learned that she wouldn't have enough credits to graduate with her class. She quit school and took a minimum-wage job in a discount department store. "My mom was hurt big time when I dropped out, but I didn't care," she says. "I was eighteen and dumb. Nobody could tell me anything." Megan's mother and stepfather were even more upset when she moved in with her boyfriend, Todd, who lived with his mother and grandparents in nearby Palmerton. "They wanted nothing to do with me, because they thought he was wrong for me," she says.

A year later, at nineteen, Megan became pregnant. She was making minimum wage working in an apparel factory, and Todd was making minimum wage at a gas station. At first, they welcomed the prospect of a child. "I didn't stop to think about how I was going to support a child for eighteen years," Megan admits.

Like many teenage relationships, this one wasn't strong enough to last. The couple broke up a few months after Andrew was born in late 1990, got back together briefly, and then split for good when Andrew was one. Todd moved out, and Megan and Andrew stayed on with Todd's family, getting by on $150 a month in welfare benefits plus food stamps.

In late 1993, just before Andrew turned three, Megan's name finally came to the top of Carbon County's waiting list for subsidized housing. She and Andrew moved into an apartment down the street from Todd's family, and Megan began thinking about how to get off welfare.

This was well before the federal welfare reform mandate imposed time limits on welfare recipients, but already Pennsylvania, like many other states, was encouraging welfare recipients to prepare themselves for work. Megan was an eager participant in the effort. She took a three-month training program to become a certified nurse's aide. Within a month of getting her state license, in August 1994, she found a job at a nursing home in Whitehall, about twenty miles away. She was paid $6.20 an hour, or about $11,300 a year. With just one child to support, she was no longer officially poor.

But her euphoria over increasing her income so dramatically was dashed quickly when she found out that she was making $100 a year too much for Andrew to continue to qualify for Medicaid coverage. Her rent went up, too, since it was pegged to her income. And she now had many other expenses that she hadn't had when she was on welfare. Most costly of all was the car she needed to get to work: besides a monthly car payment, she also had to pay for insurance and gasoline.

And then there was child care. Though the state paid most of the cost with its allocation from the federal Title XX program, Megan still had to pay about $80 a month for Andrew's care. With all these expenses overwhelming her, she made a decision she would later regret: to forgo health insurance for Andrew. She couldn't afford the $138 a month it would have cost to add him to her group plan at work.

Ron: Father of Four

Megan met Ron in 1994, when Andrew was three. She had gone out for an evening with a girlfriend, and they ended up in a bar. "He came on really strong, and at the end of the evening he said, 'Here's my phone number. If you want to see me again, you can call me,'" Megan recalls.

Megan was hesitant to get involved in a relationship again. But Ron, a cheerful young man with rosy cheeks, a beer belly, and a 1960s-era Beatles haircut, had an appeal that was hard to resist. "He's so mellow, it's sickening," Megan jokes. Two weeks after they met, she called him. Her mother took care of Andrew while Megan and Ron went to a movie. From then on, they were a couple. Ron proposed at his company's Christmas party in December 1995.

Megan and Ron have a lot in common. Both are what is known in the area as "Pennsylvania Dutch." Their ancestors came to the area from Germany ("Dutch," in this usage, is a bastardization of "Deutsch") and developed their own dialect, cuisine, and customs. All of their grandparents spoke Pennsylvania Dutch at home, and even today Megan and Ron speak with distinctive accents and sprinkle Pennsylvania Dutch words through their conversation. Justin is "gretzy," not grouchy. A doughnut is a "fastnacht." And they often end a sentence with a question (for example, "It's a nice day, say?").

Ron grew up on what amounts to a family compound on a dead-end dirt road about five miles from Palmerton. Like Megan, he was the product of a broken marriage. His father left his mother and three children even before Ron was old enough for school, and he rarely contributed to their support afterward. His mother supported the family by operating a sewing machine in a clothing factory.

Instead of going to the local high school, Ron attended the regional vocational-technical high school in nearby Lehighton, where he studied masonry and framing. But he dropped out two months short of finishing his junior year. "It was like a jail," he says. "I couldn't take it no more." After a week of celebrating his freedom, he got a $6-an-hour job at a factory and since then has worked in a series of construction jobs. Sometimes he thinks about taking the GED test, but he doesn't see much point to it. He says he's never found the lack of a high school degree an impediment to employment. "I learn everything pretty quick as soon as I get on the job," he says.

Soon after he left high school, Ron fathered his first child, now nine, and then a second one, now eight. His current income—$9.25 an hour, or a total, with overtime, of almost $23,000 in 1997—puts him well above the poverty line for a single person, but it never seems to be enough to meet all of his obligations to both sets of children and to his mother, who is disabled. "I know it sounds good, but it's not enough for us all to live on," he says. Ron pays $73 a week—about $3,800 a year—in court-ordered child support for his two oldest children, buys all the groceries for Megan and her three boys (about $400 worth a month), and helps his mother with her expenses, including the loan payment on the dilapidated trailer they share.

If Ron weren't part of Megan's life, it's not clear at all how she would make ends meet. Here's how her monthly budget looks:

TAKE-HOME PAY

$852

EXPENSES

Rent (includes electricity)	$328
Car payment	101
Car insurance	150
Phone	30
Cable TV	22
Child-care copayment	65
Asthma medicine	80
Gasoline	60
Total expenses	$836

Obviously, with $852 in take-home pay most months, and $836 in fixed expenses (not including food), Megan is always juggling bills. Things are a little better in the four months of the year when she gets three paychecks instead of two. And every now and then, Andrew's father sends her child support. (A court order requires him to pay $36 a week—$1,872 a year—but in 1997 he paid a total of only $432.) Most weeks, however, it's Ron and the federal Women, Infant, and Children (WIC) supplemental food program that make the difference between eating and not eating for Megan and her children.

So how would the couple's monthly balance sheet look if they combined their incomes and expenses? Conventional wisdom would lead you to expect them to be better off. But conventional wisdom doesn't factor in the intricacies of eligibility rules for antipoverty programs. Megan and Ron have spent hours writing down columns of numbers—their incomes on one side, their expenses on the other—trying to figure out a way to make marriage financially feasible. Here's how their monthly budget would look if they combined their incomes and lived under one roof:

INCOME

Megan's take-home pay	$852
Ron's take-home pay	1,036
Joint income	$1,888

EXPENSES

Megan's current expenses	$836
Additional rent (Megan would lose her housing subsidy)	322
Gas/electricity	150
Child support for Ron's two other children	294
Support for Ron's mother	250
Ron's car insurance	150
Ron's gasoline	60
Food and diapers	400
Child care (after loss of subsidy)	1,060
Joint expenses	$3,522

"It's hard to believe, isn't it?" says Megan. "You always hear that two can live more cheaply than one. Well, not in our case."

A Desolate View

Palmerton, population 5,394, was once a company town for the New Jersey Zinc Company, which has left signs of its occupation everywhere, both in the grand old homes that its executives built up in Residence Park and in the shoebox-style company housing that workers used to crowd into, closer to the zinc plant.

But the most obvious sign of the zinc industry's one-hundred-year presence here is the stretch of Blue Mountain that runs through Palmerton. It's been almost totally defoliated by emissions of lead, cadmium, arsenic, zinc, and sulfur dioxide from the zinc plant's smelter, and the groundwater below the town has been polluted by the seepage of heavy metals. Years ago, when smelting operations were at their peak, residents used to complain that not even grass would grow. As a result of the emissions, the Environmental Protection Agency (EPA) has said, Palmerton children have higher than normal levels of lead in their blood, as do the horses and cattle that graze on the farms outside town. For a stretch of two and a half miles beneath the town, scientists have said, 33 million tons of molten toxic waste are still burning. A 2,000-acre area of the town has been designated a federal Superfund site, with the cost of cleanup estimated by the EPA at more than $200 million.

From the windows in her living room, Megan has a view of the mountain, which is studded with the eerie black skeletons of dead trees that, for some reason, don't decompose. "I think the grass is starting to come back," she says optimistically as she gazes out one sparkling spring day.

Megan and her three boys live in a two-bedroom apartment in a converted one-hundred-year-old elementary school. It's an ingenious reuse of space, since Palmerton is unlikely ever again to have as large an elementary school population as it had in the zinc company's heyday. Each classroom in the building was reconfigured as a two-bedroom apartment. The living room is the center of family life, and Megan has furnished it nicely, though sparingly, with a couch, loveseat, coffee table, and end tables that she bought as a package for $600, on an installment plan, a few years ago. At one end of the living room, there's a small round table, just big enough to accommodate three people for meals. The kitchen is in a small alcove on the way to the bathroom and bedrooms.

Megan shares her bedroom with Justin and Brian; Andrew has his own. Although it would seem to make sense for Justin to share Andrew's room instead of Megan's, she's fearful that Andrew would hurt Justin if he slept there. "Sometimes when I sneak in and watch them play together, I find Andrew shaking him," she says.

A Difficult Child

At age seven, there's something strange about Andrew. He's got a smart mouth and talks back to his mother at every opportunity, often using words that make her blush. Although the windowsill in his bedroom is lined with Power Rangers, he spends little time playing with them. Instead, he watches TV or picks fights with Justin, who bursts into tears at least a dozen times a day because of something Andrew's done.

Megan wonders how much of Andrew's behavior is due to the violence he was exposed to during the first few years of his life. Her pregnancy with Andrew marked a turning point in her relationship with Todd, she explains. (Domestic violence experts say that's not unusual.) He became increasingly abusive, knocking her around when she didn't comply with his orders quickly enough, once pushing her out of a moving car. Things got even worse after Andrew was born.

Now she worries about Todd's continuing influence, since a custody order requires that Andrew see his father two nights a week plus every other weekend. Not long ago, Andrew was present when Todd fought with his mother's boyfriend, and Todd's mother, who tried to intervene, ended up getting stabbed. "There was blood all over the kitchen," Andrew chimes in as he hears Megan telling the story.

When Andrew returns home from his visits with his father, he's often in a foul mood. He calls Megan a "f——ing bitch," a phrase she knows he's picked up from his father. And Andrew sometimes tells Megan about seeing his father hit his new girlfriend.

A couple of medical problems also set Andrew apart from other children his age and possibly contribute to his problems at school. For one thing, he wears glasses, and other children sometimes make fun of them. And as a result of severe asthma, his recess time has to be restricted during cold weather and he's not allowed to go on field trips unless a relative accompanies him; that is rarely possible, given his mother's work schedule.

His first attack occurred two years ago, when he was five and spending summer days at a child-care center. The owner brought in some rabbits for the children to pet. "They called me at work and said he was having trouble breathing and that his lips were turning blue," Megan recalls. Tests determined that he was allergic to animal dander, mold, and pollen. (The air quality in Palmerton may also be a factor; respiratory diseases are at near endemic levels among all age groups.) The doctor prescribed Nebulizer treatments every four hours. Even so, every two or three months he'd have an attack so severe that he had to be taken to the emergency room.

Besides causing Megan a great deal of worry and Andrew a great deal of discomfort, the asthma threw Megan's finances for a loop.

Since she had forsaken health insurance for Andrew as too costly, his asthma drugs alone cost her $160 a month.

"When I didn't have insurance, I really got behind on all my bills," Megan says. "I used my rent money for medicine. What was I supposed to do? I didn't have a medical card. I couldn't afford my Blue Cross/Blue Shield at work. And my child needed medicine. The bottom line was that I got five months behind in my rent. I only got caught up because I refinanced my car."

At the end of 1997, Megan finally began buying the family health insurance policy offered by her employer. It costs her $130 a month, but she now knows from Andrew's experience that it's worth whatever sacrifice she has to make. Once she got family insurance coverage, she was able to take Andrew to a pediatric pulmonary specialist, who discontinued the Nebulizer treatments and prescribed drug treatment, via inhalers, twice a day. Andrew's been much better ever since. Although her copayment on the new medications is $80 a month, they would cost her much more than that without insurance.

"Thank God for the Family and Medical Leave Act"

Justin is an adorable two-and-a-half-year-old. He has a sweet disposition, an open, expressive face, and a curious mind. There's no sign in him yet of the terrible twos—except maybe when he acts as though the world is ending because his mom has told him he can't watch his favorite video, *Beetle Borg,* which she loathes.

Megan was at work in the nursing home when she felt the first of the contractions that signaled Justin's impending birth. She finished bathing her patients and clocked out a few hours early. He was born three hours later, weighing nearly eight pounds. Six weeks later, Megan went back to work, and he went to child care.

Exposure to all the germs that pervade the air in even the best of child-care centers made for nearly constant respiratory infections and earaches. Then, when Justin was six months old, he became desperately ill. At first, it just seemed to be a little virus—he was throwing up and having diarrhea—and the doctor told Megan not to worry. But the next day the fontanel on his head was concave, a sign of severe dehydration, and he had to be hospitalized. The diagnosis was rotavirus, which had been going around his child-care center. Older kids were able to shrug it off quickly, but not a six-month-old. He stayed in the hospital three weeks.

This was before Megan had signed up for family health insurance. To make matters worse, she also didn't have any paid sick leave to use while she stayed by his side night and day, making sure he didn't pull out his IV lines. "Thank God for the Family and Medical Leave Act, or I would have lost my job," she said. "They didn't have to pay me, but they had to keep my job for me."

While she was on unpaid leave, Ron took care of her household bills. But the medical bills were beyond his ability to pay. Sacred Heart Hospital eventually wrote off the cost of Justin's care, but the doctor didn't. Megan finished paying his $1,200 fee only last month, two years late, with the check she received from the Internal Revenue Service thanks to the Earned Income Tax Credit.

An Unplanned Pregnancy

Brian was an unplanned baby. Megan had gone on birth control pills after Justin's birth, intending to stop at two children. But her doctor took her off them a year later because he believed they were adversely affecting her cervix. (For years she's suffered from cervical dysplasia, a precancerous condition of the cervix.) She and Ron were using condoms, but Brian is proof of their high failure rate.

Megan's pregnancy with Brian was harrowing. She was sick for much of the time and lost forty pounds. (Normally a pregnant woman *gains* at least twenty pounds.) She had to be hospitalized three times in the first three months because of dehydration. Then, when she was five months pregnant, she got a scare that lasted for a month and almost caused her to have a nervous breakdown.

"The ultrasound showed that the spaces were too big between the sections of his skull," Megan says. "They told me that it was possible that he would have an open hole in his head, and that babies that have this do not live past three months of age." The doctor told Megan to return for another ultrasound in a month.

"It was hell, pure hell, for that whole month," she says. "I cried all the time. I was totally miserable."

Fortunately, the skull looked normal in the ultrasound the following month. But the month after that Megan got an ear infection that turned into mastoiditis. "I ignored it for a while, because I'm prone to swimmer's ear, but then one day I woke up and the whole side of my face was swollen and I couldn't open my jaw," she recalls. She missed two weeks of work, using up most of the sick leave she was saving to use after Brian's birth. In the end, she had just one week of paid leave to claim after his birth. She supported the family for the five weeks she received no pay with help from Ron and what was left of her IRS refund.

A Wedding Twice Postponed

It's Mother's Day 1998. Megan and Ron are dropping in on each of their mothers to deliver greeting cards. Later in the day, Ron plans to take Megan out for dinner, one of their rare "dates," while the grandmothers watch the children. Though Ron and Megan see a lot of each other, they get to spend very little time alone.

Megan's mother and stepfather—Mammy and Pappy to her children—live in a modular home in a subdivision on the outskirts of Palmerton. The stretch of Blue Mountain that abuts their trailer park was beyond the fallout from the zinc plant, so right now it's a lovely light green, its trees bursting with spring buds. Deer frequently venture out of the woods to nibble on the petunias and geraniums that residents have planted in front of their modulars. Rarely a day passes without the sighting of a wild turkey.

There's a store-bought turkey baking in the oven and a children's video playing on the TV when Ron and Megan arrive with the boys. Megan gives her mother a sentimental card, and as she reads it, her mother's eyes well up with tears. "That's the fourth time I've cried today," she says. Her own mother died eleven months ago, and this is the family's first Mother's Day without her.

Throughout the afternoon, much of the conversation is about Megan's plans for her wedding, now twice postponed, and about the couple's dream of building their own home. Megan bought a wedding dress several years ago, when she and Ron set the date the first time. It's been hanging in a closet in her mother's home ever since. Megan called off the first wedding date after she became pregnant with Justin. The reason, Megan says, was the cost of child care for a baby—about $100 a week then, without a state subsidy. Megan knew that even on two salaries she and Ron couldn't pay child-care expenses for both a baby and her older child and that she'd continue to need subsidies, for which their combined income would have made them ineligible.

They reset the wedding date for October 1997. Then Megan unexpectedly became pregnant with Brian. They postponed the wedding again, for the same reason as before. Only now, with three children, the child-care costs would be about $265 a week, and even more in the summer, when Andrew would have to go full-time instead of just before and after school.

"We've looked at it every way we can, and there's just no way right now we can afford to be married," Megan says ruefully. "My Title XX worker did the calculations, and she said we'd be just over the line. Without my day care subsidies, I'd be paying $265 a week for day care. That's more than Ron brings home after a forty-hour week."

But still Megan dreams of being married someday. Today she's talking with her mother about what kind of centerpieces she'd like at her reception. "We'll make them all ourselves, because my mom's very crafty," she explains. Her goal is a church wedding at the Neffs Union Church, which her family has been attending since her great-grandparents' time, followed by a reception at the Emerald Fire Hall for 350 people. She figures such an event would cost $4,000, a sum it will take her and Ron years to save. "We're going to open a joint savings account and put $80 in a month, and then put $1,000 in from my income tax refund for the next two years," she says.

Deep down, Megan knows that many people might think it's foolish for her to be thinking about spending so much on a wedding when she and Ron could get married inexpensively in front of a justice of the peace. But this is how marriage is done in this part of the world. And Megan says she feels she owes her mother and stepfather a traditional wedding. "Because I quit high school, they didn't get to see me go off to my senior prom, or walk up on the stage to get my diploma," she explains. "Those are the things parents dream about all through their children's childhoods, and I denied them that."

Megan and Ron haven't yet set another date. Everything hinges on whether they can figure out a way for the children to be taken care of if they lose the child-care subsidies. At the moment, they're pinning all their hopes on what sounds like a pie-in-the-sky plan. They want to build a house and move Ron's disabled mother in with them so that she can watch the children while they work. The three of them, they figure, could pool their incomes, consolidate their housing costs, and eliminate the cost of child care.

To keep costs down, Ron plans to do much of the construction work on the house himself. He estimates that they can build a three-bedroom house for $70,000. Right now, Megan, Ron, and his mother pay a total of $518 a month for housing, and Megan pays $148 for child care, for a total of $666 a month on housing and child care. Among the three of them, they figure they should easily be able to handle the monthly payments on a $70,000 thirty-year loan—about $488 a month. The hitch is that they need to persuade a bank that they're creditworthy. Later in the week, they have an appointment with a local banker to discuss their prospects.

They plan to build the house on the small plot of land now occupied by the ramshackle trailer that Ron and his mother share. It's near Trachsville, a crossroads outside Palmerton that's famous for its quaint covered bridge. "The kids love it out there," Megan says. "There's woods everywhere, and a crick to play in."

The couple spent last night walking around two huge building supply stores—a Home Depot and a Hechinger's—trying to visualize how various light fixtures and plumbing supplies and kitchen cabinets would look in the home of their dreams. The outing has whetted Megan's appetite for a home of her own. But the prospect of laying out her finances at the bank later in the week has made her a nervous wreck.

"Every time I think about it, I feel like throwing up," she says. "I'm really afraid that my credit rating will mean that we can't get a loan." Megan still owes about $3,600 for visits to emergency rooms and doctors during the two-year period when she lacked health insurance for the children.

"I wish youse luck at the bank next week," Megan's stepfather says as the couple leave for Ron's mother's house.

Up Before the Birds

It's Monday, a workday, and Megan's alarm clock goes off at 4:15 A.M. She dozes for a few minutes and then jumps out of bed to avoid falling back to sleep and throwing her whole schedule off. It's still pitch-black outside, and the birds aren't even awake. Megan's apartment is the only one in the building with a light on.

This is the beginning of Megan's second week back at work since Brian was born seven weeks ago, and her morning routine, with an extra child to feed and dress, isn't quite established yet. Before Brian was born, she used to be able to sleep until 4:45 A.M. "With there suddenly being three kids, everything is much more complicated," Megan explains. "If I try to rush them too much, they make sure everything goes the wrong way."

Megan takes a shower and has just enough time to dress herself in her nurse's aide uniform—white pants and a bright pink top—before the baby begins stirring at 4:50 A.M. She changes him and gives him a bottle of formula. He's in a delightful mood, cooing and gurgling and happy to be alive. Holding him is fun because he's just beginning to focus on faces and to turn toward familiar voices. "Guess what, pumpkin? You've got Mommy all to yourself tomorrow," Megan tells him, referring to the fact that she has the next day off, since she has to work the following Saturday.

Megan wishes she could spend more time cuddling him, but she's got to pack a breakfast for Andrew to take to his child-care center, make lunches for herself and Ron, and get the other boys up and ready. She puts Brian in his automatic swing and positions it so that he can watch her as she goes about her chores.

At 5:30 A.M., Andrew emerges from his room, rubbing the sleep dust out of his eyes. Without prompting, he brushes his teeth and dresses. Then he comes into the living room and settles into the couch, laying his head on the arm. "I'm tired," he says. But he's got several asthma medications to take before they leave the apartment, and his mother tells him to go find his inhalers. He gets up silently, rummages through his backpack, and finds the inhaler that contains a bronchodilator. He shakes it and then sucks in a deep breath while simultaneously squirting it into his mouth. He holds his breath as he counts slowly to thirty. Then he gets out his second inhaler, which contains a corticosteroid drug to block his bronchial tube's inflammatory response. He puts it in his mouth and sucks on it.

Around 5:35 A.M., Ron arrives to help Megan with Justin, as he does most mornings. (Sometimes Ron spends the night in the apartment. But Megan's lease limits guests to two weeks a month, and she's scrupulous about restricting Ron's stay-overs. If he exceeds the limit, his income would be counted as part of her household income for purposes of rent calculation.) Justin has the most trouble getting going in the morning, and he likes special attention from his daddy. This morning, Justin's diaper is a big mess. "Just my luck," Ron chuckles.

By 5:45 A.M., Justin is dressed and ready to go. He toddles over to Megan for a morning cuddle. By now, the baby is asleep again in his swing. "Oops, time to start getting coats on," Megan says, breaking Justin's cuddle short when she jumps up. The family is out the door just before 6:00 A.M. Only the baby has had breakfast. Justin and Andrew will eat at their child-care centers. Megan and Ron will do without.

Megan loads the baby and Justin into their car seats and tells Andrew to buckle himself in. She drives a mile to the child-care center that Andrew attends both before and after school. It opens at 6:00 A.M., and Andrew, as usual, is the first child there. Ron has followed her in his car so that he can wait outside with Justin and Brian while she signs Andrew in. She's too safety-conscious to leave them in the car alone, even for a few minutes, and too rushed to take the time to unload them from the car for the short time she'll be inside the child-care center.

The center is located in a storefront on Palmerton's main street, between a trophy shop and a photo studio. Megan's not happy with the quality of care here—the smell of dirty diapers is pervasive—but it's her only convenient option, since it's just two blocks from Andrew's school. Andrew spends about two hours here each morning and about one hour after school.

Ron and Megan give each other a quick kiss good-bye before he heads up to Lehighton to a construction site and she heads to Slatington, three and a half miles down Route 873, to drop Justin and Brian off at the Hill Street Children's Center. This is a model child-care center, with affectionate, well-trained caregivers and a nice outdoor play area with climbing structures, and Megan feels fortunate that her children can come here. By now, the sun is up, and the rest of the world is starting to wake up, too. Megan pulls into the parking lot at 6:11 A.M.

So far, there's only one other baby in the nursery, a seven-month-old who's sitting in a stationary walker in the middle of the room, smiling at the newcomers. The caregiver is busy mixing rice cereal for him but pauses to compliment Megan on Brian's easy adjustment to child care. "He likes to laugh," she says. "He really smiles at you." Brian has fallen asleep again in his portable car seat, and Megan sets it on the floor while she replenishes his supply of disposable diapers. Then she lifts him out of his carrier, kisses him good-bye, and lays him down in a crib. He doesn't even wake up.

Over in the area set aside for two- and three-year-olds, only one other child besides Justin has arrived, and the atmosphere is subdued. Justin sits down to a breakfast of Fruit Loops. Megan bends over to give him a good-bye kiss. "And off to work I go," she says as she heads out to her car.

"Goddamn Son of a Bitch!"

From the child-care center, it's a seventeen-mile drive to the nursing home where Megan's worked for nearly four years. She'd like to cut her commuting time and travel costs by working closer to home, but there just aren't any nursing homes close by. She's repeatedly applied for a nurse's aide job at Palmerton Hospital, but the only jobs that ever come open are on the overnight shift, which would really complicate her life. Once she and Ron are married and he can add her and the kids to his health insurance policy, she might try to get a job as a home health aide, she says. Though such jobs usually don't provide benefits, the hourly rate of pay is better. "I'd like to have a job where I could get paid more for less time, so I could spend more time with my children," she says.

Megan realizes now that she should have become a licensed practical nurse rather than a nurse's aide. But she was in such a rush to find a way off of welfare that she didn't want to devote two years to schooling, which an LPN license requires. "I should have done that while I had the chance," she says. "I'd be making $14 an hour by now. Sometimes I think about going back to school to get my LPN license, but I don't see how I could do it. I need my job to support the kids, and I don't spend enough time with them as it is, so I couldn't go to school and work at the same time."

Today she takes the back route to Whitehall, through Slatington and Friedens and Ballietsville and Ironton and Ruchsville, a landscape of old stone farmhouses and new subdivisions. The morning has gone smoothly, and she arrives fifteen minutes before her starting time. She puts her lunch in the refrigerator in the employees' lounge and goes outside for a quick smoke with one of the other aides. By the time she comes back in, a few of the other aides, mostly single mothers like herself, have arrived. They're all discussing what they did over the weekend.

At 6:59 A.M., they start clocking in. Megan heads up to the second floor. "The wacky floor, I call it," she says. Most of the residents here suffer from Alzheimer's disease or other forms of dementia. "I'm going to hit the bathroom before I get started, because I never seem to have time later," she tells her supervisor. She yawns as she heads down the hall.

Within a few minutes, all seven of the floor's aides gather around the nurses' station, discussing which patients need what, who's getting up for breakfast, and who's eating in bed. They all wear back braces, a nursing home rule aimed at lessening the strain on their backs from lifting heavy patients. "Don't forget, it's toenail day," the head nurse reminds them, referring to the scheduled visit of a podiatrist.

Megan drags several laundry bins out of a closet and a couple of garbage cans, one for regular waste and another for biological waste, such as dirty diapers. She adds two packs of adult-size diapers to her rolling cart and then heads off down the hall. At 7:07 A.M., she changes her second diaper of the morning, only this one is worn by an adult, not her baby. She'll change a few dozen more by the end of the day.

Megan often thinks about the similarities between the work she does at the nursing home and the work she does at home. "Alzheimer's patients are a lot like children," she says. "We change them, bathe them, and feed them. And if they're doing something they shouldn't be, we try to distract them, just like you do with children."

If a patient is lucid, Megan engages him or her in friendly banter as she goes about her work. "You're sneaky sometimes, aren't you?" she says to her first patient, a man in his late sixties who wears a helmet because he's prone to falls. "You're trying to get out of bed before I'm ready. Do you want to give me a heart attack? You must be really hungry this morning. Usually I feel like I'm rushing you, but the shoe's on the other foot this morning, say? Now, let me get your chair before you fall out of bed. You stay there, okay? No more heart attacks for me today. I'm too young."

She helps the man into a chair called a "Mary Walker"—something like an adult version of a baby walker—and then tunes his TV to a morning newscast before she turns to his roommate. "Delays in all directions, north and south, on 22," the newscaster is saying. The two men in this room listen wordlessly. They're not going anywhere.

"Okay, Walter, you're all set," she says to the second man, with whom she doesn't banter, since he doesn't seem to enjoy it. It's taken her twenty minutes to get these two changed and bathed and out of bed.

In the room next door, one of the patients is mumbling unintelligibly. On the wall across from his bed is an embroidered sampler with an abbreviated version of that old familiar prayer: "God grant me the serenity to accept the things I cannot change, courage to change the things I can, and wisdom to know the difference." The mumbler usually stays in bed until lunchtime, so he doesn't need to be dressed, but Megan needs to ready his roommate for the "Breakfast Club," a group of residents who eat together down the hall, with assistance from aides. After Megan's ministrations, he wheels himself out of the room in a wheelchair, wearing a baseball cap with his name on it. Two more patients ready for the day, another twenty minutes gone.

Megan moves on to her first female patient of the day. "Good morning, Shirley," she says to a seventy-nine-year-old great-grandmother. "How are you? You seem to be in a fairly decent mood today. Are you? I'm glad to hear that."

Given Megan's cheerful cooing, the response that comes out of Shirley's mouth is a shock. "Goddamn son of a bitch!" she says as Megan tries to put support socks on her bare feet.

"Shirley, you have to wear these. They help your feet," Megan tells her.

"Come on, you son of a bitch," Shirley grumbles. "What the hell's the matter with you?"

"Are you mad at me, tootie?" Megan says. "We got to get this nightie off so I can get you dressed."

"Aaaarghhhhhh!" Shirley shouts at the top of her lungs as she simultaneously pinches Megan on one of her breasts. "Get the hell out of my way."

Megan, who has been through this before, is undaunted. "You know I have to get you washed for breakfast," Megan tells her.

"You goddamn dirty son of a bitch," Shirley responds. "Aaarrrggh!" she shouts again as she pinches Megan on the other breast.

"Hey, that's not nice," Megan says.

"You dirty son of a bitch," Shirley counters again.

Megan laughs. "Shirley, Shirley, Shirley. Why do you pinch me like that? You know that I love you."

"Oh, I sometimes wonder," Shirley responds, sounding surprisingly lucid.

"I tell you that every morning, don't I, that I love you, and still you don't believe me," Megan says.

"Oh, shut up, you son of a bitch," Shirley says. And to emphasize her point, she spits on Megan.

"Don't start your spitting," Megan scolds. "It's not necessary."

"I'd like to bite you, you son of a bitch," Shirley says. "Get the hell out of my room."

Just then, a nurse ducks her head in the room. "Hello in there. Are you killing Shirley?" she asks Megan playfully.

"No, I think she's killing me," Megan says. "I'm going to be all black and blue."

Once Megan had to go to an emergency room after Shirley scratched her, and both she and Shirley had to have tests for HIV, since Shirley's bite broke Megan's skin. By the end of the day, Megan will have black and blue marks on her breasts from Shirley's pinches, but she shrugs them off as part of the job.

Shirley is more bark than bite, Megan explains. "She's a real sweet woman," she says. "It's just that she really doesn't like to be bathed. Whenever I try to bathe her, she tries to bite me. Sometimes I let her. She doesn't have no teeth, so it doesn't really hurt, and it makes her feel better."

The last patient to be readied for breakfast is Gerald, one of Megan's favorites. Another nurse's aide had stopped in the room earlier to turn on his television and, inexplicably, had tuned it to *Sesame Street*. "Youse don't want to watch *Sesame Street,* do youse?" Megan asks Gerald and his roommate and switches the channel to *The Today Show*. He flirts with Megan shamelessly, calling her his wife.

It's now 8:40 A.M., and Megan has washed, diapered, and readied eight patients for breakfast. She spends the next thirty minutes ducking in and out of rooms, urging patients to finish their eggs or their bran cereal or their prune juice. Then she joins the other aides who have gathered around the head nurse to hear about each patient's overnight problems and new medication orders. One patient is being transferred to a hospital for three days for a catheter repair; another is about to be put on morphine. Shirley has a dangerously high blood sugar level, and whoever put Marilyn's false teeth in last used too much adhesive and they can't be removed.

At 9:00 A.M., Megan goes outside for the first of her two ten-minute breaks and smokes another cigarette, shivering coatless in the forty-degree morning air. "They're all sweethearts, really," she says of her patients. "They can't help the way they are."

"I'd Knock Him Out"

At 3:00 P.M., Megan clocks out and begins the reverse commute. Even though it's a few miles out of her way, she retrieves Andrew first, for a couple of reasons. One is that she doesn't want to leave him in his center a minute longer than she has to. "I really hate that place," she says. Another is that it's the only time they have together all day without the distractions of the two younger children. A third is pure convenience: Megan doesn't have to worry about leaving Justin and Brian in the car alone while she runs in to get Andrew. He chatters all the way to his brothers' child-care center, where he's well known from his attendance during the summers.

When Megan arrives in Justin's classroom, he's sitting on a portable potty and isn't quite ready to leave. He had been making progress toward being potty-trained until Brian was born and has since regressed. This attempt is unproductive, and Megan puts his diaper back on him. As she puts his jacket on him, he throws his arms around her and gives her a big kiss. "Bye-bye," he tells the caregiver and the four classmates who remain as his mother carries him to the Busy Babies Room, where Brian has spent the day.

Justin also spent his infancy in the Busy Babies Room, so it's quite familiar to him. He checks on his favorite toys as his mother talks with the caregiver about how Brian's day went. Andrew stands by Brian's crib, stroking his cheeks and rubbing foreheads with him, and Justin soon comes over to shower him with kisses, too. "I put him in the little swing today so he could look around, and he slept for more than an hour," the caregiver reports about Brian.

His mother goes over and lifts him out of his crib. "Hi, you little pumpkin," she says. "How are you?" He starts wailing as Megan puts his jacket on him. Meanwhile, another mother arrives to pick up her infant and is distressed to learn that he's been running a fever all day. Megan doesn't even allow herself to think about whether there might be something contagious in the air. She used up all her sick leave during her pregnancy and recuperation and can't afford to miss work again so soon to take care of a sick baby.

Back at the apartment building, Megan unloads the two youngest from their car seats. It's always a challenge getting all three—plus assorted diaper and school bags—up to the third floor without a mishap. Brian needs to be carried, of course, and Justin wants to be, too, but Megan has only two arms. Disappointed, Justin climbs up the two flights of stairs on all fours, the lights embedded in the heels of his shoes flashing with each step.

Inside the apartment, Andrew immediately turns on the TV, and his mother just as quickly turns it off. "No TV until you do your spelling," she says. Within a minute, it's on again. This time Justin's the culprit. "Not till Andrew finishes his homework!" she says. "Go play with your toys."

"I want *Beetle Borg!*" he wails.

Megan loads Brian into his automatic swing, and he falls asleep instantly. This gives her a chance to sit down and try to unwind. But she rests for only a few minutes before she starts to go through her mail. "Boy, that comes around fast," she says of her car insurance bill, which costs her $130 each month because she had an accident a few years ago.

Miraculously, Andrew and Justin are now sitting side by side on the couch, looking at a book together. "What does c-o-m-p-u-t-e-r spell?" Andrew asks. "Sound it out," his mother responds. She gets up to look into Andrew's backpack for his homework folder. Her face falls when she sees the daily report from his teacher.

Since early in the school year, Andrew's teacher has been sending home daily progress reports in an attempt to help Andrew stop disrupting the classroom. Andrew's teacher was so alarmed at his behavior that she asked Megan to have him tested for attention deficit disorder and hyperactivity. He has yet to be tested, however, because his doctor doesn't think it's necessary.

In the daily reports, the teacher rates Andrew on a scale of one to five on several different classroom activities, with one being "very good" and five being "very poor." "There's usually at least one four or five every day," Megan says. Today there are *twelve* fours and fives, a sign that it's been a very bad day. Furthermore, there's a note. "Andrew needs to bring his own scissors to use," the teacher has written. "He used his scissors to cut up crayons today. Please discuss the purpose of scissors and showing respect for school property."

Megan tries to contain her anger. "If you can't take care of things that are given to you to use, you're not going to be able to use them," she tells Andrew. "How would you feel if you gave something to someone to use and they treated it like that?"

"I'd knock him out," Andrew responds.

Brian has awakened while Megan's been talking about Andrew's school problems, and she picks him up to give him a bottle. Justin comes over and tries to climb on her lap, too, showering her with kisses and trying to displace the baby. "No, Justin, not now," she says.

In response, he hits her and then sweeps all of Andrew's school papers off the coffee table, looking at her defiantly as they waft across the room.

The small size of the apartment makes all this conflict hard to stand, but Megan manages not to lose her temper. "It takes a lot out of you dealing with all those old people at work and then coming home to these wild animals," she says with resignation.

"I Don't Know What We'll Do Now"

Another day dawns. Megan has the day off, since she's working next Saturday. Ron's taking a couple of hours off of work, too, so that they can go to the bank together and apply for a home loan. They've gotten all their financial papers together—their W-2s, their income tax returns, their rent receipts. They drop Andrew and Justin at their child-care centers but keep the baby with them. Ron's mother meets them at the bank, since she's going in on the loan, too.

Megan has dressed with special care so that she'll make a good impression on the loan officer. Her stomach is churning as she and Ron enter the old granite bank on Palmerton's main street. Ron is confident that they'll have no problem getting a loan, but Megan isn't so sure. She knows her credit history better than he does. Although she paid off the biggest doctor bill, she knows she's still got more than a dozen smaller ones, and her payment history is not going to look good to the loan officer. "I'd just hate it if it's my credit that kept us from getting the loan," she worries.

As it turns out, the loan application process doesn't even get that far. The loan officer tells them that the bank will lend them $70,000 for a new house, without a down payment, only if the land they own is worth $30,000 and they can pay the closing costs—about $5,000—in cash. There's no point in even talking further until they can prove that, he says. The loan officer gives them the name of a real estate appraiser who can look at the land. But the couple knows that at the moment they don't even have the money to pay the appraiser's fee. "I don't know what we'll do now," Megan says.

Once home, Megan and Ron start discussing plan B. They could lease space in a trailer park in Lehighton, buy a modular home, and put it there. The financing companies that loan money for such homes have more lenient standards for borrowers but also charge higher rates of interest. That option isn't very appealing to either Megan or Ron—it's a trailer park, after all—but Ron can't move into Megan's current apartment, since it's so small. Three-bedroom apartments in the area rent for $700 or more a month, so that isn't an option either.

Ron is still characteristically upbeat, certain that they'll find a way to buy their own house and solve the child-care problem. One possibility he suggests is to pour a foundation on his mother's lot and install a modular on it. It won't be the house they've dreamed of, but it would be theirs, he points out, and Ron's mother could live with them and take care of the boys. They might be able to get married.

But Megan is glum, tired of having to postpone her marriage, tired of getting by on six hours of sleep a night, tired of changing diapers all day long, tired of seeing so little of her children.

She starts to think of all the mistakes she's made in her life, dropping out of high school, getting pregnant while she was still a teenager, staying too long with a man who abused her.

"This isn't how I planned my life to be, which is why I get depressed sometimes. I've made plenty of mistakes, but I've learned from them, too," she says. "I know I've got to make the best of it. My boys are depending on me. I just wish it were easier."

2

OAKLAND, CALIFORNIA

Five days remain until her next payday, and Magda Rodriguez has just $60 left in her coin purse. Things are going to·be tight.

Magda sits down at her kitchen table with a cup of coffee and begins making a list of the expenses coming up this week. As she writes, her oldest son, Manuel, stands behind her, playing with her long, thick, dark hair. His brother, Jorge, sits at the table coloring a dragon and wearing a determined look on his face.

Magda's list looks something like this:

She'll need $12 today to wash two weeks' worth of dirty clothes at the laundromat down the street. She hopes that she still has some detergent left and doesn't have to buy more.

She'll need $14 for four days of fares on the Bay Area Rapid Transit (BART) train that she takes to work.

It's time to buy another monthly bus pass, which costs $45. Magda can't part with that much this week, so instead, she'll have to spend at least $10 paying by the ride.

Then there's the $1.20 that Manuel and Jorge each need every day to ride the bus to school, or a total of $12 between them for the week. That would be pocket change for many people, but it's a budget item for Magda.

That leaves about $12 for any other expenses that pop up over the next five days, such as a gallon of milk, which she's just realized she forgot to get at the store. Thankfully, she's already stocked up on essentials like eggs, cheese, beans, rice, and tortillas. "Just the main things we need to live," she says.

This is the kind of arithmetic that Magda Rodriguez does several times a day, every day of the week. In her life, there's no such thing as a spontaneous purchase. She doesn't buy herself a new blouse just because she sees one she likes. She doesn't buy her children ice cream, even though they beg for it each time they hear the bell on the ice cream vendor's cart as he passes by. Last week, when Manuel turned nine, she couldn't even afford to give him a birthday cake because a bill she had forgotten about had come due, wiping out her small reserve.

And this isn't even the most difficult arithmetic Magda has to do. The harder calculations for her are those involving time: how can she make sure that Manuel and Jorge see enough of her so that they don't feel they have a mother in name only? Because Magda works different shifts every week—and sometimes different shifts every *day* of every week—the time she can give her sons is unpredictable. An hour in the early morning, typically, and maybe a few minutes at night, if they're still awake when she gets home.

One of the ironies about this family's situation is that it's not even officially poor. If Magda stays in her current job through 1998, she will earn a total of $17,680, well over the official estimated poverty threshold of $13,001 for a family of three. The rub is that the family lives in the San Francisco Bay Area, where the high cost of living makes a mockery of the official cutoff point for poverty.

Taquerias *and Chinese Take-outs*

Magda, twenty-seven, and her two boys, Manuel, nine, and Jorge, seven, live in the Fruitvale section of Oakland, a densely populated area that's as ethnically diverse a neighborhood as can be found in California. On almost any given block, there are Mexican *taquerias,* Vietnamese-run nail salons, African American–run barbecue stands, Chinese take-outs, and produce markets featuring vegetables unknown to most Americans. As of the last census, the area's population was 24 percent white, 34 percent black, and 23 percent Asian. Twenty-seven percent of residents reported that they were of Hispanic origin. Of the Hispanic population, 70 percent reported lacking a high school diploma or GED certificate. The per capita income of the neighborhood's Hispanics was only 58 percent that of white residents' and 75 percent that of black residents.

One of the things a visitor notices right away about the Fruitvale area is the number of young children who call it home. At almost any time of day, dozens of women are pushing strollers or leading toddlers by the hand on Fruitvale Avenue, one of the main streets. Of all Oakland's neighborhoods, the city says that the Fruitvale area has the highest concentration of children and youth, their parents attracted by the relatively affordable rents and the easy access to public transportation. These aren't yuppies or urban pioneers. More than 50 percent of the young children in the area live in families with incomes below the poverty line.

The Rodriguezes live in a one-room apartment with a small kitchen nook and a bathroom. It's about the size of a motel room. At first, the landlord refused to rent it to the family, telling Magda that the unit was too small for three people. But Magda persuaded him that her boys were small and that they would spend little time in the apartment except to sleep. The rent is $390 a month, plus about $110 in utilities.

It's been a year since the family moved in, yet the furnishings are sparse: one twin-sized bed, a small round kitchen-type table and three chairs, a television stand, and a TV. The two boys usually sleep together in the single bed, and Magda sleeps on a piece of foam on the floor. There's no chest of drawers, so they store their clothes in plastic garbage bags in the apartment's single closet. Two bare light-bulbs in a ceiling fixture provide the only light. The apartment's window looks out onto the roof of another building, about eight feet away, but there's a nice hedge of fuchsia-colored camellias in between, and at the moment, they're exploding in color.

To the family, the apartment's biggest drawback is that there's no place for the boys to play. Magda is very protective and rarely lets the boys go outside by themselves, because Fruitvale Avenue is a busy street. But both boys are overflowing with energy, so on this beautiful spring day, it's hard for them to keep still. They're kicking a soccer ball from one side of the small room to the other, and it's ricocheting off walls and knocking over treasured trinkets. As soon as she finishes talking with her visitor, Magda promises them, she'll walk them to the nearest park, ten blocks away. In the meantime, she tells them, if they promise to be careful, they can ride their bicycles up and down the sidewalk in front of the apartment building. They shriek with joy and head downstairs to the storage shed to retrieve their bikes.

"Every Marriage Has Problems"

Magda was born in 1969 on a ranch near Colotlan in the state of Jalisco, Mexico. Her parents were subsistence ranchers, raising corn, hay, beans, vegetables, and animals on rented land. Their only cash income came from the occasional sale of a steer and whatever their children could earn. They had ten children. "I'm the number five," Magda explains in imperfect, though understandable, English.

Magda worked part-time all through junior and senior high school making hand-tooled leather belts, a craft for which the region is famous. She was paid by the piece. "Not too much money, but enough to help our parents with shoes and clothes and food," she says.

The family was very, very poor. "They were always short of money, so much so that once, when I was a teenager, I told my mother maybe I shouldn't be in school anymore because we couldn't afford the books and the paper and the uniforms," Magda recalls. "But my mother, she told me, 'You need to be in school.' She always tried to push us to stay, telling us, 'When you start something, you must finish it.'"

Magda married right after graduating from high school, just a few months shy of eighteen. Her husband, Pedro, was two years older. She moved into the cinder-block house he had built himself—basically one room with a sleeping area, a cooking area, and a primitive toilet. While he went to work as a car mechanic, she stayed home and made belts. (He didn't want her to work outside the home.) Their first child, Manuel, was born nine months after the wedding.

As time passed, Magda found that married life wasn't what she had expected.

"I knew there would be problems," she said. "Every marriage has problems. But I never expected that my husband would beat me and kick me and call me bad words. It made me feel so sad when I started having these problems."

In Mexico, there are few places a woman can turn to if she's having trouble with her husband. Most Mexicans "think marriage is forever, no matter what happens at home," Magda says. So Magda made the best of her situation.

In May 1991, with Manuel a month shy of two, Magda gave birth to her second son. As Manuel began to talk and ask questions about the world, Magda became increasingly concerned about the effect on him when Pedro hit her and abused her verbally. She had recently found out that Pedro had grown up in a household in which his father regularly beat his mother, and she wondered whether that was why he treated her the same way. So Magda worked up the courage to tell her husband that "he must stop, that otherwise Manuel would end up like him."

"He said, 'It's okay if he's like me,'" she recalls. "'I want my son to be like me.'"

Soon after this conversation, Pedro hurt Magda so badly that she needed medical treatment. Pedro had broken one of her fingers, and it was swollen and twisted. After the doctor put her finger in a splint, Magda went home and told her husband that if he ever hit her again, "Me and my kids are going away."

"He Will Kill You"

About four months later, Pedro beat her again. She was holding the baby, and after he had knocked both of them to the floor, he pushed them out of the house and locked the door. She took the baby to her parents' house, and they saw the bruises on her face. "'You must not go back,'" she says her father told her. "'You need to stop this now. Otherwise, he will kill you.'"

But Manuel, her firstborn, was still with her husband. Magda went back home to tell her husband that she was leaving him and that she wanted Manuel with her. Her husband refused to let him leave. "'If you don't come home and stay here with us, you will lose him,'" she says he threatened her. "'I'm only letting Jorge stay with you right now because he's feeding from your breasts. But when he grows up, he will live with me also unless you come home.'"

"I begged him to let Manuel come and stay with me," Magda continues. "I told him he could see him anytime he wanted to. But he still said no. So I told him I was going to make a legal complaint against him for beating me. And he said: "'Go ahead. I will fight you. I have money, and you don't, and without money, you can't win. And anyway, the men who work in the courthouse are my friends, and they won't listen to you.'"

Which is exactly what Magda found out when she went to the courthouse. "I explained to them the problem," she said. "After I finished, the man said, 'Who is your husband?' I told him the name, and he said, 'You know what? We can do nothing for you.'"

Every day for the next month, Pedro took Manuel with him to the garage where he worked. Magda would sometimes stand in a doorway down the street from the shop so that she could catch a glimpse of Manuel and assure herself that he was okay. Finally, she went to a lawyer for advice.

"I told him my problems, that these things had happened to me and I didn't know how to get back my child," Magda says. "I was crying the whole time.

"He asked me, 'Do you have any money?'

"I told him no. Then he told me he felt sad for me, but he couldn't help me.

"But he also told me, 'Magda, I'm going to tell you something, but don't tell anybody I told you. Go back with him, and stay for a while. Let him think you've come back to him, that everything's okay, that you're going to be a dutiful wife. And when the time is right, take your son and leave. If you love your son, you must try to do this.'" Magda's parents urged her to follow the lawyer's advice.

Two days later, before she had made up her mind, Pedro pulled up in front of her parents' house. He pushed Manuel out of his car and toward the house.

"I grabbed him and put my arms around him and hugged him and cried," Magda recalls. "I asked him, 'How are you, Manuel?'

"At first, he said he was okay, but then he started crying, too, and he said, 'I'm not really okay. I'm sick. My father took me to the doctor, and he said I'm not okay. And my father said to tell you, you have to come home and take care of me.'"

Magda went over to her husband's car and asked him what was wrong with Manuel. "He said, 'I don't have to explain anything to you,'" Magda remembers. "'I am just telling you, if you love your son, you must come home and take care of him. He is sick because you are not at home with him.'"

Magda and the boys rode home with her husband. On the way, she says he told her, "'If you take Manuel away, I'm going to come after you and take him and Jorge, too, and you will never see either of them again.'"

For the next two days, Magda's husband didn't let Manuel out of his sight. He continued to take him along to work, even though Manuel was still ill with what turned out to be pneumonia. At night, he slept next to him, with his arm over Manuel's frail shoulders to prevent him from leaving the bed. He hid the couple's savings and changed the locks on the doors. And he told Magda: "If you leave me, nothing in here is yours, not your clothes, not these boys."

Magda took the lawyer's advice and pretended to be happy to be home. "'I'll do whatever you want me to do,'" she remembers telling him. "'Whatever you want is okay.'" While he was at work, she cleaned and laundered and cooked his favorite meals, all the while plotting her escape.

On the third day after her return, her husband let Manuel sleep when he left for work around 8:00 A.M. Magda knew he would be home for lunch at noon, so she had four hours to get away. She packed a canvas bag with clothes and diapers and dug her personal savings from belt-making out of their hiding place.

Manuel balked at leaving. "He told me, 'No, we can't go out,'" she said. "'My father will be mad at us. He told me I must make you stay here, that if you took me somewhere he would come after us and do something bad to you.'"

Magda pulled the boys out of the house and took a taxi to Colotlan, and from there, a bus to Guadalajara, about six hours away. She went to the home of her mother's sister, where she stayed for a month while she thought about where to go.

In Magda's mind, she didn't have many options. If she went back to her parents' house, Pedro would find her and take the boys. And it was inconceivable that she would be able to set herself and the boys up in their own household in a place where Pedro wouldn't find them. In Mexico, it's very difficult for single mothers to find housing or work that pays enough to support a family.

Four of Magda's brothers and sisters had already emigrated to the United States, and they offered to send her money and sponsor her for a visa. In April 1992, she and the boys took a bus to Los Angeles, and then a plane to Oakland, where they moved in with one of her brothers and his family.

Looking for Work

Although Magda had a work permit, she couldn't find work because she spoke no English. (Even if she had been successful in her job search, she hadn't thought about who would take care of her children while she worked.) After watching her search unsuccessfully for a month, her brother and sister-in-law suggested that she take care of their twin daughters while they worked. "They said the arrangement would help all of us," Magda said. "They needed a baby-sitter, and I needed work."

So for the next three years, Magda took care of her two nieces, who were the same age as Jorge, for $120 a week, plus free rent. She and her boys occupied one bedroom in her brother's three-bedroom apartment, and he and his family occupied the other two.

"The first year was so difficult," Magda recalls. "I was so sad that my marriage hadn't worked out, and I was homesick. I didn't know anyone, and I didn't speak the language. I was glad we had a place to live, but it was my sister-in-law's house. She's a really good girl, and I don't want to complain, but it was her rules and her kitchen. When she would come home from work, suddenly there would be two mothers there, and the kids would start fighting over everything. There was so much stress."

By the fall of 1994, Manuel was old enough for kindergarten, and the twin nieces and Jorge were old enough to attend Oakland's public preschool. Her brother and sister-in-law no longer needed Magda as a full-time baby-sitter, so she started looking for a job again.

One day, at a laundromat, she met a woman who told her she cleaned houses "in the rich area," as Magda puts it, pointing up toward the Oakland hills, where homes can cost millions of dollars. The woman asked Magda whether she would like a job for $5 an hour. "My brother told me that's not too much money for that job, but you can learn how to do it and then find a better-paying one," Magda says. So when the children left in the morning for preschool, Magda began leaving the apartment to help clean the houses in the hills.

It was harder work than Magda had imagined. "The houses are so big!" she exclaimed. "The first day I worked for her, we went into a big house, and she told me, 'We have only two hours to clean this house. You must hurry.'

"'Two hours!' I said. 'We can't clean a house like this in two hours.'

"And she said, 'That's all they're paying me for, so we have to do it in two hours.' I worked so hard."

Magda stayed in that job for four months and then started looking for a position with a janitorial service, where the pay would be better.

"For two weeks, I went down to the office every morning and asked whether there was work," Magda said.

"The man asked me, 'Do you have experience?'

"I said, 'No, but you can show me. Just give me a chance.'

"He said, 'No, I can't afford to take time to teach you. Time is money.'

"And I told him, 'Please, I really need a job. I got two kids and no husband, and I have to support them.'" The janitorial service supervisor, whose name was Scott, didn't speak Spanish, and Magda still didn't speak much English, so Magda laughs as she thinks back to how these conversations were conducted in "Spanglish."

Magda made friends with some of the cleaners, and they advised her to continue to come in every day and to ask whether anyone had called in sick.

"Scott would say when he saw me coming, 'Here's that lady again. She must really want to work.' And I'd tell him, 'I really need work. My babies need to eat.'"

Scott was apparently charmed by her persistence. "Finally, one day, somebody went home sick, and Scott told the owner, 'I've got this lady here who really wants to work, so why don't we give her a chance?'" Magda says. So Magda got her first real job, at $6.90 an hour, cleaning offices in downtown Oakland. "It was my lucky day," she says.

At first, she just worked intermittently as a fill-in for cleaners who were sick. Then Scott took her on for three full weeks as a substitute for a janitor who was on vacation. "I tried really hard to do a good job, and at the end of three weeks, Scott said to me, 'I really like your work. You really learn fast.'" He recommended Magda for a permanent job, and the owner agreed.

Magda worked for the service for two years, while continuing to live with her brother and sister-in-law. She usually worked the night shift, from 5:30 P.M. to 2:00 A.M., while her relatives watched her boys. In return, she watched their girls after school. Magda slept from about 2:30 A.M. until 7:00 A.M., when she had to get up to get the boys ready for school. "Getting enough sleep, that was a big problem," she said.

In April 1997, Magda decided it was time for her family to have its own place. She found the little apartment in the Fruitvale area, persuaded the landlord to rent it to her, and moved in.

But within a few weeks of moving in, the janitorial service went belly up, and Magda was without a job. There was no janitorial work to be found, so she took a job in a Mexican restaurant, at $4.60 an hour, plus tips, which were meager, since the clientele was largely poor. A month or so later, the owner told her that her granddaughter needed the job, and Magda was unemployed again.

For the next ten months, she picked up a little money cleaning houses and baby-sitting for a girl in her apartment building while she tried to find another job as a janitor. She was lucky if she earned $150 a week. "It was a terrible time," she said. "Sometimes we didn't have enough to eat."

In February 1998, she finally found a job as a janitor at a grocery distribution center. The starting pay was $8.50 an hour, or about $318 a week, before deductions. Magda was thrilled.

It has taken Magda more than an hour to tell this much of her life story, and all the while, Jorge and Manuel have been outside, riding their bicycles up and down the sidewalk. Suddenly, Jorge comes running in the door, shouting excitedly in Spanish. He grabs his mother's arm and pulls her out the door. Together, they run down the outside corridor that leads to the staircase to the ground level. Magda also begins shouting in Spanish.

A few minutes later, Magda and the boys return to the apartment, pushing the bicycles in front of them. Both Jorge and Manuel are breathing hard, their cheeks streaked with tears. It turns out that two older boys had come along and tried to take their bikes. Manuel bravely held on to both of them while Jorge ran upstairs to get their mother. When the thieves saw Magda, they let go of the bikes and ran away.

"That's why I don't like this place we live," Magda says. "There's no place for them to play."

"*Monsters as Big as Dinosaurs*"

Shaken by their experience, Jorge and Manuel no longer want to go to the park. Instead, they turn their attention to some children's books that their visitor has brought them. They sit side by side on the bed, and Manuel reads out loud to Jorge from *Afraid of the Dark,* a Berenstain Bears book, and then from *Danny the Dinosaur* and *Clifford, the Big Red Dog.*

Both Jorge and Manuel are exceedingly appealing boys, friendly, polite, and handsome. Manuel is mature beyond his years; he seems to have taken it upon himself to be the man of the house. He's very protective of his younger brother.

Both boys seem to take pride in their appearance, wetting their hair with water before they comb it and being sure to tuck their shirts into their pants, even if they're just going outside to play. To-day Jorge is wearing a brand-new soccer uniform even though he doesn't have a game scheduled. It's the first real soccer uniform he's ever had—a canary yellow shirt, bright green shorts, and yellow socks—and he's really proud of it. He received a scholarship to play on one of the teams offered by the Rockridge Soccer Club. But there were none available for Manuel.

"He's so sad, because he can't play," Magda said of Manuel. "The coach said he will try to find a place on a team for him, but that I might have to pay $65. That's a problem for me."

After the boys make their way through the pile of books, Manuel agrees to talk about what his routine is like on the days his mother works. He's eager to list his responsibilities.

"When my mom has to go to work real early, I get myself and my brother up at eight o'clock, and my mom's friend, Don Eduardo, comes at eight-thirty," he says. "Sometimes I have to help my brother get dressed if he's lazy. Then I lock the door. I have my own key. And then Don Eduardo drives us to school. We have breakfast there."

School runs from 9:30 A.M. to 2:40 P.M., Manuel says. "Then Don Eduardo comes and gets us at school and takes us to his house. His son, Eddie, is my friend, and we play and get our homework done. Sometimes we skate. I don't have skates, but he lets me use his skates because he doesn't know how to use them. Sometimes we watch the Spanish channel on TV, or the *Coffee Kids Club.*

"If it's a day when my mom has to work late, we eat dinner there, and then he brings us home at nine. Sometimes I drink a cup of milk before I go to sleep, and I get one for my brother, too. I like to read before I go to sleep, and sometimes I read to my brother, too. Then I turn all the lights off, except for the bathroom, and we go to sleep.

"That's when I miss my mom the most, just before I go to sleep. Sometimes I wake up when my mom comes home, but usually I don't."

Jorge wants to talk about his daily routine, too. "Sometimes I get scared when my mommy isn't here," he says. "I get scared that there are monsters outside, monsters as big as dinosaurs, and that they're going to come inside and eat us."

Learning English, Word by Word

The next day, Magda is almost an hour late when she arrives for her English class, which she's taking in an attempt both to prepare herself for a better job and, eventually, to take a citizenship test. She and the boys were up at 7:00 A.M. to get ready for the day. Then they took the number 40 bus across town, up Telegraph Avenue, to the boys' school, about a thirty-minute ride, and Magda walked them to their classroom. Then she took a bus back, another thirty-minute ride, to a stop a few blocks from the Clinton Park School. The front wall of this neighborhood center adult school, operated by the Oakland Unified School District, is painted with a mural extolling the virtues of education: *"En el Libro to Libertad."* "It sort of means 'From Learning to Liberty,'" Magda explains. The mural depicts immigrants of every race and hue reaching out for knowledge. Some are carrying books under their arms, one holds an artist's paintbrush, another a covey of nails.

Because she's late, Magda has missed a lesson on intonation, but the teacher, Gail Leong, is understanding. She knows that her students have all sorts of other obligations that prevent them from attending class regularly. That they're here as much as they are testifies to their strong desire to learn the language of their adopted country. There are almost two dozen students in the room, ranging in age from nineteen to more than seventy. They come from China, Laos, Vietnam, El Salvador, Mexico, Russia, Ethiopia, and Cambodia.

Some have been here just a few months, others twenty years. All they have in common is that they're strangers in a strange land.

When Magda arrives, they're deep into a lesson about the meaning of the word *could*. Soon, the teacher calls a fifteen-minute break. About two-thirds of the students leave, mostly to rush off to jobs. Many of the rest pair off for private conversations, and the babble of largely non-Roman languages enlivens the room. A few stand by the bulletin boards reading their classmates' autobiographies, which Ms. Leong has displayed on bright construction paper, much as elementary school teachers everywhere do the first month of the school year. The students' words are at once heartbreaking and hopeful.

"My family is very short," writes a sixty-nine-year-old Russian man named Felix, in a context that makes it clear he means "small." "I am all alone. My profession was an electronics engineer. I don't work now because I'm old and ill. My activities are visits to my doctors."

A middle-aged Cambodian woman has written: "My niece and I live in Oakland. There are only two people in my family. Every morning after breakfast, my niece goes to school and work. I go to English school. After I get back from school, I prepare dinner. Sometimes I get dizzy and have a headache. Then I can't cook. Sometimes I can't do homework because I get dizzy. I hope the teacher understands this."

Magda has yet to write her autobiography because she doesn't feel her written English is good enough. "Soon," she promises.

The lesson for the second part of the class is on how to report accidents and seek medical treatment. Only eight students remain.

Ms. Leong holds a caricature of a man with an arm in his sling. "Have any of you ever broken your arm?" she asks. Most of the remaining students are too shy—or too embarrassed about their English—to speak out loud. Ms. Leong knows from experience that Magda will take the lead in the situational exercises she has prepared, and she looks at her. "I haven't, but my son did," Magda volunteers.

"What happened when he broke his arm?" Ms. Leong probes.

"He was in the park," Magda explains. "He was on that thing you slide on. He went down with his head first."

"So he was playing on the slide, and then what happened?" Ms. Leong prods.

"He fell down," Magda says.

"And then what happened?" asks Ms. Leong.

"He broke his arm," Magda finishes.

For the next half hour, the class discusses other possible medical emergencies that might send one of them or one of their children to an emergency room in the next few weeks. All the while, they're learning about the "past continuous" tense, one of those things that native English speakers know intuitively from an early age, even if they can't put a label to it.

Magda flips through her looseleaf binder to find a blank sheet on which to record the term. But there are no more blank pages. Jorge has covered page after page with brightly colored drawings of birds and flowers and trees and dinosaurs. Magda suppresses a laugh.

"What Can I Do?"

Magda is no stranger to emergency medical situations and their consequences. It had taken her almost a year to pay off the $300 emergency room bill for Jorge's broken arm. (At the time, he wasn't covered by Medi-Cal, California's Medicaid program, because Magda hadn't realized her children were eligible.) And then, a few months after that, Jorge had become violently ill, with a temperature of 103 degrees, a severe headache, and projectile vomiting. Magda took him to Oakland Children's Hospital, where he spent three days being fed intravenously. He had a rotavirus that had caused him to become severely dehydrated.

The illness turned out to be a blessing in disguise, because as a result of it, both children found their way onto the Medi-Cal rolls for a while and the whole family found its way into counseling. Magda was distraught over Jorge's hospitalization, afraid that he might die, and a hospital social worker had been sent to talk to her. All of the troubles she had been carrying on her shoulders came tumbling out. His illness was only one of them.

"I asked her if I could get some help with Jorge," she explains now. "We had so much trouble with him, all the time. He was so aggressive. He don't like to respect any rules or listen to anyone. He was in trouble at school every day, sent to the office twice a week. They would call me and say, 'Your son has been sent to the office. Come and get him.'"

His behavior in class affected his learning. "By the end of kindergarten, he didn't even know the alphabet," Magda says. "Too many problems with him. I didn't know what to do."

The hospital social worker found a therapist near Magda's apartment who would counsel her and the children in their own language and charge Magda according to a sliding scale. At the first visit, Magda poured out her heart, revealing for the first time to anyone outside her family how her husband had treated her. She shared her conflicted feelings over leaving Mexico and her anguish over Jorge's behavior, which had become unmanageable. "I had never told anyone these things before," Magda said.

Magda and Jorge have been seeing the therapist nearly every week since, for the last nine months, and both have benefited, Magda says. "The therapist says that Jorge's problems are because of my job, that he doesn't see me enough," Magda says. "He was angry with me for being gone so much. He does these things to get attention. He feels all alone, that nobody likes him."

All through the next summer, Magda worked with Jorge on the alphabet an hour a day, helping him master all the letters. And now, on weekends during the current school year, she sets aside an hour a day to sit with him to review his schoolwork.

She feels guilty that she's at work most days when he gets out of school, because it means that she can't help him with his homework. "But what can I do?" she asks. "I have to work."

"This Is My Day"

Magda has an hour and fifteen minutes between the end of her English class and the time she has to set off for work. Today officials at her union, Local 1877 of the Service Employees' International Union, have asked her to drop by the union office to pick up information about an upcoming members' vote on a dues increase, which the union wants so that it can increase its organizing efforts.

It turns out when she gets there that she's actually expected to attend an hour-long meeting. She tells the organizer as nicely as she can that she can't stay very long, that she has to go home and eat lunch and get ready for work. She stays for twenty minutes before excusing herself. As penance, she agrees to spend two hours the following Saturday staffing a "get out the vote" phone bank at the union office. "But my boys will have to come along," she tells the organizer.

Back home, she hurriedly eats a bowl of leftover oatmeal. Then she sweeps her carpeted floor with a broom, makes the bed, washes the breakfast dishes, and tidies up.

"This is my day, every day," she says. "Get the kids to school. Go to language school. Come home quick and clean and cook. And then go to work."

Because of her limited income and her erratic schedule, child care is one of the banes of Magda's existence. At the moment, she's got things worked out, but the arrangement is by no means ideal.

Most weeks, she pays a friend named Don Eduardo, who has children at the same school, $15 a day—about one-fifth of the amount she herself earns—to watch the boys at his house until 9:00 P.M. and then drive them home. He puts them to bed and then goes back to his own children. Manuel and Jorge are alone in the apartment for an hour and a half.

"Manuel sometimes says, 'Mama, I don't like to stay alone. I get scared,'" Magda admits. She knows that the neighborhood is dangerous, so much so that she worries about her own one-block walk late at night from the bus stop to her door.

"Too much trouble," she says. "Too many people who use drugs and alcohol. Two months ago, some kids shot the owner of the furniture store down the street. He died on the way to the hospital." But she reassures the boys that they are only alone for a little while, and that if they don't open the door to anyone, they'll be safe. And she sometimes calls them from the BART station before she boards a bus for the last leg home to let them know she's almost there.

If, for some reason, Don Eduardo can't watch the boys after school, they go to one of her brothers' houses and then spend the night. On those occasions, Magda takes the bus across town the next morning, bearing clean uniforms, and helps the boys bathe and dress before walking them to school. "But it's better for them when they can spend the night in their own place," she says.

Once school's out in a few weeks, she's going to have an even bigger problem with child care. If she wants to continue at language school, which she sees as key to the family's future, she'll have to find a baby-sitter or child-care center where they can spend the days.

But she'll still have the problem of evening care, since she's still likely to be working mainly evening shifts. It will be hard to find that much money in her budget for two shifts of child care.

As she's talking about her child-care problems, Magda glances at her watch and jumps up. "Time to go to work," she says, throwing her purse over her shoulder. To get to work, she has to take a bus to the BART station, ride for ten minutes on BART, and then take another short bus ride, if the connection works out. If it doesn't, she has to walk ten blocks. As it turns out, today she misses her connection and has to walk.

"Oh, Mommy, Please!"

A few weeks have passed. School ended a week ago, and the report cards have just arrived. Manuel has received top grades in every subject, and he's beaming with pride over his teacher's comments. He wants to show off his report card.

"Manuel is a joy to have in class, as well as being an exceptional student," the teacher has written. "He has really shown that he can read and write in English, and he is my best second-grade math student. He has really made progress the last two years. It has been a pleasure to watch him grow more mature and confident."

Manuel's excellent report card is proof both of his hard work over the last two years and his innate drive to succeed. He had entered kindergarten not knowing a word of English. "He was in an English-only kindergarten, and it was so difficult for him," his mother recalls. "He would come home crying every day. I would ask him, 'What happened?' And he would say, 'I don't understand nothing.'

"Things got better in first grade. The teacher explained everything in English, but his workbooks were in both English and Spanish, and I could help him better. When Manuel couldn't understand something in English, I would explain it to him in Spanish. And I think it helped him a lot that he had the same teacher this year for second grade. He took a lot of time with both him and Jorge."

As his mother is talking about him, Manuel takes me by the hand and pulls me into the kitchen nook. "Look at what my teacher gave me," he says, pointing to a colorful clock mounted on the kitchen wall.

"He gets so many awards," his mother says proudly, "for good listening, good homework, good math skills."

If Manuel is the type of student that a teacher looks forward to seeing every morning, Jorge is the type that makes a teacher feel relieved to go home at the end of the day. Jorge jumps up to try to hide his report card. "He knows it's not so good as his brother's," his mother explains.

When Jorge finally relents and allows his report card to be examined, it's clear that he's performing below first-grade level in most areas of instruction. And the teacher's comments over the year indicate his continuing frustration with Jorge, although things seem better at the end of the year than at the beginning.

"Jorge has a great deal of intelligence," the teacher had written at the end of the first trimester. "He needs to mature to the point where he can take school seriously. I hope he develops some maturity this year so that I can recommend him as a second-grader in June."

Then, after the second trimester: "Jorge has made some progress this term. He is still very difficult in a group situation. He will definitely have to go to summer school."

And at the end of the school year: "I am beginning to see Jorge make some progress in the core curriculum. It gives me hope for the future. The main concern continues to be his aggressiveness toward the other children. Summer school is a must."

The good news is that he's being advanced to second grade.

Although only Jorge is required to go to summer school this year, Magda is enrolling Manuel, too. The Oakland school district's summer school, which is free, runs for four weeks, four hours each morning. "I'm so happy that Manuel got such a good report, but I want him to keep busy this summer," she says. "They lose too much just being at home all summer."

Magda is also trying to find some recreational programs for the boys in the afternoons, but cost is an obstacle. "There are some art classes they can go to for $2 each every day, and I'm not sure I can manage that, plus bus fare," she says.

"Oh, Mommy, please," Manuel begs.

"If I have the money, you can do it," she says. "But I only have so much money. If I can do it, I will do it."

"Where I Go, My Boys Go"

Another month has passed, and Magda has lots of good news to report. She invites her visitor to come along to the laundromat, so they can talk while her clothes are being washed and dried.

Between kicks to a soccer ball, the boys help her load two weeks' worth of dirty clothes and bedsheets into plastic garbage bags. Manuel empties the pockets of his winter coat and finds a couple of pennies, a box of crayons, and a plastic bag containing eight markers. "My teacher gave these to me," he says proudly of his cache.

Magda tells Manuel to bring the markers and some paper along to the laundromat so that he and Jorge will have something to do. The boys help her carry the bags full of laundry downstairs, and she loads them onto an old grocery cart that's parked behind her apartment building. They set off down the street. Washtime, the laundromat, is three blocks away.

About two dozen people are already inside the laundromat. A couple of single men are drinking beer out of bottles concealed by paper bags. A family is eating fresh-made tamales from the liquor store across the street. Several women are eating ribs and cole slaw from a barbecue stand up the street. Children are running around everywhere.

Jorge and Manuel load the wash into washing machines while Magda gets enough change for three large-capacity loads—a total of $7.50 in quarters. The dryers, which cost $.75 for a 30-minute cycle, will require another $4.50.

Once the washers are turned on, the boys sit down at a folding table with their crayons and paper, and Magda starts to share her news.

First, she's solved her summer baby-sitting problems in the best way possible: her fifty-eight-year-old mother has come from Mexico for a three-month visit. Magda and her three Bay Area siblings all chipped in to buy her a ticket.

This makes Magda happy for several reasons. The boys will get to know their grandmother, and Magda won't have to worry about gaps in their care. This past week, for instance, she worked three different shifts—12:30 P.M. to 8:00 P.M. for two days, then 8:00 A.M. to 4:30 P.M. for two days, and then 2:00 P.M. to 10:30 P.M. on Friday—

and there's no way Don Eduardo, her regular baby-sitter, would have been able to cover them all. Without their grandmother there, Jorge and Manuel would have had to spend many hours alone.

But there's still the cost of their care to worry about. Besides helping pay for the ticket, Magda feels she should pay her mother the same amount of money she would have paid her regular baby-sitter. "It's only fair," she says. "She'll need spending money while she's here."

Another piece of good news is that Magda has passed her probationary period at work, so she's become eligible for health insurance through a health maintenance organization. "Next week, I get the papers to be a member of the Kaiser health plan," she says proudly. "That's a good one. They will take money from my check, but when I go to the doctor, I won't have to pay anything. The boys haven't had insurance for a while, so I'm very happy." (The boys had lost their Medi-Cal coverage when Magda went to work for the janitorial service, since her projected annual income was just over 133 percent of the federal poverty guideline, the eligibility ceiling at the time. California's new health coverage program for near-poor children, Healthy Families, had not yet started up.)

And the last bit of news, which makes her beam with happiness, is that she's got a boyfriend. Tony, thirty-two, is a doughmaker for a pizza company. He came here from Mexico sixteen years ago as a migrant laborer. Magda has known him for about four months, but they've only recently become boyfriend and girlfriend.

"The first time Tony invited me out to dinner, I said, 'Well, if you want me to have dinner, my sons have to go, too. Where I go, my boys go.' And he said, 'That's okay.'

"At first, my boys were too jealous," she continues. "When he started to come around, Jorge would say, 'I don't like Tony to come here.'

"Even Manuel is jealous. Tony likes to kiss me on the cheek when he comes to visit, and Manuel runs over to put his hand on my cheek to prevent it. He tells him, 'Don't kiss my mother!' And Tony says, 'Why not? I love your mother.' And then Manuel says, 'Okay, you can love her, but you can't kiss her.'"

More recently, though, the boys have come to regard Tony as their friend, Magda says. "The other day we went to a park to watch Jorge play soccer," she said. "Jorge said to us, 'I'm going to tell my team that Tony's my dad.'

"Tony asked him, 'Why are you telling them that?' And Jorge said, 'Because they laugh at me because I don't have a father.'

"I think my boys really need a man in their lives, besides my brothers."

Tony's presence in the family's life has eased some of the pressures on Magda. For one thing, he has a vehicle, a fifteen-year-old van, and he's happy to drive Magda and the boys to the grocery store or to visit her brothers. In addition, he had been upset to learn that Magda was sleeping on the floor and bought a secondhand sofa bed as a present for the family. Right now, Magda's mother is sleeping in the single bed, and Magda and the boys are sharing the sofa bed, but once Magda's mother leaves, Magda will use the single bed and the boys will have the sofa bed to themselves.

It's not yet clear whether the relationship is going to endure and end up in marriage, or even in living together, Magda says. On the one hand, if she and Tony pooled their incomes, they could afford a bigger place, and she wouldn't have to worry so much about making ends meet between paychecks. On the other hand, she and her boys have been on their own for a long time and are managing to make it, even though they go without a lot. Magda's trying to figure out how to bring more money into her household so that she won't be tempted to move in with Tony for the wrong reason. She has to believe that he's the one for her before she makes a commitment like that.

"It would be good if I got a second job, but right now I can't do that because they keep changing my hours at the warehouse," Magda says. "Maybe when I get a permanent shift I can think about it. But I already see so little of the boys that it would be hard on them. Jorge, especially, needs to spend more time with me. That's what the therapist says. He's getting better, but it's slow."

The dryers have stopped, and it's time to get the clothes out. Jorge is still working hard on his drawing, a bright yellow tyrannosaurus rex with green stripes and a big grin. But when Manuel sees his mother get up to fetch the clean clothes, he puts down his markers and goes over to help, like the good boy he is.

For thirty minutes, Magda and Manuel stand side by side at the folding table, smoothing out wrinkles, matching socks and rolling them into balls, and putting everything into neat piles.

Manuel whistles "This old man . . ." as he works.

3

RANDOLPH COUNTY, ILLINOIS

The message imprinted on the doormat on the Keebler family's front porch announces to all visitors that a sentimental soul lives within. "A house is made of brick and stone," it reads. "A home is made of love alone."

If the doormat were to list all of the ingredients that went into making this particular house a home, it would have to include hard work and hope, a song and a prayer, and a lot of help from friends.

Nancy Keebler, thirty-four, and her two children, Alice, twelve, and Benji, five, moved into this neatly kept, aluminum-sided house fourteen months ago, from public housing. It cost $27,000, which Nancy would never have been able to afford on her income of $10,620 a year except for a thirty-three-year loan subsidy provided through a homebuyers' program created by the National Affordable Housing Act of 1990.

By most anybody's standards, the transformation of a vacant, worn structure into a cozy family home with lace curtains at the windows would be seen as a positive example of a social program that works. But ironically, restrictions imposed by the homebuyers' program on the Keeblers' use of the house inhibit the family's prospects for moving out of poverty anytime soon.

Because her youngest child is severely disabled and no child-care provider in the area will care for him, Nancy can't work outside the home. After mulling over all of her options, she came up with a creative plan to raise her family's income above poverty level. She would open a licensed child-care facility in her home. That way, she could both take care of Benji and become self-supporting.

"There's a big demand here for good day care," she says. "This is a working town, and parents don't have enough options for their children."

But Nancy's plans came to a standstill when she learned that restrictions attached to her federally subsidized mortgage forbid her to use her home as a business. She can't understand why a program designed to help poor people would make it harder for them to improve their situation. "You'd think that the agency that gave me the mortgage subsidy would be glad that I want to earn more money and get off welfare," Nancy says.

Hydrangeas and Abandoned Cars

The Keeblers live in a small rural town in southern Illinois that began as a market center for farmers in the nineteenth century. It's managed to maintain its rural feel as the twenty-first century approaches, even though most residents now work in the factories that have sprung up within a seventy-five-mile radius or in the prisons that pepper southern Illinois. It's the kind of community whose residents are likely to answer that it's "a good place to raise children" when asked what they like about living there (and in the next breath will bemoan its lack of cultural and recreational amenities).

As in many small rural towns, its small downtown business district has been hurt by the giant Wal-Mart store that sprang up on the outskirts of town a few years ago. Downtown, you can still rent a video, buy furniture, or rummage through the second-hand clothes at a thrift shop, but there's no pharmacy or five-and-dime. Along the tree-lined residential streets, there are both substantial brick homes with huge hydrangea and lilac bushes in the front yards and small frame homes whose yards are cluttered with abandoned cars and doghouses.

In the Keeblers' neighborhood, the last census found that fewer than 4 percent of households received public assistance and about two-thirds received some form of Social Security income, which includes retirement, survivors', and disability benefits. Married couples predominate. Of those households in which children were present when the last census was taken, about one in six was headed by a single mother, as the Keebler household is. Largely because of the high proportion of married-couple families and the low welfare rate, the town had a young child poverty rate of only about 9 percent, well below both the national and state rates.

Schizophrenic Mother, Absent Father

Nancy Keebler grew up in a series of Illinois towns much like the one she lives in now. The closest city was always Carbondale, an hour or two away. The closest *big* city was always St. Louis, Missouri, two to three hours away, depending on which relatives she and her grandmother were staying with at the time. Nancy's sixty-five-year-old grandmother cared for her from the time she was born until she was ready to enter first grade. Her mother was schizophrenic and spent time in a state mental hospital. Her father was a bar owner with erratic working hours and marginal parenting skills. All four of the couple's children lived with relatives on and off throughout their childhoods.

Nancy remembers not even recognizing her parents when she was sent to live with them at the age of six. "I had hardly ever seen them before," she says. The family lived in a tiny two-bedroom house, so small that they had to walk through one bedroom to get to the other. Nancy and her mother shared one room and her older brother, Bobby, slept in the other. Her father usually slept at his bar.

Nancy's parents divorced when she was in fourth grade, and her mother and Nancy and her brother went on welfare. (Two older sisters were already grown up and out of the house.) From Nancy's description of her childhood, it sounds as though she pretty much raised herself. Her mother had a paranoid form of schizophrenia and didn't like to go out. "When she was home, she kept all the doors locked and the shades pulled down," Nancy remembers. "She thought there were 'bush people' waiting outside to come in." Relatives would step in when they saw that the household was running low on food, and Nancy's father always made sure that she had a good Christmas, a happy birthday, and new clothes for the first day of school.

Nancy graduated from high school in 1982 and then took nurse's aide training at the local community college. After completing the three-month nurse's aide course, she got a job for $4.25 an hour in a local nursing home. "I loved being a nurse's aide," she says. "I love older people." She and her father pooled their savings and came up with a down payment on a two-bedroom trailer, where they lived together and shared expenses.

Since there were no longer any children in her mother's home, Illinois terminated her mother's welfare benefits. With no money to live on, she moved to Chicago to stay with an older daughter. She died in August 1985 of lung cancer, at age fifty-eight.

About four months after her mother's death, Nancy found out that she was pregnant. "I started getting pains in my abdomen, and at first the doctor couldn't figure out why," she says. "It turned out I was about five months along."

The pregnancy was unplanned. The baby's father was a young man she'd begun seeing after her longtime sweetheart moved to North Carolina. "I was devastated when he left, and I started dating his best friend, I guess out of loneliness," she says. "I thought he really cared about me, but once he found out I was pregnant, he basically said, 'See ya.' My sister wanted me to give the baby up for adoption through her church, but I didn't think I could do that."

Nancy had a difficult pregnancy. Overweight to begin with, she gained eighty-six pounds in the final four months of pregnancy and developed toxemia. In April 1986, she gave birth to Alice, a healthy seven-pound, eight-ounce girl. Nancy took the baby home to the trailer and went on welfare. She and her daughter received $230 a month plus food stamps.

The trailer was 10 feet wide by 54 feet long—540 square feet in all—and living there with a baby was difficult. "My brother had moved in, and our nephew was living there, too, and there just wasn't enough room for me and the baby," she says. "A double bed took up all the floor space in the largest bedroom. The room was so small that I had to put half of the baby's crib in a closet."

After six months there, Nancy and Alice moved into a small apartment in a public housing complex in a nearby town. Nancy stayed home with Alice, getting by on welfare benefits and food stamps. When Alice was about two and a half, Nancy returned to work at the nursing home where she'd worked before. This forced her to confront a problem that working parents everywhere, but especially in rural areas, know all too well: the difficulty of finding safe, affordable child care.

Nancy was on the midnight shift, the hardest shift of all for a mother needing child care. She felt lucky when a neighbor offered to let Alice spend the night in her trailer, for just $1 an hour. Since Nancy was earning minimum wage, she couldn't afford to pay for a second shift of baby-sitting while she slept, so she tried to catch snatches of sleep in the afternoons while Alice played nearby. That arrangement came to a near-fatal end when she woke up one afternoon to find Alice unconscious on the floor, surrounded by loose prescription pills and several near-empty bottles.

"She had pushed a chair over to the refrigerator, climbed up, and gotten into my medicine," Nancy recalls. Emergency medical treatment saved Alice, but Nancy realized that she and Alice couldn't continue on that schedule.

"I called the nursing home and told them that either they'd have to give me a different shift or I'd have to quit," she says. Fortunately, Nancy was given the 3:00 to 11:00 P.M. shift.

Nancy was grateful when her neighbors agreed to continue to watch Alice while she worked evenings. The price was right, and the location convenient. But three months into her new shift, her world caved in. Alice told her that the baby-sitter's adult son was molesting her.

Nancy became hysterical. She took Alice to the local clinic, where the doctor examined her and told Nancy it looked as though Alice didn't have an intact hymen. He notified the Illinois Department of Children and Family Services, as is required of physicians if they suspect sexual abuse, and the agency began an investigation.

A more sophisticated examination at a teaching hospital near Chicago found no physical evidence of molestation. But based on Alice's account, plus her sexually precocious behavior, a state investigator concluded that she had been molested, and Alice entered the state's child-abuse caseload. "They told me they believed something had happened, but they couldn't say what, or who did it," Nancy says.

The baby-sitter and her son failed lie detector tests, but no one was ever prosecuted for molesting Alice. "The prosecutor told me Alice was too young to testify," Nancy says.

The incident made Nancy terrified to leave Alice with anyone for nearly two years. She quit her job, went back on welfare, and gave her full-time attention to Alice and her father. Her father's health had been bad for years (he had emphysema), and he needed help both at home and at his bar. Nancy tended bar for him when he was too sick to go in. An elderly aunt took care of Alice.

One of the bar's regular customers was a tall, quiet man about twenty years Nancy's senior. Barry was a former railroad worker who'd retired early because of heart disease and was living on a meager disability benefit. Nancy and Barry fell in love and married in November 1990.

Nancy's father's health began worsening just as the marriage was getting under way. So that she could nurse him, Nancy virtually lived with her father through the last few months of his life, though doing so strained her marriage. About the same time her father died, she found out that Barry had a girlfriend. He told her he wanted a divorce. "I was devastated," she recalls. "I didn't want to be on my own again."

Because Barry had adopted Alice, after the divorce Nancy began receiving about $200 a month from the Social Security disability program in lieu of child support. For a few months, that was Nancy's sole source of income, and rent consumed $125 of it. Although she was still reluctant to leave Alice with a baby-sitter, Nancy went back to work at the nursing home, making $5.25 an hour. Alice was in kindergarten classes for part of the day, and a cousin volunteered to baby-sit Alice for the rest of Nancy's shift. The family connection persuaded Nancy that Alice would be safe.

Even though they were divorced, Nancy continued to see Barry. "We were the kind of couple who got along great as long as we didn't have to live together," she says.

In the spring of 1992, she became pregnant with Barry's child.

A Devastating Diagnosis

Nancy was not a good candidate for a trouble-free pregnancy. A few years before, she'd been diagnosed with early-stage diabetes. It hadn't yet progressed to the point that she needed to inject herself with insulin, but she was on oral medication. It took her a while to find a local obstetrician who'd monitor her pregnancy since she was on Medicaid and few doctors in rural Illinois would accept Medicaid patients. She finally found one in a town thirty miles away, but as soon as he learned she was diabetic, he told her he couldn't treat her.

He referred her to a high-risk OB specialist in Carbondale, more than an hour away from her home.

As often happens in pregnant women with mild diabetes, the hormonal changes associated with pregnancy made her diabetes worse. By her seventh month of pregnancy, she had to begin injecting herself with insulin every day.

One bitterly cold night in early December 1992, six weeks before her due date, she began having labor pains. Nancy hadn't expected to go into labor so soon and didn't even have enough money to buy gas for the trip to Carbondale. Nor did she have a phone in her apartment on which she could call the out-of-town friend who'd agreed to care for Alice while she was hospitalized. So she threw a coat on over her nightgown, loaded a sleepy Alice into the car, and headed over to the local convenience store to use a pay phone.

"And there on the ground was a $20 bill," she says, her voice still filled with wonder as she recounts what she regards as the miracle that enabled her to gas up for the trip. She called her friend to meet her in Carbondale and then drove herself and Alice to the hospital there. "By the time I got there, my contractions were only three minutes apart," she remembers.

Nancy was in labor for thirteen hours. As the baby began moving through the birth canal, the doctor could see that the cord was wrapped tightly around his neck. "As soon as he came out, they took him over to a corner of the delivery room and bagged him, and then they took him to intensive care," Nancy says. "His blood sugar had bottomed out, and he had to have a transfusion. They didn't know if he was going to make it or not."

Two days later, the hospital discharged Nancy. A nurse gave her $5 for gas money to get home. Benji stayed in intensive care. He weighed six pounds, three ounces, a good size for a preemie, but because of the stress he'd suffered in the womb and during and after delivery, it wasn't clear what his prognosis was.

"It was really hard to leave him there, especially because I didn't have the money for gas to come back and see him," Nancy says. "But the hospital let me call collect every day to check on him."

Because she couldn't afford to drive to Carbondale regularly, Nancy was able to see Benji only once while he was hospitalized and had to give up her hope of breast-feeding because she couldn't deliver her milk. When Benji came home from the hospital two and a half weeks after his birth, he had lost more than a pound. But Nancy had no inkling yet that he had suffered lasting damage from his difficult birth.

"He cried a lot, and I had to hold him all the time," she says. "My friends would tell me, 'Well, all babies are different, and you've just got one who likes to cry.'

"But his crying really scared me. He would throw his head back and stiffen his whole body. It looked like he was having a seizure. Gradually, over time, I began sensing that something was really wrong, but I couldn't put a name to it."

Benji was getting regular checkups from a local doctor and developmental checks at the local WIC clinic, but for his first year of life, nobody raised any red flags. It wasn't until his one-year physical at the WIC clinic that anyone mentioned that something might be seriously wrong.

"They measured his head and said that it hadn't grown since he was six months old," Nancy says. "They told me to take him to his doctor. He measured his head, too, and agreed."

Benji was referred to specialists at St. Louis Children's Hospital. Barry went with Nancy and Benji to St. Louis to find out what was wrong. The diagnosis was spastic quadriplegic cerebral palsy.

"They may as well have told me he was going to die," Nancy recalls, beginning to cry.

More Bad News

After doctors at Children's Hospital put a name to Benji's condition, Nancy set about educating herself on what it meant and looking for services that would help maximize his potential. Benji began receiving physical therapy at a nearby community hospital. There Nancy learned about a state-funded program for disabled children from birth through three—Prime/Care—which began sending a case manager to the apartment twice a month to work with Benji.

Soon after Benji turned two, Nancy by chance noticed an item in the local newspaper about an upcoming annual visit by specialists from Shriners Hospital in St. Louis. She took Benji to see whether they could do anything for him. A doctor from Shriners told her of an operation that would prevent Benji's leg muscles from contracting and help him maximize the use of his legs. In 1995 he had surgery to cut his abductor muscles and heel cords. He spent eight weeks in a body cast recovering. "The doctors at Shriners think he might walk someday," Nancy says hopefully.

At the moment, the best Benji can do is stand upright, with the help of leg braces, and propel himself by leaning into a wheeled walker. But he lacks the muscular control to keep the walker from running away from him, so its usefulness is limited outside the house.

From her Prime/Care case manager, Nancy learned about an Illinois state agency called Specialized Care for Children. The agency is a payer of last resort, providing help with the purchase of specialized equipment that Medicaid won't pay for. A caseworker there enrolled Benji in a program that will deliver diapers to his door as long as he needs them and the family's income remains low. The caseworker also helped Nancy acquire a Rifkin Chair, a highly stable, oversized high chair that enables Benji to sit up while he eats. (He slides off of regular chairs.)

Still, getting equipment to help Benji maximize his potential is almost always a battle. Nancy had to file an appeal to get the Illinois Medicaid program to pay for his first set of leg braces (which cost $600). Then, when she asked the agency to purchase an oversized stroller for him, the agency took so long to approve it that Benji was too big for it by the time it arrived. More recently, she had to enlist lawyers from the Land of Lincoln Legal Aid Society and social workers from Shriners to help her fight the Medicaid program so that Benji could have a wheelchair. Unfortunately, he'll outgrow his wheelchair in another year or two. Nancy's already dreading the next battle over a replacement chair.

Although federal law requires local school districts to do whatever's necessary to ensure that disabled children can attend school, Nancy has had a few battles on that front, too. As Benji was beginning his second year at the local district's special education preschool, Nancy had to bring someone from her doctor's office to plead with school officials to hire an aide to help load Benji onto the school bus every day, since Nancy was finding it increasingly difficult.

"She had to go in and tell them that I'm a diabetic and pass out sometimes, so I can't really be carrying him up the steps of the bus," Nancy says. "That got them to listen. They gave him a bus aide."

But district officials have already made it clear that they will not require the school bus company to buy a wheelchair-accessible bus when Benji becomes too heavy for an aide to lift, Nancy says. How will he get back and forth to school? "They said something about maybe hiring someone to drive him in a car," Nancy answers.

Benji is one of about half a dozen disabled preschool-aged children who receive special education services through the local district. In general, Nancy has been happy with the services Benji receives at preschool during the school year. He has weekly physical and occupational therapy and engages in typical preschool-type activities, such as drawing, building with blocks, listening to stories, learning to count and identify colors, and singing songs. On his last report card, his teacher wrote:

> Benji is very friendly, polite, and excited about all school activities. He is cooperative and is interacting more with his classmates. He still is easily distracted by sounds and other activities. He identifies all colors, rote counts to fourteen, follows some directions, recalls and relates details of events. Benji has good vocabulary skills and is improving with verbal responses to questions. He continues to have difficulty with most fine motor skills (cutting, copying, puzzles). Benji is handling his wheelchair much better in school and is more consistent in using the bathroom. He continues to need much urging to perform tasks and still expects things to be done for him.

In the fall, Benji will continue in the special education preschool for a third year and also attend regular kindergarten for two and a half hours a day. Nancy is concerned that the school doesn't realize how much help he'll need when he's mainstreamed. "At the least, he's going to have to have an aide to take him to the bathroom and help him get to lunch," she says.

Last week, Nancy's pleasure over his largely favorable report card dissipated when she received the report from a sophisticated psychodiagnostic evaluation of Benji performed at a hospital a few months ago. Benji was found to have an estimated mental age of eighteen months, "placing his cognitive abilities within the mentally retarded range," the evaluator noted. The evaluation labeled Benji's socialization skills as his most well-developed skills, with an age equivalent of two years, eight months, still well below his actual age then of five years, three months. The evaluator also detected serious vision problems that hadn't been diagnosed before, raising questions about how much Benji can see.

The findings were devastating to Nancy. Though she didn't want to believe them at first, she knows that they're probably correct.

"I sat there with him and watched him through all the tests, and I was surprised at all the things he couldn't do," Nancy says, fighting back tears. "I just didn't know all that he didn't know."

"Babies Need Holding"

What does all this mean for Benji's daily functioning?

On this hot summer day, Benji is propped up on the couch, his legs ramrod straight in front of him. He's eating French fries and fish sticks with his right hand and using the left to balance himself. *Sesame Street* is on the TV screen. It's almost 100 degrees outside, so the air conditioner is on full blast.

At first glance, Benji looks like a normal five-year-old, and a tall one at that. Only after a few minutes pass does it become clear that something is off. He seems to be looking at the TV screen, but he doesn't appear to be *seeing* it. When he's asked how his day is going, he turns his head slowly in the direction of the questioner and, in carefully enunciated words, says: "Fine. Thank you for asking." But there's no personality animating the words, and his eyes don't seem to connect with the visitor's.

After Benji has finished eating, he slides down from the couch and propels himself to the kitchen, where his mother is getting herself some diet lemonade. Though he has little control over his legs, his arms are strong, so he moves by assuming a frog-like position and then using his arms to drag his legs along. He usually wears leg braces, but he hasn't been able to wear them for the last week because his feet are dotted with open sores. A teenager who watched him for a few hours last week let him crawl around outside, and he developed blisters, which have since popped.

When his mother goes down to the basement to put her laundry into the washer, Benji sits at the top of the stairs and bleats, "Mama, Mama," over and over, until he gets a response.

"What do you want, Benji? A lovie?" Nancy asks him when she gets back upstairs. She bends down and picks him up, grimacing at the strain his forty-five pounds place on her lower back. She carries him over to a rocker and sits down. He folds his body against hers and lays his head on her breasts.

Nancy says Benji loves to be held. "We often play a game at night," she says. "He'll say to me, 'Hold me, hold me.' And I'll say to him, 'Why should I hold you?' And he'll say, 'Because babies need holding.'"

After a few minutes of cuddling, Benji slides down on the floor again and propels himself through the living room and down a short hall to the door to his sister's bedroom. He begins opening and closing it methodically, seeming to enjoy the bang it makes each time it closes. He must do it one hundred times. "Is that bothering you?" Nancy asks her visitor. "It bothers some people, but I've gotten to where I don't even notice it."

Periodically during the day, he erupts in fits of giggling that can last an hour or more. There's no apparent provocation, nor does he share whatever private joke has set him off. Nancy worries about this more than about most anything else, "but the doctors have told me that it's probably just the way he is and not to worry unless it seems as though he's in another world," she says.

The local school district offers no special education programs in the summer, and Nancy is concerned that without regular occupational therapy and mental stimulation for three months, he will regress. "I asked them what I should do with him, and they suggested Bible school," Nancy says, making it clear with her expression that she considered that suggestion no help at all. "My church doesn't even like to have him in Sunday school. That's one of the reasons I've stopped going there myself."

Because Nancy has no way to get him there, he no longer receives physical therapy at the community hospital. There's a special transport service for the elderly, but not for a disabled child.

Alice: "A Walking Time Bomb"

Benji's condition isn't the only problem Nancy's had to cope with over the last few years. Alice is an extremely difficult child. She spent most of her kindergarten year confined to a corner of the classroom. "The teacher told me that she had to keep her there, or she'd just walk out of the classroom in the middle of a lesson," Nancy said.

One problem was that she was so large for her age—112 pounds by kindergarten—that any misbehavior was quite noticeable. It also made it hard for her to get along with other children. Her size intimidated them, and they reacted by making fun of her. The teacher referred Alice for testing for hyperactivity and learning disabilities, but the school district didn't follow through.

Before first grade began, Nancy moved the family to another town so that Alice wouldn't have to attend the same school as the children of the baby-sitter in whose home she'd been molested. Alice finished first grade with D+ grades in reading and writing and a D- in mathematics, but her teacher wrote nothing out of the ordinary in the comment area of the report card. "Encourage Alice to read daily this summer and practice handwriting skills," was her only advice.

By second grade, Alice was really acting out—misbehaving at school and screaming at her mother at home. Her teacher wrote in an evaluation:

Alice has very low self-esteem. Many times I hear her make comments such as: "Why are my papers always so bad?" or, "I never get a good grade." Many of Alice's problems she causes herself. Many times she pushes into children in line. She is either hugging or picking up other students. Also, rather than talking out a problem, she will give the child either a pinch or a kick.

She has trouble making friends because she offends the child first, then says they don't like her because she is fat. She is very self-conscious about her size and weight. I feel that many days she cannot learn or get along with the other students because she is so preoccupied with her own inner feelings.

She cannot sit down in a chair for longer than five minutes. She usually lays across her desk with her knees in her chair and her posterior end high in the air. If she is not in this position, she is walking slowly around the room. She interrupts others constantly.

At her desk, she tears up all supplies—paper, pencils, scissors, crayons, etc. I had to take them all away. She would eat her glue, break and peel her crayons, tear up her eraser in small pieces, mark all over her arms and dress with her Magic Markers, use her tape to tape small pieces of shredded paper together. She started taping her mouth closed because I told her not to blurt out. She even attempted to tape herself to the chair. That's when I took the tape away. She broke one pair of scissors. The next pair I took away because she tried to cut her clothes and her hair.

When I work with Alice one to one, she is very pleasant. She will try very hard to please. She thrives on praise. In reading, she listens well if she believes she has your undivided attention. Math is a different story. It is difficult to get her to concentrate. She is likely to blurt out, "I don't get it," and then shutdown occurs. She has trouble doing any type of memory work, whether it is spelling words, vocabulary words, math problems, or basic sight words.

Even though Alice is having many problems academically, I am most concerned about her social growth and development. Alice is beginning to be a "tagged" child, which I am fighting to keep from happening. Partly because of Alice's own behavior and also because of children's own cruelty, they are starting to jump away when Alice comes near them, or they step back in line so they don't have to be near her. She has the talent for being in the wrong place at the wrong time.

Alice is a very lovable, troubled little girl. I feel she would have a better chance at learning if she felt better about herself. She can't concentrate on her lessons or much of anything because she is so worried about failing at everything. Her attitude each day, as I see her, is one of defeat before she even starts. I don't want to see Alice shut down. She has potential. Her greatest assets are her beautiful singing voice and [being] very lovable.

The image of her daughter taping herself to her desk broke Nancy's heart. "It was like she was telling us this was the only way she could make herself sit still," Nancy says.

Nancy sought advice from the teacher, who recommended that Nancy call the Illinois child protection agency for help. In recent years, many state child protection agencies, including the one in Illinois, have begun trying to provide help to children in stressful situations, not just abusive or neglectful ones. A social worker referred Nancy and Alice to a private agency called Cry for Help for counseling. It took only a few sessions for Alice to reveal what was bothering her. She had been molested again, two years ago—by the twelve-year-old daughter of the cousin whom Nancy had trusted enough to baby-sit Alice while she worked.

"Alice told the therapist that the girl would put on Madonna's videotape *Truth or Dare* while she had oral sex on her," Nancy says, weeping as she recounts the details. "For it to happen to her one time was bad enough. But a second time, and her not being able to tell me for two years? How much can a child take?" (Five years later, Alice still struggles with the memories. "Not too long ago she came to me and asked me, 'Because of what Cindy did to me, does that mean I'm gay?'" Nancy says.)

Since Alice got mostly Ds and Fs in school that year, Nancy asked school officials to require her to repeat second grade and to test her for learning disabilities. "She didn't like me very much for a while, but it put her with a better class of children," Nancy says. "They don't make fun of her as much."

Diagnostic testing found no identifiable learning disabilities. But the Children's Depression Inventory, based on self-ratings, gave her high scores in negative mood, interpersonal problems, anhedonia (a diminished capacity to experience pleasure), and negative self-esteem. Her teachers rated her in the ninety-eighth percentile in hyperactivity, and above the ninety-eighth percentile for the following traits: anxious, socially withdrawn, unpopular, self-destructive, obsessive-compulsive, inattentive, and aggressive.

As a result of that evaluation, school officials classified Alice as behaviorally disordered. The label entitles her to receive thirty minutes a day of special education services, such as individualized instruction and review of material, and Nancy believes she's benefited from the extra help.

Although Alice's second-grade teacher reported that the special help made her more manageable at school, she was no better at home. She threw temper tantrums, woke up frequently with night terrors, engaged in constant power struggles with her mother, and reported hearing voices. Nancy began to be afraid of her. "She used to tell me, 'So-and-so told me to kill you.' And once she pushed Benji's stroller right out into the street, on purpose," Nancy says.

Nancy took her to a psychiatrist. He put Alice on an antidepressant and, later, on antipsychotic drugs, for more than two years. Within the last year, she's been weaned from her psychotropic medications, and the voices have not returned. Her teachers report a better attitude at school. Last spring, she received third place in a schoolwide "young authors" competition, and an A in music.

But she still fails to complete assignments regularly, and her quarterly report cards are still marred by several Ds and Fs. Her health and self-image remain a concern. She's only recently turned 12, yet she weighs 234 pounds and wears a woman's size 24 dress. "With her family's medical history, [Alice] is a walking time bomb," says the physician assistant who treats her.

For the last two weeks, Alice has been visiting her mother's sister in Chicago. She'll stay for another month or so. Both her mother and Benji miss her terribly, but Nancy acknowledges that without her at home, the house is a much calmer place. "She needed a break from me, and I needed one from her," she explains.

An Unbalanced Budget

It's the third of the month, and today's mail has brought a Social Security check for $252, the monthly stipend the two children receive because their father is disabled. Benji's monthly SSI (supplemental social insurance) check—$388—arrived two days ago, so Nancy has a total of $640 to spread among her creditors until she gets the rest of her monthly income—$83 from welfare and $100 from baby-sitting—in 12 days. Altogether, her income right now totals $885 a month, or $10,620 a year. In 1997 the poverty threshold for a family of three was $12,802.

This is only the second month that Nancy has income from baby-sitting. In an attempt to bring more money into the home, she's agreed to care for Timothy, an affectionate three-year-old, while his mother works the afternoon shift, 3:00 to 11:00 P.M., at a nearby factory. Because Timothy's mother uses a state subsidy to pay for his care, Nancy has had to agree to limit her charges to $8.98 a day, or about $1 an hour. So the most Nancy can expect to earn each month from baby-sitting is $162.

When Nancy reported her baby-sitting income last month, as required, to the state Department of Public Aid, the agency reduced her monthly welfare check to $81 from $131. The family's food stamps were also cut, to $95 a month from $131. So Nancy's really just bringing in an extra $86 a month by baby-sitting—less than $.50 an hour, or a little over $4 a day. It's not very much, Nancy acknowledges, but it's almost like free money, since she's usually at home taking care of Benji anyway. An added benefit of baby-sitting is that because it gives her earned income, she'll be able to apply for an Earned Income Tax Credit next year.

Here's what the family's budget looks like this month:

INCOME

Social Security benefits	$242
Benji's SSI benefit	388
Public aid	83
Baby-sitting earnings	162
Subtotal	$875
Food stamps	95
Total	$970

EXPENSES

House payment	$81
Cable TV	38
Water and gas	80
Electricity	300
Installment payment for vacuum cleaner	16
Phone	80
Car insurance	43
Food	350
Total	$988

Although Nancy's budget doesn't look very good on paper, the reality is even worse. For one thing, her budget doesn't include any payments on the $6,000 she owes the state student loan program. For the time being, she's given up trying to keep current on her required $50-a-month payments and, as a result, has been receiving increasingly threatening letters from the program's collection agency. (The loan was for $4,500, but interest and collection fees have increased it to over $6,000.)

The unpaid debt means that Nancy can't borrow to go back to school to get an LPN credential, something she once aspired to. And though she doesn't know it yet, it probably means that any tax re-

funds she's owed for the next few years, including the Earned Income Tax Credit she hopes to receive for the first time next year, will
be seized to satisfy the debt.

Most worrisome to her at the moment is that there's no cushion
in her budget for emergencies, or even for the periodic extra
expenses that come with owning a home. For instance, in two
months, Nancy has to come up with $200 to pay the first half of
her annual real estate tax bill; another $200 is due the following
month. And just two months after that, her annual homeowners'
insurance premium of $305 is due. Nancy's just realized that she
should have established an escrow account and had one-twelfth of
the tax bill and of the homeowners' insurance premium rolled into
her monthly mortgage payment. But as a first-time homeowner, she
didn't know that was the customary practice. And she's not sure
how she would have come up with the money every month anyway.

"I just can't seem to keep current with my bills," Nancy says.
"There was a time, I guess, when I was caught up, but I can't remember when. It seems like something's always coming up. All
spring I had sinus problems, and I had to take Claritin D. It costs
$32 for a month's supply, and Medicaid doesn't pay it. And then my
van went out. It had to go into the shop, and I had to pay for some
repairs. It's things like that."

The van is a story in itself. Just before Christmas 1996, Nancy got
a call from Mary Donner, the physician assistant who regularly takes
care of her children. Mary's Sunday school class wanted to sponsor
a family for Christmas, and she had suggested the Keeblers. Nancy
was both embarrassed and pleased, because she knew she wasn't going to be able to do much for her children that Christmas. "They
gave my kids a fantastic Christmas," Nancy says, "and Mary and I
became friends."

As Mary got to know Nancy, Mary learned that the old car that
Nancy's father had left her when he died had recently stopped running, and that Nancy had no way to get Benji back and forth to
physical therapy or doctor's appointments. So Mary and her husband bought the family an '85 Plymouth Voyager for $1,500.

"It wasn't nothing to write home about, but it was a miracle to
me," Nancy says. "How many times does somebody go out and buy
somebody else a car?"

Mary explains her involvement with the Keeblers this way: "I don't know anyone in this world who's been more blessed than I have been, nor anybody who struggles more than Nancy. There's something really remarkable about Nancy, really endearing. She never expresses any bitterness about her situation. And she's so appreciative of any help—not just appreciative, but awed that someone would want to help her. Her response is always, 'Why are you doing this for me? I don't deserve this.'"

But with the car came problems of the sort you'd expect of a twelve-year-old car with 170,000 miles on the engine. "Only a week or so after I got it, the transmission went out," Nancy says. "I went back to the man who sold it to me and told him I thought he knew he was selling me a problem. I told him that he should make it right with me, and that if he didn't, God would take it into account. Well, he didn't do anything, but Mary and some of my friends went around town to a bunch of churches and raised $700 to buy a rebuilt transmission."

The car worked more or less well for seventeen months. But a few weeks ago, the engine locked up, and Nancy's mechanic told her it couldn't be fixed. She sold the car for scrap for $50. She hasn't gotten up the nerve to tell Mary, because she fears Mary will think she'll expect her to buy a replacement.

"It'll all work out somehow," Nancy says. "It had better, because I've got to have a car. I've got to get Benji to physical therapy twice a week."

A House That's Also a Home

Even with the extra expenses that come with homeownership, it's hard not to view the little house with the decorative well in the front yard as the best thing that ever happened to the Keebler family.

"I thank God every day for my house, that he got me out of public housing," Nancy says. "There are some nice people in [public] housing, but more and more there seem to be people without goals who spend their time causing problems for other people. Where I live now, everybody keeps to themselves and minds their own business. It's nice."

Fourteen months after the family moved in, the house has the feel of a home. On the front door, Nancy has hung a plastic angel that bears the message, "A mother is a blessing of love." Curtains hang above all the windows—a pink eyelet valance in the bathroom, off-white lace valances in the living room, and a cheerful green print in the kitchen that coordinates with the linoleum on the floor and Nancy's new set of dishes.

In the bedroom that Nancy and Benji share because he has to be turned several times during the night, Nancy has hung a cabbage rose wallpaper border and artfully arranged family photos and a doll collection. The living room furniture—a brown velveteen-covered couch and matching swivel rocker—was a recent gift to the Keeblers from a family that was getting new furniture.

Nowhere in the house is anything out of place, except for whatever toys Benji happens to be playing with at the moment. "I don't believe in making a child play in his bedroom," Nancy explains. "I believe he should be able to play wherever he wants to, as long as it's safe."

How Nancy ended up with her name on the deed to a house is testimony to her resourcefulness. Alice's child protection caseworker had sent Nancy a flyer about a new federal homebuyers' program. The caseworker was concerned about the Keeblers' ability to continue to live in public housing. Their two-story apartment was totally unsuitable for a child who couldn't walk and a mother with serious medical problems of her own. The bedrooms and bathroom were on the second floor, and Nancy had to carry Benji up and down several times a day.

"Life is full of miracles," proclaimed the flyer for the homebuyers' program.

> Like finding out you can own a home. For over sixty years, the Farmers Home Administration has helped over 20 million people become homeowners. And we can help you get into a home of your own as well. With an FHA loan, your down payment could be as little as a few months' rent. And you don't need to have perfect credit or a high-paying job to qualify. Depending upon the house you buy, your monthly payments may not be much more than your rent.

It sounded too good to be true, but Nancy, who believes in miracles, decided to check it out. She found out that she would have no trouble getting over the first hurdle: the program was open only to families with an income of no more than 80 percent of the area's median family income.

The next hurdle was much higher and designed to weed out the unmotivated. To even apply, Nancy had to complete more than a dozen workshops relating to all aspects of home purchase and ownership, from finding the right house to avoiding foreclosure. Because of the difficulty of finding care for Benji, it was hard for Nancy to attend them all, but she did, except for the last one. (And for that absence, she had a good excuse. The neighbor who took care of Benji during the workshops had been hospitalized, and Nancy was caring for *her* three children.)

The final hurdle was coming up with a down payment amounting to 3 percent of the purchase price, or $810. Nancy had only $200 in savings, but Alice's caseworker found her a grant for the rest from a program designed to help people with disabilities move into accessible housing.

Then came the fun part—finding a house. Nancy found the two-bedroom house that fronts on a state highway all by herself. The price was $27,000, well within the amount she'd been told she could spend.

"I'd been looking at this house for a long time, because I could tell it was empty, and I thought the neighborhood was nice," she explained. The house was about forty years old and had had only one owner. No repairs or improvements had been made for years, so it was in pretty bad shape. But the Western Egyptian Economic Opportunity Council, which administers the homebuyers' program in Nancy's area, found Nancy a zero-interest loan of $17,800 to pay for repairs, a new furnace, a two-hundred-square foot addition, and modifications to make it wheelchair-accessible. If she lives there ten years, she won't have to repay the repair loan.

With the federal mortgage subsidy, the Keeblers' monthly payment is less than half of what they paid for public housing. (It will rise if their income rises.) Nancy's already looking forward to the day she can burn the mortgage. "I'll be sixty-six years old when it's all paid for," she says, laughing.

"I'm a Follower"

But there are a lot of years to make it through before then, and Nancy feels weighted down by the pressure to come up with a plan to increase her family's income without jeopardizing health coverage for herself and the children.

During the national welfare reform fervor of 1995, Illinois imposed a five-year lifetime limit on welfare benefits. "Public Aid's pushing everybody to get off welfare, and even though we only get $83 a month now, if I lose it, I've got to have a way of replacing it," Nancy says. The welfare payment isn't as important to Nancy as the Medicaid coverage that comes with it. Both Nancy's and Alice's eligibility for Medicaid is linked to their status as welfare recipients. (As long as his family is considered low-income, Benji's disability assures him of continuing coverage.) Without Medicaid, Nancy doesn't know how she'd pay for the daily insulin injections that keep her alive or for her frequent hospitalizations.

Nancy has tried to work numerous times in the past but has always run into baby-sitting problems: none of the licensed child-care providers in town will care for Benji. (They say he's too heavy for them to lift, but Nancy suspects they just don't want to deal with all of his problems.) When Benji begins attending school full days next year, Nancy might be able to get a lunch-rush job at a fast-food restaurant or at Wal-Mart (assuming she has a way to get there). But for now she's concluded that working in her home is the only way she can both earn income and take good care of Benji.

Almost as soon as the family moved into the house, Nancy started thinking about how well suited it would be for a home-based child-care center. It has a full basement that would make a nice playroom, with easy access to the backyard.

Alice's child protection caseworker encouraged Nancy to develop her idea and brought her information about state regulations. Illinois requires baby-sitters to obtain a state license if they're caring for more than three children, including their own. With a license, Nancy could care for up to seven children, she learned. If she charged $1 an hour for each of them, and each was with her for forty hours a week, she could gross $280 a week, she figured—an income that would raise her family above the poverty line and entitle her to an Earned Income Tax Credit of up to $2,000.

But Nancy's planning came to a standstill recently when she learned that restrictions attached to her federally subsidized mortgage forbid her to use her home as a business. She probably shouldn't even be baby-sitting for one child.

Nancy has written to the head of the program and to her congress-man to ask that the rule be changed, to no avail. "My friends tell me I ought to make a fuss, that it's the squeaky wheel that gets the oil," says Nancy. "But I don't want to stir up anything if it means I could lose the house. And anyway, I'm not a leader. I'm a follower."

"I Admire the Fact That She Keeps Going"

This morning, Nancy is wearing a T-shirt bearing the message "God Is My Co-Pilot." At 10:00 A.M., a teenager, Linda, arrives to take care of Benji for a few hours so that Nancy can clean the house of a friend, Becky Grant. Linda's the same baby-sitter who let Benji crawl around outside last week and get blisters all over his feet, so Nancy spends a few minutes making sure she understands how important it is that he stay inside today (and then she writes it down for good measure). When she crosses the room to kiss Benji good-bye, he's al-ready whimpering. "It's okay, sweetie, Mama's just going to be gone for a few hours," she reassures him. "Linda will take good care of you."

Nancy's been cleaning Becky's house once a week for the last month, ever since Becky lent her $200 to pay some bills. "She gives me a $20 credit every time I clean and pays the baby-sitter, too," Nancy says. The two women are good friends. Without Becky's sup-port over the last five years, it's not clear that Nancy and her chil-dren would be doing as well as they are. In fact, it's possible that Nancy wouldn't be alive. Becky was the person Alice called when she found her mother lying unconscious on the floor of the bath-room last summer, her blood sugar level dangerously high. Becky took care of Alice and Benji while Nancy was hospitalized for a few days.

Becky met Nancy five years ago, about a week after Nancy had given birth to Benji. "I saw this young woman across a room, and I could tell that she was in need somehow," Becky recalls. "She looked miserable. People think I'm strange, but the Lord talks to me, and he told me to help her."

A few weeks later, Becky went by Nancy's apartment to check on how she was doing. "By then, Benji was home, and he was crying all the time," Becky recalls. "They were new to the area, and she really didn't know anyone. So every now and then, I'd just go by and see her, just to give her support. We became friends, and then we got a Bible study going, four or five of us, so we saw each other a lot."

Maybe a half-dozen times over the last five years, Becky has sensed that Nancy was in the throes of a financial crisis, even though she never brought it up. That's how the most recent loan came about.

"One day, I could sense that she was upset about something, and I asked her what was going on," Becky says. "She said, 'It's my bills. I just don't know what I'm going to do.'

"I said, 'How much would it take for you to get caught up?' And she said, 'About $200.'

"I told her, 'I'll go down and pay the water bill and give you $100 to pay the other bills, and you can work it off.'"

Becky is not a rich woman by any stretch of the imagination. Her husband is a factory worker, and she baby-sits part-time. But she's a born giver. The Keebler family is just one of many around town that benefit from her kindnesses. (Another is the family of the teenager who's baby-sitting for Benji today. "See, by paying her to baby-sit Benji, I'm helping her and Nancy, too, and neither thinks they're accepting charity," she says.)

Why does she do it?

"The reason I'm willing to do this for her is because I've been there," Becky says. "I've been in a situation where I've felt like there's no tomorrow, and people have helped me out, and I feel like I'm paying them back by helping Nancy."

And why Nancy? Because Nancy is the type of woman who inspires people to want to help, Becky explains. "She's had a lot of things to overcome," Becky says. "I love Benji to death, but he's a challenge. I don't think I could handle a child who can't stand to have me out of his sight. She's got a lot of strengths. I admire the fact that she keeps going."

"On a Roller Coaster"

When Nancy gets home from cleaning, Benji is asleep on the floor under a blanket, and Linda is on the phone, as teenage baby-sitters are wont to be. Nancy pays the baby-sitter with money that Becky's given her and then sits down at her kitchen table to test her blood sugar. While she had been cleaning, Becky badgered her about taking better care of herself, and her message seems to have registered. A month ago, Nancy's blood sugar had soared to 800 milligrams per deciliter (mg/dL) of blood (70–110 mg/dL is normal) after she cut her hand with a knife and developed an infection. She had to be hospitalized while her blood sugar was stabilized and her medication adjusted.

As she sets up her portable glucose monitor, Nancy admits that she hasn't tested her blood sugar in a week. Why not? "It's just too depressing to see readings of 200 and even 300 when I'm taking my insulin injections and eating like I should," she says. "It makes me feel like I'm on a roller coaster, with no control."

The memory in the blood glucose machine shows that Nancy's last reading was 149 mg/dL. "That was a really good reading for me," she says. "It's when it gets over 200 that my doctor worries. That's when organ damage occurs."

Nancy pricks her finger with a lance and squeezes the blood onto the litmus paper. Sixty seconds pass as the machine analyzes her blood. The reading flashes on the screen: 291.

"It must have been that hamburger you fed me," she says, trying to laugh it off. "You see why I don't test more often? Now I'll be depressed all day."

Nancy has a strong family history of diabetes and its complications. A first cousin her age, also diabetic, has just had two fingers amputated, and another diabetic cousin is about to have several toes amputated. Nancy's already showing signs of nerve damage in her feet and hands. She worries about going blind, having her kidneys fail, or losing her ability to walk—all possible consequences of severe diabetes, along with an early death.

Mary Donner, the physician assistant who treats her, says of Nancy's condition: "She doesn't seem to want to grasp how serious her illness is. I just had a twenty-nine-year-old patient, very much like Nancy, found dead in her trailer last week. Neither I nor the doctor have been able to get through to Nancy how devastating this illness is, and the need for her to get it under control, for the sake of her kids. I've said to her: 'Nancy, I know how much you love your children. You would die for them. Why can't you see how important this is?'"

Nancy's response? In a barely audible voice, and with tears welling in her eyes, she says: "I do worry about what would happen to my children if something happened to me."

A Belief in Prayers and Miracles

The future carries with it a whole different set of potential complications for the Keeblers than it does for many other poor families.

As Nancy tries to earn enough to raise her family out of poverty, she has to be sure not to earn so much that she jeopardizes Benji's SSI status, which depends both on being disabled and being poor. If he loses SSI eligibility, he also loses Medicaid coverage, and with Benji's health problems, private insurance would cost a fortune, if he could even get it.

Nancy's own health problems will make it difficult for her to get medical insurance when she loses her Medicaid coverage after her welfare eligibility is exhausted in five years. (She'll lose her eligibility even sooner if she begins to earn too much money to continue to qualify.) With her health problems, she probably couldn't even get private insurance, and even if she could, she certainly couldn't afford it.

Then there's Alice's future to think about. Nancy worries that Alice might become schizophrenic, like Nancy's mother. "I don't want to think that that's what's wrong with her, but I don't know," Nancy says. "She doesn't hear voices anymore, which is good, but I keep worrying that they'll start up again."

And Alice's weight puts her at risk for a whole host of medical conditions, not the least of which, with her family history, is diabetes. "She'd eat all the time if I let her," Nancy says. "I just don't know how to make her stop."

Then, of course, there's the most obvious concern: Benji's disabilities.

"My most fervent wish for the future is that Benji will someday walk and be a normal child," Nancy says. "Benji's showing progress, though it's real slow. But I believe in prayers and miracles.

"You know, there's a guy who writes a column in a newspaper, Percy Ross, about how he gives away money to people who need it. Well, I wrote him a letter once. I told him that I needed a good running van that I could have Specialized Services put a wheelchair lift in for me. I even sent him a copy of Benji's evaluation so that he would know I wasn't lying to him about Benji's problems.

"But I never did hear back from him. Like Benji's dad said, he probably gets requests like that from millions of people. I guess our problems aren't as bad as other people's."

Despite everything, Nancy is fundamentally optimistic. "If I could start over, there are a lot of things I would have done differently with my life," she says. "For one thing, I wouldn't have had a baby without being married, and I would have finished college. Because of those two mistakes, I struggle every day to survive.

"I get depressed, like everybody else, but I'm not depressed all the time," she continues. "I accept the way my life is, but I don't think that's the way it has to be. I don't believe in fate, that this is the hand you're dealt, so that's the way things are going to be.

"Life is full of choices. Whatever choice you make, whether it's right or wrong, if you believe in God, he's going to stay with you and see you through it."

4

HONOLULU, HAWAII

According to the federal poverty guidelines, the five children in the Likio family of Honolulu, Hawaii, are no longer officially poor. But their lives are hardly what you'd call comfortable.

Occasionally, lack of medical and dental care allows minor illnesses or dental problems to develop into major ones.

Sometimes they don't have enough to eat.

Almost always, their clothes are someone else's castoffs.

Yet each of the five children in this family has been affected differently by the material deprivation that has characterized their lives since birth. One is floundering, while others have flourished. For some, it's too early to predict how things will work out.

The oldest, Keanu, now twenty and living away from home, seems least likely to overcome the disabling effects of his family's extreme poverty during the first decade of his life. He dropped out of school in the tenth grade and has already fathered four children by a woman twelve years his senior. He's been in trouble with the law several times, and his mother fears for his safety.

The second child, Kalani, eighteen, has all the makings of a success story. He was the first person on his mother's side of the family to finish high school and now attends Hawaii Pacific University. But he's continually torn between his desire to earn a degree and the knowledge that his family would be better off in the short run if he quit school and went to work.

The third child, Kawailani, sixteen, qualified for a coveted slot at an elite private school when he was just five. But he begged his parents to let him give it up at the end of sixth grade as the desire to fit in with the other kids in his public housing project grew too strong to resist.

The fourth child, Keola, thirteen, has found a focus in Polynesian dancing and sports. But she, more than her brothers, yearns for the accoutrements of middle-class life—cable TV, a telephone, some nice clothes, regular spending money.

Since she's only ten, the youngest child, Elena, remains sublimely innocent of how poor her family really is. Yet she's the one who has suffered what may be lifelong ill effects from poor nutrition and inadequate medical care.

The Likios' story shows how hard it can be for a family to break out of poverty even when one parent works full-time and has a vision for a better life. But the family's story also provides some insights into how a poor family nurtures hope. "When I was growing up, there was never any talk in my house about going to college," recalls Jeanette Likio, the children's mother. "There was never even any expectation of graduating from high school. All of the kids in my family dropped out as soon as we could, in eighth or ninth or tenth grade.

"I decided what I wanted for my kids was for them to graduate from high school and go to college. Education is the key to everything."

Poverty Amid Plenty

It's midmorning in Honolulu. Scores of video camera–toting tourists are heading out to the Atlantis submarines, at $89 a trip, for an up-close look at Oahu's coral reef. A few shoppers are already emerging from the Ferragamo boutique, their shopping bags bulging with $450 purses and $350 pairs of shoes.

Five miles from the tourist glitz of Waikiki Beach, Jeanette Likio wrestles a baby crib, a stroller, and four battered kitchen chairs into the back of a pickup truck. The items are going to a poor family that gets help from the social service agency she works for. When her visitor points out the irony of her mission today—her own six-member family has only one kitchen chair, which means some of them sit on the floor to eat—she breaks into a broad grin. "Maybe I should get one of our workers to fill out a voucher for me, yeah?" she jokes.

Jeanette is a family development specialist for the Head Start and Early Head Start programs run by Parents and Children Together (PACT), a social service agency that helps poor families in some of Honolulu's grimmest housing projects. She helps parent-child educators, home visitors, and teachers obtain second-hand items for needy families, as she's doing today. She sets up child abuse, substance abuse, and domestic violence prevention workshops for parents. She trains parents to be advocates for their children. She even drives the agency's twenty-passenger school bus on field trips.

Unbeknownst to most of her coworkers, Jeanette struggles daily with many of the same problems that afflict her agency's clients, including substandard housing, unpaid bills, and the lingering effects of teen parenthood and domestic violence.

Jeanette, thirty-six, a short, stout woman with a melodic accent, is the sole regular breadwinner for her household of six. In 1997 she earned $23,278—just above the official poverty threshold of $21,886 for a family of the Likios' size. Her husband, Bobby, thirty-nine, seems bedeviled by memories of his abuse-filled childhood and hasn't held a steady job in years, though he earns a little money by umpiring kids' softball games and collecting and selling shellfish. Most of Bobby's earnings go directly to their children, in $1 and $5 handouts that take the place of regular allowances.

"I Realized We Were Poor"

Jeanette spent her early childhood on Kauai, one of Hawaii's bigger islands. The oldest of four children, Jeanette remembers her early childhood as a time of simple pleasures, when she was blissfully unaware of her family's station in life. "We played with seeds and berries and chased the pigs and chickens," she says. "We didn't have any proper toys."

When Jeanette was in sixth grade, her family secured an apartment in Palolo Valley Homes, the public housing project in Honolulu where they all still live. Family life was chaotic when she was growing up, Jeanette says. "My parents were always drinking, and my cousins were always smoking *pakalolo* [marijuana]," she recalls. "Everybody was always swearing and hitting each other. At our aunties' houses, it was the same. At my friends' houses, too. It was the norm. I didn't know there was another way to live."

At fifteen, Jeanette became pregnant, a common fate for girls growing up in Palolo Valley Homes, then and now. She dropped out of the tenth grade. The baby's father was Bobby, a "Waikiki boy" who spent his days surfing and making puka necklaces for the tourist trade.

Bobby had been born in 1958 in Western Samoa. When he was six, his mother and father and three younger sisters moved to Honolulu so that his mother could get medical treatment for a heart condition. For financial reasons, Bobby and several older siblings were left behind. For almost six years, the children bounced from one relative's home to another, by Bobby's account each one worse than the last. "I still have nightmares about the treatment I got," he says.

When Bobby was twelve, his parents finally sent for him and his brother. They flew alone to Honolulu, where they were met by a family they hadn't seen for almost six years. The sisters spoke English; Bobby and his brother spoke Samoan and pidgin English. "I could hardly talk to my sisters," he says. "They'd say to me, 'You're not really our brother.'"

Still, Bobby was happy to be with his family, and he fell in love with Hawaii. "At first, I thought, 'This is heaven,'" he says. "Nobody in the United States is allowed to treat their children the way my uncles treated me."

Bobby's parents enrolled him in sixth grade, which was appropriate for his age. But it was a big challenge for Bobby, since he hadn't attended school for several years and couldn't read or write English. As he made his way through middle school, he began skipping school to surf. "Surfing became my pride and joy," he says.

Feeling he could never make up for the school years he'd missed, Bobby quit school in ninth grade and left home to escape his father's beatings. For years, he slept on the beaches on the North Shore or on friends' couches. "Sometimes we stole food to survive," he says. Of the two dozen youths with whom he hung out, he's the only one who's never been sent to prison. Two are dead from street violence.

Jeanette: From Welfare to Work

After their child, Keanu, was born, Jeanette and Bobby fell into the same kind of domestic routine followed by many of the other young couples in the housing project: Bobby went off surfing during the day and Jeanette stayed home to care for Keanu. Jeanette and Keanu continued to live with her parents, and Bobby with friends. The couple's major source of income was Jeanette's welfare check; sometimes Bobby qualified for general assistance. As of the last census, about half the residents of their neighborhood depended on public assistance or Social Security for income; only one-fourth had income from wages or salaries. For years, Hawaii has had a welfare dependency rate significantly higher than that of the United States as a whole, second only to California's.

As Keanu became a toddler and the couple got more serious about each other, Bobby, nearing twenty, began feeling that it was time to settle down. So, in 1978, he joined the Army Reserve/National Guard. "There went the hair and the surfboard," he says with a laugh.

Bobby loved the National Guard. The military provided him with his first trip ever to the mainland—to Fort Benning, Georgia, and Fort Knox, Kentucky, where he first saw snow—and a half-dozen other trips over the fifteen years he served. It opened his eyes to a world he had heard about but never before seen. The training didn't give him any marketable skills, he says, "but I learned ironing, sewing, sweeping, waxing floors, washing dishes, and polishing shoes. Even today, if my kids need something sewn, they come to me." The pay wasn't great, but there was always the promise of retirement benefits twenty years down the road.

Soon after Jeanette got pregnant with her second child, her name reached the top of the waiting list for a two-bedroom apartment of her own in Palolo Valley Homes, and Bobby moved in with her. A son, Kalani, was born in 1979, and another son, Kawailani, followed in 1981. The couple married in 1983 when Jeanette was pregnant with their first daughter, Keola. The couple's last child, Elena, followed in 1987.

As they matured, Jeanette and Bobby both took on leadership roles in the Palolo community. When Keanu was five and begging to play baseball, Bobby signed him up with the Palolo Little League. Soon after Keanu joined the team, the coach had a heart attack, and Bobby, who had never played ball himself, became the team's coach and Jeanette the manager. "I had to teach him the rules," she says with a laugh.

That first year, the team was second to last in the league. The next year, it took second place. In each of the next six years, it won the championship. "No team could touch us," Bobby brags, his eyes lighting up as they survey the trophies that adorn the living room.

When the children entered Head Start, and later elementary school, Jeanette became active in parents' organizations. Her involvement in the local PTA led to a part-time job as a teacher's aide in Project Follow Through, a federally financed program for impoverished schools. She did so well that the school hired her for a more demanding position with emotionally disturbed special education students. And she became chairwoman of the policy council of the local Head Start center, which was then run by Parent-Child Center of Hawaii (the precursor to PACT). In 1987, when she was pregnant with Elena, the Parent-Child Center hired her as a "parent involvement assistant," at a salary of $700 a month.

"She was only twenty-six years old, but she knew a lot," says Jo Jo Teixeira, a coworker and friend who often gives Jeanette a ride home from work. "I don't know how she knew so much—just from being a mom, I guess, and from being active with Head Start. She knew the regs inside out. In fact, she taught the staff. And it's still the same today. We learn from her."

Diana Buckley, who hired Jeanette, says of her: "Jeanette had great spirit. She could connect with all types of people. She had incredible insight into people and was always able to hone in on the real issue. And she wasn't prone to pick sides but rather acted as a peacemaker and natural diplomat among people with differing views. She was a tremendous link and articulate spokesperson between the parents and the agency and other policymakers."

Working at the Parent-Child Center gave Jeanette the boost in confidence she needed to seek a GED. Without even taking any cram courses, she passed the test on the first try. Later she took a few classes at a local community college, working toward an associate's degree. She did well but never finished.

"There were too many other demands on me," she says, almost apologetically. "I couldn't do my job, and take care of my kids, and go to school." Even without a degree, she was doing well at work, mastering computer skills, becoming more confident about leading meetings, and tackling writing projects. She was being given more and more responsibility and getting regular raises.

Bobby: "It's Too Late"

While Jeanette was making steady progress in her job, Bobby's work experience was erratic. Things started to fall apart for him in 1992, when he required knee surgery. It left him unable to pass the annual physical for the Reserves, and he was forced to take a medical discharge the following year and forgo any hope of retirement benefits. He began seeing another woman and using an illegal stimulant known as "ice" (crystal methamphetamine), a major problem among Polynesians in Hawaii. Then he got in a dispute with a supervisor at the public housing project where he worked as a nighttime security guard, and he quit. Since then, he seems to have been overcome with self-pity and feelings of worthlessness.

"I've been hurting so much, I didn't know what to do," Bobby says. "I thought, 'Man, every time I get into something I really like, to help build up my family, something brings me down.' The whole thing made me fold into my self and shrink."

When he was using drugs, he sometimes took out his rage on Jeanette. Finally, a few years ago, Jeanette took the children and moved into a shelter. The children were miserable there, so after a week Jeanette moved back home and threw Bobby out. "I told him we weren't going to put up with it anymore," she says. "No fooling around. No abuse. No drugs, no alcohol."

Once home, the children missed their father terribly and begged Jeanette to let him return home. After a month apart, the couple reconciled, though Jeanette today describes the marriage mostly as a relationship of convenience. She has little patience with Bobby's seeming lack of ambition and his inability to find work. He spends his days fishing, playing men's slow-pitch softball, umpiring kids' softball games, and running errands and cleaning house for a disabled neighbor. "I always tell the kids, 'It's okay if we're poor,'" he says. "I've been poor from the beginning. Mom's been poor from the beginning. As long as the Lord is with us, we can survive."

But there have been signs in the last year or so that Bobby is trying to pull his life back together. A year ago, he rededicated himself to the Catholic religion into which he was born and hasn't missed weekend Mass since. He no longer uses drugs. He says he's trying to build up his self-confidence and start looking for security work again, though with an overall unemployment rate of 6 percent in 1998—and much higher for residents of Polynesian descent—Hawaii isn't an easy place to find work. Its economy, heavily dependent on tourism, is in a deep recession, with few prospects for growth.

"If I had the education Jeanette had, maybe I'd have gotten somewhere," he says. "I didn't finish high school. But I can't do that over. It's too late."

"Another Way to Live"

It's the eve of Jeanette's thirty-seventh birthday. She's bone-tired from a long day at work, starting at 7:00 A.M. with a meeting and ending at 5:30 P.M., when she finishes up the last of her paperwork. She snacks on some leftover tuna salad from the office refrigerator and tucks an orange into her purse before locking up.

Traffic is terrible on H1, Honolulu's main thoroughfare, but today she's getting a ride home, so at least she doesn't have to endure an hour-long bus ride and then the long walk up the hill to Palolo Valley Homes. Jeanette begins to relax as the car makes its way up the valley to the housing project. "I just love how these mountains look at this time of day," she says.

It may just be the most beautiful setting for a public housing complex anywhere. The 424-unit low-rise complex fills a beautiful valley just fifteen minutes from Waikiki. A stream runs through it, and in the hills above, there's plenty of space for children to roam. Mountains rise steeply on three sides, their color changing from purplish black to green to reddish gold as the sun makes its way to the ocean horizon on the west. At night, lights begin twinkling in the mansions that perch on the surrounding hillsides, creating a magical air.

The sun is low in the sky as Jeanette walks up to her front door, moving a tricycle out of the way and straightening the jumble of shoes on the stoop. (In the Polynesian tradition, family members and visitors leave their shoes outside the front door.) Pasted on the front door is a bumper sticker that proclaims, "There's No Excuse for Domestic Violence," a not-so-subtle reminder to Bobby that Jeanette won't tolerate any abuse. (As a joke, someone has blacked out some of the letters on the bumper sticker, altering the message to read,

"There's Excuses for Domestic Violence." Jeanette doesn't think it's very funny.)

The Likios live in a 965-square-foot apartment in the complex, which has a reputation as a rough place. Four out of nine preschool-aged children in the area are officially poor; among preschool-aged children of Asian or Pacific Islander descent, like the Likios, far more children live below the poverty line than above it. One of three adults is, like both Jeanette and Bobby, a high school dropout.

The Likios' two-story unit is in a multifamily building that faces an identical building across a patch of grass. From the outside, most of the units are indistinguishable; only the Likios and one other family have planted gardens in their tiny front yards. As in many public housing projects, there's little privacy. On any given night, you can hear the raised voices of a couple arguing a few doors down, the piercing cry of a newborn next door, the throb of rap music from across the courtyard.

Once inside, Jeanette exchanges her work clothes for a *lavalava* skirt, created on the spot from a large colorful cloth. She settles into their old worn couch, upholstered in a garish orange floral print, and puts her feet up. Her oldest daughter, Keola, sits down beside her and begins rubbing her back.

The Likios' apartment includes a living room, kitchen, tiny bedroom, and half-bath downstairs, and three small bedrooms and a bath upstairs. The lights are fluorescent, the walls concrete block, the floors linoleum, the screens torn. The family currently pays $454 a month in rent. (The rent is pegged to the family's income and rises as Jeanette's salary goes up.)

Jeanette has furnished the apartment with items gleaned from dumpsters, bought from thrift shops, or handed down by relatives and friends. The only household item purchased new was the big-screen TV that Bobby bought a few years ago, back when he was working full-time. But for the last few years, the family hasn't been able to afford the cable hookup needed for reception in this mountain valley, so the TV is usable only for viewing videos. Even so, it's rarely turned on, since the electricity bill is a constant worry. Even without heat or air conditioning, electricity costs at least $100 a month, no matter how vigilantly Bobby switches off lights every time he leaves a room.

When it comes time to sleep, only the children settle into beds. Bobby stretches out on a living room couch, Jeanette on the living room floor. (Right now, Elena is sleeping on the other couch because her mattress was ruined when a neighbor's toilet overflowed, sending water cascading through the ceiling of her first-floor bedroom.)

The two girls, Keola and Elena, are excited about having a guest. They don hula skirts, put on a videotape of a Samoan dance performance two of their brothers were in last year, and dance along. Both have long, black hair that hangs below their waists, in classic Polynesian style, and their performance is mesmerizing. Keola, in particular, is a graceful dancer and has earned a place as one of the leaders of her *halau* (hula dance school). When she dances, she has the focused look of a professional, with every hand gesture meaningful, every sway of the hips a message.

No matter how tight the household budget, Jeanette had always made sure that there was money for the children's *halau* fees—$25 per month per child. But when Bobby left his last job, it got tougher to find the money. As resourceful as her mother, Keola found a Christian *halau* that charges no fees, though participants commit to seemingly endless fund-raising projects. Today Jeanette has dragged home a large garbage bag filled with her coworkers' empty soda cans, which the girls will take to the recycling center to turn into cash for the *halau*.

"I want my kids to dance hula not only because it's a cultural experience, but because it's an avenue to other things, to the larger world," Jeanette says. "I like them having friends in the project, but I want them to have friends outside, too, so that they see there's another way to live."

Despite the obvious lack of material comforts in this household, family life feels rich. The four youngest Likio children are the personification of politeness, self-respect, and hope. They treat each other and their parents lovingly and respectfully; no coarse words are spoken here. "I always tell my kids to be role models for the other kids in Palolo," says Jeanette. "We're poor like everyone else, but we don't have to act ignorant or show attitude."

As on most evenings in the Likio household, the children's friends come and go. One of Keola's friends, Marjorie, thirteen, is here so much that she's treated like a family member. She takes her turn washing the dishes and running to a store or a snack wagon to pick

up food. Her mother works a 6:00 P.M. to 6:00 A.M. shift as a security guard, and there's no one to stay at home with her, so the Likios
have basically taken her in, even though it means another mouth to
feed.

"She was hanging out on the street before she got friendly with
Keola," says Jeanette. "She's better off here with us. We talk to her
just like we talk to our children."

The Grandchildren: Sorrow and Joy

Jeanette and Bobby's two oldest grandchildren, Malia, four, and
Keanu Jr., three, are also with them much of the time. They're the
source of both joy and great sorrow for Jeanette, who worries so
much about their home life that she sometimes thinks about trying
to *hanai* them—the Hawaiian practice of informal adoption, usually
by a family member. For now, she just lets them spend as much time
at her house as their mother will allow.

Malia sleeps here every night, by Jeanette's side on the linoleum
floor. Although she's almost five, her speech is unintelligible. A
month ago, her mother finally enrolled her in a Head Start program,
two years after she'd become eligible. Jeanette hopes she'll get
speech therapy there. Keanu Jr. started Head Start at the same time.
Maybe his earlier start will provide him with a true head start,
Jeanette hopes. He also has speech problems.

As darkness descends, stomachs start to grumble. It's two more
days until the monthly food-stamp voucher is due in the mail, so
there's little to eat. Even the twenty-five-pound bag of rice—rice is
served with every meal—is almost empty. Three-year-old Keanu
emerges from the kitchen with an orange in his hand. "That's the
last orange!" his aunt, Keola, shrieks. "I wanted that for breakfast!"

Jeanette remembers the orange she put in her purse as she left
work and retrieves it for her grandson. Then Elena starts begging for
money so she can buy something from the *manapua* wagon. (These
ubiquitous snack wagons, which sell cigarettes, candy, soda, and fast
food, are kind of like mobile convenience stores, open nearly around
the clock. They even accept food stamps.)

Elena rummages through her mother's purse and finally finds a
folded-up $1 bill, which she waves in the air triumphantly.
"Mommy, can I please have this dollar?" Elena asks.

"That's my last dollar, my honey," Jeanette responds. "What am I going to do for lunch tomorrow?"

"Please, Mommy, I'm hungry," Elena begs.

Jeanette relents. "Go look if the snack wagon's still open," she says. Elena returns ten minutes later with a *musubi*—a rice cake flavored with chopped-up Spam—and a can of Coke.

Late in the afternoon, Bobby had gone down to the beach to fish, but when he arrives home, he's empty-handed. Wordlessly, he goes to the refrigerator and takes out nine small fish, caught on a better day, and begins scraping off the scales. The only other food in the refrigerator is a box of cereal and several half-full jars of condiments. The freezer holds a box of chicken wings and necks and a few plastic bags filled with *opihi,* mollusks that Bobby has collected from the rocks at the breakwater. "Better put the chicken on, too," Jeanette tells him when she sees how small the fish are.

Now that the family is getting food stamps—$363 worth a month—food is less of a problem than it was last year. "It's really only the last few days before we get our voucher that we run out," Jeanette says apologetically.

Like many families trying to wean themselves from government aid, the Likios have cycled on and off food stamps several times. Sometimes they've left the food-stamp rolls voluntarily, when Bobby was working and Jeanette would start to believe that they could make it on their own. Even if things were going to be tight, she'd think it would be worth the squeeze just to avoid the humiliating periodic process of requalifying. "It breaks you as a person," Jeanette says. She still remembers the first time she applied for welfare and the state worker asked who had fathered her child and how often they slept together.

But every time the family has voluntarily given up food stamps, Jeanette has eventually had to swallow her pride and apply again a few months later when she realized they were diverting too much money to food and falling behind in their other bills. "When we didn't have food stamps, I would have to juggle, juggle, juggle, even more than I do now," Jeanette says.

The most recent time the family went off food stamps, it was involuntary. In 1996, for the first time, Jeanette filed for and received an Earned Income Tax Credit, the federal income supplement for the working poor. She received a check for $2,000. When she later went

to the state welfare office to fill out the monthly eligibility paperwork for food stamps, a state worker told her that she'd have to
spend the $2,000 immediately or lose the food stamps. "It seemed
like a dumb rule to me, but I knew by then that we needed those
food stamps," Jeanette says. Jeanette didn't know it, but the worker
was wrong. Federal rules in effect at the time allowed the refund to
count as a resource in determining eligibility for food stamps only if
unspent after twelve months. Jeanette took the worker's advice,
however, and went out and spent the tax refund on a seven-year-old
Geo Storm.

"When I took in the receipt from the car to show the worker that
we had spent down our assets, she said the car was worth too much,
that my assets were still too high," Jeanette says. "And they cut off
the food stamps."

A few months later, another blow landed. The family received a
notice that their landlord, the Hawaii Housing Authority, had ne-
glected to adjust their rent the year before to take into account
Jeanette's most recent raise. (Residents pay one-third of their gross
income as rent.) It was the housing authority's fault, but the family
would suffer the consequences. They would have to pay back rent of
more than $1,000.

"I told my manager I couldn't pay the whole thing up front, that
I'd have to pay it in monthly installments," Jeanette says. "So we began paying $80 more a month until we could catch up."

For months, the loss of food stamps and the extra rent payment
added up to a diet consisting mostly of saimin noodles, bought on
sale at eight packages for $1 and supplemented with whatever fish
Bobby could catch. "The only good meal the kids got every day was
at school," Jeanette recalls. "I would cry because I knew my poor
Kalani wasn't getting enough to eat. He would give up his food for
his baby sister."

In the summer of 1997, after the asset rule on automobiles
changed, the family began receiving food stamps again and eating
more or less normally, at least for most days each month. (Ironically,
the car that cost them food stamps now sits idle in a parking lot because Jeanette and Bobby can't afford insurance.)

The monthly food-stamp voucher won't arrive until tomorrow, so
tonight is one of those nights when dinner is skimpy. "If you guys
don't mind, we're going to eat Polynesian style on the floor," Bobby

says as he spreads a bath towel on the floor and begins doling out the stewed chicken parts and fried fish onto plastic plates.

The Biggest Worry: Medical Bills

Despite periodic bouts of hunger, the family's biggest worries are dental and medical care. Through her job, Jeanette has dental and medical insurance that provides 80 percent coverage for herself. But it would cost her $415 a month to insure the rest of the family, money she simply doesn't have with a take-home income of $1,393 a month.

"The thing we really miss is dental care," Jeanette says. "Poor Keola has gum disease. Her gums are all red, and they bleed. We try a lot of home remedies, like Listerine and baking soda and peroxide, but they don't seem to help. And I'm worried about Elena's teeth coming in crooked. I don't want her to grow up like me, with crooked teeth that other kids laugh at." The children used to get dental care through a state-operated clinic, but a few years ago it restricted its services to children with disabilities.

Although Jeanette has dental insurance for herself, she says she doesn't visit a dentist regularly "because I'd feel guilty getting dental care when my kids can't." The last time Jeanette went, the dentist pulled three molars. Recently, Kawailani had a toothache that wouldn't go away. A dentist charged $60 to pull Kawailani's infected molar. Jeanette doesn't like to think about whether her own teeth or Kawailani's could have been saved if she'd had enough money for more sophisticated treatment, like root canals and crowns.

As for medical care, the local clinic charges $28 a visit, so usually a child is really sick by the time he or she is examined. "First we do a lot of self-doctoring," says Jeanette, who has herself been suffering from an untreated hacking cough for the last two weeks.

At least three times in recent years, the children have faced medical crises. The first was when Kalani, then twelve, fell off a second-floor balcony and broke his elbow. "They had to do surgery to put it back in place," Jeanette says. "Now he's got pins holding it together." The family's income at the time was low enough that the children were covered by Medicaid.

Four years ago, Kawailani woke up with pain in his hip. Jeanette took him to the clinic, and a doctor there said he needed to see a specialist. "By then, we didn't have Medicaid anymore, so I was really worried about the cost," she says. But the clinic arranged an appointment at Shriners Hospital for Crippled Children, which doesn't charge for care. Kawailani turned out to have a slipped capital femoral epiphysis—dislocation of the upper growing end of the thigh bone—which is common among adolescent boys of Polynesian descent. He underwent surgery and spent weeks in a cast. He was also restricted from playing baseball for two years and football for four. "They said we have to watch the other hip because if one goes it's likely the other will," Jeanette said.

The most recent medical crisis came in the summer of 1997, when Elena woke up one morning with pains in her legs and back. Jeanette took her to the clinic, where they diagnosed her condition as bronchitis and sent her home. The next day, Elena was worse. She couldn't even get out of bed. Jeanette and Bobby had to carry her to the car for a trip back to the clinic. "She was in terrible pain," Jeanette recalls. "And when they took a urine sample, it was bright orange."

Elena was hospitalized for three days. The diagnosis was rheumatic fever. The disease was uncommon in the United States until the last decade, when it began increasing among children who are poorly nourished and don't receive prompt treatment for strep infections. The result of her infection is that, until she's eighteen, Elena must receive a monthly shot of penicillin in her hip to prevent damage to her heart. The clinic has agreed to provide the shots at no cost, but the Likios still have a $5,000 hospital bill to worry about.

The Likio Girls: "A Good Lesson"

For the most part, the Likio children don't complain about their family's place in the world. "We've taught them to be happy with very little," Bobby says. Yet it's clear that each in his or her own way has already internalized the fact that they are poor.

Of all the children, Elena, just ten, is the least aware of the family's economic status because her world is still circumscribed by her elementary school, her neighborhood, her dance club, and her softball team. Without exposure to television's situation comedies, she has little sense of how her family's circumstances differ from those of other families. She's a congenitally sweet child, curious about the visitor's children, whose names she memorizes instantly. Like her brothers, she's quite large for her age and is often mistaken for an eighth-grader though she's just in fifth.

When Elena overhears her parents talking about their finances, she's surprised to learn that the family once had a phone, since she has no memory of one. But she remembers well the long months during which they ate nothing but saimin noodles and fish, because she hates both. "I'd always say, 'Do we have to have *that* again?'" she says, screwing up her face in disgust.

Knowing that her mother still worries a lot about bills, Elena tries not to ask for new things very often. When her father mentions that he plans to start looking for work, Elena brings him a copy of the local paper's classified ads, open to the "Help Wanted" section.

Two years ago, the local health clinic nominated Elena for a spot on United Airlines' annual "Keiki" flight for underprivileged children—a flight over the islands during which the child passengers are treated like royalty, with entertainment by clowns, party food, and plenty of favors to take home. Elena was thrilled by the experience, and her parents didn't spoil the day by telling her she was chosen because they were poor.

In contrast, thirteen-year-old Keola, on the cusp of womanhood, is keenly aware of the family's finances. "When I was small, like Elena, it didn't really bother me that we were poor," she says. "Sometimes I'd really want a Barbie or something, and I couldn't have it, and that would upset me. But most of the time, I got enough to eat. Even the time when all we ate was saimin, it was okay with me, because I'm the only one in the family who likes it."

But recently, the family's economic status has begun to impede Keola's athletic opportunities. All of the family's children have been on baseball or softball teams since they were five, and Keola has as much raw talent as her brothers. But last year, she was forced to stay home when the rest of her team played in a fast-pitch tournament in Kona, on a neighboring island, because her family couldn't pay her share of the expenses. "The coaches offered to pay themselves, but I didn't want that," Jeanette explains. "I didn't want them to think we needed their charity. They already look down on us because we live in Palolo. When they drop her off after practice, it's always at the park, and then she walks home. They won't even drive into Palolo."

Like teenagers everywhere, teenagers in Honolulu are status-conscious, and more and more Keola's been begging her mother for Fila shoes and Nike shirts instead of whatever is available at the Salvation Army's second-hand store. "If I'm really lucky, my mom will buy me something from K-Mart," Keola says.

She's also becoming more aware of how the family's lack of money restricts her social life. There's simply no extra money for bowling, or movies, or admission fees to Honolulu's many tourist attractions. "My friends like to hang out at the mall, but my mom won't let me go because we don't have the money," she says.

"You know why, my honey," her mother interjects. "Do you want to tell the story?"

"You tell the story, Mom," Keola says, looking down in embarrassment.

"Well," says Jeanette, "one day, one of Keola's friends begged her to go to the mall, and she went, even though she wasn't supposed to. They were at Long's Drugs, and she took some batteries, and hair clips, and a set of earphones, worth a total of $10.75, and she got caught. The store detective wrote her up, and the police came and took her to Juvenile. They called my mom, who called me at work and said, 'You've got to pick up your daughter from the police.'

"I left work and went over to pick her up. She was in a cell block, crying. I was crying, too, because I felt so sorry for her. She told me what happened, and I said, 'Do you understand now why I tell you guys not to go to the malls without money? It's too tempting.'

"I guess if there's anything good that's come out of it, it's that it was a good lesson for all of us. Wasn't it, my honey?"

Tears are running down Keola's face, and her mother's, too.

Kawailani: Worries About Mom

Kawailani, the family's third-born, was marked for success even before he entered elementary school. He did well on developmental tests and was offered a spot in the kindergarten at the elite Kamehameha School, a private school established by the Bishop Estate, a foundation, to educate promising children of Hawaiian ancestry. The school spends $16,000 a year on each pupil, almost three times the state's public school average. Kawailani stayed through the sixth grade, when he and his parents decided it was too stressful for him to continue commuting between two worlds. They worried that other boys in Palolo Valley were harassing him because of his privileged status.

"He had to wear a uniform and real shoes and have his hair cut a certain way, and the kids in the neighborhood would accuse him of acting like a muckety-muck," Bobby explained. Now Kawailani is a junior at the local high school, where he has a 3.2 average. He still has a few friends from his days at Kamehameha School. But they won't come to his home, his mother says, because they're afraid of the neighborhood.

People around Palolo still talk about a poem Kawailani wrote a few years back that won a prize in the middle school's poetry contest. "It was one of the most poignant pieces of writing I've ever read," says one of the school's counselors, who keeps it on a school bulletin board to inspire other adolescents. The poem is called "Just Because."

> *Just because I Samoan,*
> *No mean I hard core and carry one knife.*
> *Just because I Hawaiian,*
> *No mean I play ukulele all day in the back*
> *   yard.*
> *Just because I Potagee,*
> *No mean I take a bath once a week.*
> *Just because I play football,*
> *No mean I dumb and no care about school.*
> *Just because I live in da housing,*
> *No mean I get welfare, do drugs, get rip clothes*
> *   and wear Moses slippers.*
> *Just because I live in Palolo,*
> *No mean I in one gang and carry one gun.*
> *Just because I Samoan, Hawaiian, Potagee,*
> *   play football, live in the housing and in*
> *   Palolo,*
> *Doesn't mean you know who I am.*

Most summers, Kawailani goes to summer school to polish his math and English skills so that he can have a better chance of getting a scholarship to college. But last summer, he was lucky enough to get a job with the local youth employment program, called Alu Like, for children of Hawaiian ancestry; the program paid him $5.25 an hour to work part-time as a recreational aide for a summer fun program. Through the summer, Kawailani earned about $500, which his parents let him keep for school-related expenses through the year. "But every time he got a paycheck, he'd stop at a Chinese takeout and bring us home some dinner," his mom recalls proudly. And he bought each of his siblings a new outfit before school started up in the fall.

"My mom was so stressed out by money, because we were off food stamps," he says. "All we had was her paycheck, and it wasn't enough."

Kalani: First to Graduate

Kalani, the second-born, was reminded of his family's poverty every time he signed up for a sports team. It was always hard to scrape together the money for the necessary equipment—a baseball glove, socks and cap in the spring, and football pads and shoes in the fall. For two seasons, he wore football shoes to play baseball, something that many American high school athletes would rather die than do. As his senior year in high school began, Kalani faced the prospect of missing his last football season because he didn't have medical insurance. Just before the first game, the coach found an insurance policy that would cover football-related injuries only—for $80 for the season. But Kalani didn't think his family could come up with even that much, and he told his mother he was going to quit. "My mom said, 'Oh, no, you're not. It's your senior year. We'll find the money,'" Kalani recalls. Eventually, his maternal grandparents lent the family the fee.

A trim, handsome, six-footer who exudes self-confidence and charm, Kalani has always been popular with girls. The bamboo and rattan display shelves in the family's living room are crowded with portraits of him at one formal dance or another, always with a pretty girl by his side. How did he manage to pay for these events? He flashes a big smile. "The girls would pay for me," he says. "One of them would ask me to the dance, and I'd say, 'I'm sorry, I'm not going. My family's having a hard time right now.' And she'd say, 'Okay, I'll pay for you.'" Jeanette always managed to find him dress clothes at a second-hand store.

When Kalani walked up to the podium to pick up his diploma from Kaimuki High School in the summer of 1997, Jeanette wept. In the audience were his brothers and sisters, his three living grandparents, and Jeanette's closest friends from work, each of whom draped a fresh flower lei around Kalani's neck in tribute to his hard work. He was the first person on Jeanette's side of the family to graduate from high school, and he was soon to become the first family member to enroll in a four-year college, using a Pell grant and a scholarship for native Hawaiians to pay the $7,000 yearly tuition at Hawaii Pacific University.

Later that summer, Kalani got his first glimpse of the business world in a summer program for disadvantaged Hawaiian youth called Alu Like at the TekPlace. Among other accomplishments, he designed a web page and learned to tie a tie.

Today Kalani struggles constantly with feelings of guilt because he isn't helping to support his sisters and younger brother. "There are a lot of times when there isn't enough money at home, and I keep telling my mom that maybe I should just work for a year and put university on hold," he says. "If I did that, it would make it easier for my younger siblings. But she won't let me. She wants me to graduate."

Keanu: "He Doesn't Want to Better Himself"

And then there's Keanu, Jeanette and Bobby's firstborn. In the last family photo in which he appears, taken in 1994, Keanu has his arms around two siblings. The fingers on one hand are arranged in a gang sign. So are the fingers on one of his youngest sister's hands, because he told her to position them that way. Then age seven, she had no idea what the sign meant.

At twenty, Keanu is no longer a member of the household. But he lives right next door, with his thirty-two-year-old girlfriend, Kenika, the mother of his four children, who range in age from a few weeks to four years. She has four other children, plus a grandchild. Twelve people live in her four-bedroom apartment, Jeanette says, "except when the brothers come out of jail, there are fifteen."

How Keanu has turned out is the great tragedy of the Likios' life. And Jeanette often blames herself.

"A lot of his problems are of his own choosing. But I think part of it is the way we were living when he was young, and the place we live," Jeanette says. "I was a teenage mom, and I didn't know much about how to raise a child. I used to do what my parents told me, what my aunties told me, what Bobby told me. I didn't know any better until I got involved with PACT and learned about child development and parenting.

"Now I just hate to think about what Keanu was exposed to his first few years. He used to have sores all over him when he was a baby, from people carrying him around while they smoked cigarettes. Today I don't even let people smoke in the house."

Keanu did poorly in school from the start. Teachers didn't seem to like him. Jeanette believes he was typecast as unpromising because she was a teenage mom. "I remember someone from his school calling me once and telling me I had to come to a meeting that night," Jeanette recalls. "'What kind of meeting?' I asked. 'A meeting for parents of high-risk kids,' she said. 'What do you mean by high-risk?' I asked. 'Well, the way you live,' she said." Jeanette was furious.

In his early teens, Keanu started hanging out with the Palolo Valley Boys, a gang whose members wear red and identify with the mainland Bloods. Hawaii's gangs hadn't yet begun carrying guns—they still used fists to settle disputes—but his associations brought him into frequent conflict with the police. Once he was Maced in the parking lot next to the Likios' building, provoking Jeanette to file a complaint with the police commissioner. "It should be illegal to Mace children simply because they don't move when an officer says move," she says, still indignant years after the incident.

Then he took up with Kenika, who's just a few years younger than his mother. "She used to allow him and his friends to hang out at her house and drink," Jeanette says. When he was fifteen, Keanu came home one night and told his parents that Kenika, then twenty-seven, was pregnant with his child.

More bad news was yet to come. At sixteen, the local juvenile court sent Keanu to a boys' home for fighting. The sentence forced him to give up a spot in Job Corps, which Jeanette had hoped would be his salvation. He later worked for about six months at a gas station, but he hasn't held a steady job for about three years. He owes thousands of dollars to the state for back child support. For a long time, Jeanette kept after him about going back to school or getting a job. "I've told him about a lot of resources, about a lot of programs that would help him," she says. "He's stopped hearing me. He doesn't want to go. He doesn't want to better himself."

Now Jeanette's trying to motivate Kenika, whose dependency on welfare must end, by law, in four years. Kenika's benefits have already been cut once as Hawaii began phasing in its version of welfare reform. After another steep cut next year, the benefits will drop 10 percent annually in each of the following three years. Then they'll end altogether.

"I talk to them both a lot about welfare reform," Jeanette says. "She's got eight kids, and one of her kids already has her own kid. I say to them, 'What are you going to do to start to support these kids? Don't wait until the five years are up, or you won't be able to feed them.'"

So far as Jeanette knows, Keanu's been arrested only once, for assault, since he's become an adult. But Jeanette talks as though she knows that serious trouble is inevitable.

"Every day I pray for him," she says. "Every time I hear gunshots, I say to the other kids, 'Where's your brother?' He sometimes comes to our house to hide out, which puts all of us in danger. I tell him, 'I know you're coming here to try to protect your kids and Kenika, but what about your brothers and sisters? What about them?' Mostly, though, I'm afraid for him."

Sacrifices and Dreams

What does the future hold for the Likio family? Both Jeanette and Bobby have trouble seeing much beyond the present, except for their mutual determination that their three youngest children will finish high school.

But after thinking quietly for a few moments, Jeanette says: "I think the family will be intact. I think we'll still be talking things out. Bobby has come a long way from where he used to be. I guess he realized what he made us go through. He feels shame.

"As for the kids, the older they get, the more understanding of our situation they get. They have sacrificed so much, going to school barefoot sometimes, always wearing second-hand stuff, having to meet their friends in the park because they don't want to come up to Palolo.

"What my goal is for my kids is to have an opportunity to live healthy and fulfilling lives. How to reach that goal, I don't know."

Bobby insists that he's content with things the way they are. "As long as my kids are happy, and we have food to eat and clothes to wear, I'm happy," he says. "All I want from life now is for my kids to achieve more than I did and go further than me. I never have that thought, 'What's the use of living if you're poor?' Maybe this is the way God wanted us to be."

But then he breaks into a smile as he describes a recurring dream.

"Sometimes I've been sleeping on the couch, and I hear a knock on the door, and I think it's Ed McMahon, and he's saying, 'Mr. Likio, you've won the sweepstakes,'" he says.

"It's happened over and over again.

"But when I wake up, it's only a dream. It's just one of the kids' friends at the door."

5

LOUISVILLE, KENTUCKY

Orlando Saylor could be a poster child for the possible negative effects on young children of growing up poor.

Twice in his early childhood, Orlando's brain was deprived of oxygen because of delays in receiving medical care that his mother believes were directly related to his family's poverty. The incidents left him with learning disabilities, a speech impediment, and memory problems so serious that he may never be able to live on his own.

His father, a chemical worker, was a violent man who regularly beat his mother, rendering her virtually catatonic for months at a time and hardly able to take care of her children.

Lately, the educational establishment seems to have given up on Orlando. He's been suspended for behavioral reasons several times this school year—a total of twenty-one days by mid-February 1997. At the moment, he's suspended for being with a group of students who were smoking. He can't go back to school until he writes an essay on the evils of nicotine. He has no idea where to begin.

"It's like I can't do anything right," he says of school. "It's like they don't want me there."

Bologna and One-Pot Meals

Orlando, fifteen, a freshman in high school, lives with his mother, Carlotta Saylor, forty-one, and four brothers in a run-down public housing complex in Louisville, Kentucky. An older sister, Sandra, twenty-four, lives with her husband and baby a few miles away.

The other children in the family are Freddy, twenty-one, who's struggling to finish high school, three years behind his peers; Stephen, seventeen, a high school junior; Kevin, ten, a fourth-grader, and Martin, eight, a third-grader.

Although Orlando's mother is unmarried, that label doesn't quite tell the whole story about the structure of this family. The man who fathered Freddy, Kevin, and Martin has been part of Carlotta's life for most of the last twenty-four years and helped support the children until he became disabled two years ago. He and Carlotta have what used to be called a common-law marriage.

The public housing project where the Saylor family lives is one of Louisville's oldest. It's a 362-unit low-rise blond brick complex with the dreary look of a former military barracks. Built in the late 1940s for the newly forming families of World War II veterans, it's wedged between two railroad lines and surrounded by factories, warehouses, and an electrical substation. The small business district nearby consists of two mom-and-pop groceries and a liquor store that Carlotta and other community activists have been trying to shut down for years. There isn't any other housing in sight.

Child poverty is endemic in the neighborhood. In the last census, 94 percent of the children under age six—418 of 447—lived in families with incomes below the poverty line. Only seven families headed by black women had incomes *above* the poverty line. Married couples were a trace element among all black families with children—just 14 of 356. According to the Census Bureau, not a single adult in the area had a bachelor's degree, and the majority of adults had neither a high school diploma nor a GED.

"This is considered one of the worst places to live in Louisville," Carlotta says matter-of-factly. "The crime rate is real bad. But to me, it's just a neighborhood. It has problems like every neighborhood."

On this dreary February day, even the twenty-two inches of snow that fell overnight, making much of Louisville look magical, can't dress up the neighborhood. Garbage spills out of the dumpsters that residents must pass to reach their front doors. A water-logged mattress and matching box spring lie abandoned, too heavy from soakings by winter rains for garbage collectors to haul away. The snow will soon give way to seas of mud, Carlotta predicts, since little grass grows here.

The Saylor family's apartment is on the second floor of a building identical to the dozen or so others in the complex. When the weather is nice, Carlotta likes to sit on the tiny concrete porch, watch the children play, and visit with her neighbors. But now it's the dead of winter, so her two garage sale chairs are chained to the porch railing.

The apartment is at the top of a narrow, unlighted staircase, which feels like a tunnel. At the top of the stairs is a small living room, which has one window, concrete-block walls, and a linoleum floor. Though the housing authority is supposed to paint every five years, the walls were last painted when the Saylors moved in seven years ago. In several spots, the orange undercoat is showing where the tan top coat has peeled away.

Down a corridor strung with drying laundry are four tiny bedrooms, a bathroom, and a kitchen. Most of the floor space in the boys' bedrooms is taken up by their bicycles, since there's no place to store them safely outside.

The family pays $289 a month in rent nine months of the year, and $443 a month in the summer, when Carlotta's income is higher. Although their rent is supposedly subsidized, it's hard to imagine that the market rate would be any more than they pay.

Since she's entertaining a visitor, Carlotta lights a votive candle to add some cheer to the living room, which is furnished sparsely. There are two wooden-armed, cushioned chairs, a formica-covered end table, a beat-up old desk, and a small hutch—all hand-me-downs from friends and family. The console TV was bought sixteen years ago on a rent-to-own plan, making it cost three or four times what it was worth. Two VCRs—also bought on a rent-to-own basis—sit atop it. Only one works, and it's missing the top of its case.

Carlotta's added a few decorative touches to her walls—a landscape from her parents' living room, two paintings on mirrors—but it's just not possible to make concrete-block walls feel cozy.

The Saylors' income last year was $16,845, well under the federal poverty threshold in 1997 of $21,886 for a family of six. Most of it—$694 a month—came from the Social Security survivors' benefits that Stephen and Orlando receive because their father is dead. Stephen also gets a Supplemental Social Insurance (SSI) stipend of $141 a month because of severe asthma. The rest of the family's income comes from Carlotta's two jobs—as a part-time preschool aide during the school year and a full-time day camp counselor in the summer. The family has more disposable income in the summer, when Carlotta brings home just over $1,000 a month. During the other months, her gross monthly pay amounts to about $550.

Until July 1997, the family received about $200 a month in food stamps. But they were cut off for reasons Carlotta doesn't understand. According to published state guidelines, the family's income is well within the guidelines for eligibility. State guidelines in 1998 permitted a family of six with a gross monthly income of $2,955—almost $36,000 a year—to receive up to $582 a month in food stamps. Winter or summer, the Saylors should qualify.

"All I know is they told me I was making too much money," Carlotta says. "I guess I should go back and try again. Since we lost the food stamps, we've had to cut way back. We're eating a lot of bologna and one-pot meals. What really bothers me is that food costs more when you pay with cash, because you have to pay sales tax."

"We Got What We Needed"

Carlotta grew up in a loving family in which both parents worked full-time. They instilled a strong work ethic in their children, sending five to college and three into careers in the Marines. All but one of Carlotta's now-grown siblings have good jobs.

"My father worked real hard, and my mom, too," she says. "He was a supervisor at the GE plant, and she was a custodian for the Jefferson County School Board. We didn't go without. We might have had to wait for what we *wanted*, but we got what we *needed*."

Carlotta was the sixth of twelve children. Because her parents both worked the second shift, the older children in the family were in charge of the younger children after school, and the discipline they imposed became the model for how Carlotta runs her household today. "We'd come home, change our clothes, eat our snacks, and do our homework, and then we'd all do our chores," she said. "The TV wasn't allowed to come on until all the chores were done. My mama would call us when it was time to eat dinner, and again when it was time to go to bed. We were all in bed by eight o'clock."

Carlotta's grandmother was also a strong influence on her life, and even today, whenever she's faced with a challenge, Carlotta tries to remember what her grandmother taught her over Sunday dinners that typically lasted a whole afternoon. "My grandmother instilled in us that you don't complain about your situation," Carlotta said. "You try to make it better.

"I can't let being poor affect my outlook on life, because if it affects me, it affects my children. That's why you have kids out there seeking drugs and prostituting themselves, because their parents give them the idea that that's all that's possible for them.

"I tell my kids that money isn't the only thing. It's important. But it's not the only thing. Here's an example of what I mean.

"Last Mother's Day, the kids didn't have any money to buy me anything, but they did something even better. They cooked my breakfast, my lunch, and my dinner.

"As I said, money isn't the only thing."

A Prisoner in Her Own House

Carlotta dates the beginning of her problems to the spring before her senior year in high school, when she became pregnant with Sandra. "Back then, they didn't want you in school if you were pregnant, so I had to take a leave," she says. Sandra's father stayed in school and graduated. (The couple broke up before the baby was born, and he never provided any support.)

Carlotta gave birth in February and then enrolled in a night school to make up some missing credits. She returned to her high school in September, expecting to graduate the following June, a year later than her peers. But in early spring of her senior year, she says the vice principal called her to his office.

"He said, 'You've got a baby. You don't need a diploma,'" she recalls. "I cussed him out, which I shouldn't have, because it got me suspended. I would have had to say I was sorry to get back into school, and I wasn't ready to do that. I was too strong-headed."

So Carlotta went to work selling tickets and candy at a movie theater. She worked there for almost three years, until the theater closed for remodeling. By the time it reopened in late 1977, she was pregnant with Freddy and couldn't stand on her feet as long as the job required. At age twenty, with a preschooler and another child on the way, she went on welfare.

Freddy's father was a man named Harry, nineteen years older than Carlotta. Because of his age, her parents disapproved of the relationship. "He was in my life until Freddy was a year old," Carlotta says. "That's when they chased him away."

Carlotta and her children lived with her parents until Sandra was four and Freddy was two, when they moved to a house that her grandmother owned. The house didn't have heat, so during the winters they stayed with friends. After two years, their name finally rose to the top of the waiting list for subsidized housing, and they moved into a privately owned, federally subsidized complex called Village West (since renamed City View).

In the meantime, Carlotta had become involved with a man named Steve, a relationship that was to define much of the rest of her life. Steve fathered her next two children, Stephen Jr., born in October 1980, and Orlando, born in August 1982. The relationship sounds like a case study in the dynamics of domestic violence.

"He kept me away from my family," Carlotta says. "He wouldn't let me answer the door. He wouldn't let me clean the house. He wouldn't let me take a bath or brush my teeth. If I did my hair, he poured a bucket of dirty water over my head."

Worse, though, was the physical abuse.

"I hated payday, which was on Wednesday, because he'd go out and get drunk and then come home and beat me," she says. "The beatings continued until the money for booze ran out."

Carlotta stayed with Steve, she says, because he convinced her that his behavior was her fault, a not uncommon tactic of abusive men, according to therapists who treat victims of domestic violence. "He tore down all of the self-esteem my parents had instilled in me," she says. "I'd think, 'If I just loved him a little more, he wouldn't hit me anymore,' or, 'If he'd just stop drinking, he'd stop hitting me.' I blamed myself for what he did to me."

Carlotta's feelings for Steve began changing the day she returned home after rushing Orlando to a hospital with a life-threatening illness. "The first thing he did when I came in the door was hit me," she recalls. "I said to him, 'When I left here, I had two children with me, and when I came back, I only had one. You never even asked me where he was.'

"That was the day my feelings for him started to die."

Still, she lacked the will to change her situation. Finally, someone forced help on her. "They wanted to put me in the hospital, but I refused to go, because there was no one else to take care of the kids," she says. As a compromise, she agreed to put the children into child care and go to counseling herself. She was diagnosed as severely depressed and put on medication.

As she began to emerge from her depression, she got involved with a mothers' club, which provided her with a modest social life and her first contacts outside the home in years. "We went bowling and out to lunch and to workshops on parenting issues," she says. "I loved it, because it got me out of the house."

Finally, with the help of one of her brothers, Carlotta got Steve out of her apartment. "The last time he came after me was my twenty-seventh birthday," Carlotta recalls. "He came up to the house and tried to get in. I told him to go away, but he broke in through a window. I picked up a Louisville Slugger and started fighting back. Neighbors came from everywhere with bats and two-by-fours and chased him away. That was the last time he touched me."

Carlotta last saw Steve in court, where he came to face charges of assaulting her. "The judge asked me what I wanted, and I told him I wanted Steve to stay away from me," Carlotta says.

"The judge told Steve, 'If anything happens to this woman, I'm going to blame you. If she gets hit by a bus, I'm going to blame you. If she gets scratched by a cat, I'm going to blame you. I don't want you near her ever again.'"

"Steve asked him, 'What about my kids?'" Carlotta recalls.

"The judge asked him, 'Did you ever hit her in front of the kids?'

"He said, 'Yes.'

"And the judge said, 'Then they're not your kids anymore.'"

Tears come to Carlotta's eyes as she concludes the story. "I truly believe that judge saved my life," she says.

Steve died of throat cancer in 1985, at the age of thirty-two. "The only good thing he ever did for me was see to it that the kids got Social Security when he died," Carlotta says.

In the years since his death, Carlotta has gradually regained her self-confidence. "It took me a while to start believing in myself again," she says. "He had put me in this little hole, and I couldn't get out. But I finally realized that a lot of the things that happened to me wasn't my fault."

"He's Good to My Kids"

Among the people who came to Carlotta's aid the last time Steve beat her was Harry, Sandra and Freddy's father, whom her parents had driven out of her life because he was so much older. The two became involved again, and Carlotta gave birth to two more of Harry's sons—Kevin, in January 1988, and Martin, in July 1989.

Although Carlotta calls Harry her fiancé, she admits that it's unlikely they'll ever marry. Harry doesn't consider himself financially fit enough to be a husband, Carlotta says, and she's still reluctant to commit. "When you go through what I went through with a man, it makes you shy away from relationships," she says. (Harry declined to be interviewed.)

Even without benefit of marriage, Harry plays an important role in the family. He worked in security jobs for most of his adult life, and contributed to the children's support, until the work became too stressful. "His nerves were getting bad," Carlotta says. "He said the younger generation was getting out of hand. He said he didn't want to have to shoot nobody's child, and it was getting to that."

Most recently, Harry worked as a cook at a Hardee's restaurant. But in 1996 a disc in his back ruptured, causing him constant pain. He also suffers from diabetes, hypertension, and prostate problems; he's had prostate surgery three times. "I guess he's going to have to go on disability," Carlotta says. "He wants to work, but the doctor says he can't."

Since Harry has no income and is five years away from being eligible for Social Security retirement benefits, Carlotta helps him financially now. He's awaiting a ruling on his application for disability benefits.

"Harry has always been there for me," Carlotta says. "I could always count on him when I needed him. He's good to me, and good to my kids."

Juggling Motherhood and Work

Carlotta and her boys were last on welfare in 1982, when she began working part-time at the Village West laundromat. After Kevin was born five years later, she returned to school to try to get an office specialist certificate and a GED. She got the office specialist's certificate from the now-defunct Waterson College Career Center, but not the GED, because she couldn't bring herself to take the test. "I'm scared to death of tests," she says. "Just that word *test* makes me start feeling sick."

As the children got older, she added more hours to her workweek, until she was finally working full-time at the laundromat, on the 4:00 P.M. to midnight shift. She was earning enough money—about $166 a week in 1990 dollars—to permit a move to the public housing complex where they still live, which at that time was considered a step up from Village West.

Four years ago, though, she gave up the laundromat job when she arrived home early one night and found the boys having a party. "I realized that I couldn't stay on top of what was happening at home if I was gone that many hours a day," she says. "For a long time, I hadn't been here when they came home from school, and they were usually asleep by the time I got home, so it was hard keeping up with what was going on in their schools."

For a year or so, the family made do with the boys' Social Security benefits and food stamps. Carlotta threw herself into mothering and volunteer work. She joined an advisory board at the neighborhood's family resource center, the residents' board of the housing project, and an advisory board for the police. She became an informal mentor to many of the young mothers in the neighborhood. At various times in the last few years, she's taken in several women who have fallen on hard times. She once had three friends, plus their eight children, living with her. One had lost her home to a flood, one had no electricity, and the other "just needed to learn to be a mom," Carlotta says.

"I didn't just give my friends a roof over their heads," Carlotta says proudly. "When they left my house, they all left on their own feet, because I gave them resources."

But all the time she wasn't working, she felt pulled toward work, and not just because the family could use the extra money. "I feel much better about myself when I work," she says. "It feels good to get a check from an employer and take it to the bank and get it cashed."

After a year of not working, Carlotta found a part-time job, twenty hours a week during the school year, in the recreation center at the housing project. She works in the Pee Wees program, a preschool program for three-, four- and five-year-olds for whom the local Head Start centers have insufficient room. Carlotta can walk to that job and be home when her boys get out of school.

"We color, paint, do our ABCs and 123s, learn 'Yes, ma'am' and 'No, ma'am,'" she explains. "Basically, we try to give them the skills they're going to need once they're in school."

Going back to work brought more money into the household. But that meant that the family's food stamps were cut by $189 a month. Fortunately, the next summer Carlotta found a forty-hour-a-week job in the city of Louisville's summer camp program, which also operates out of the project's recreation center. She's worked in the program every summer since. An important perk of that job is that her two younger boys get to attend the program for free.

"There Ain't Nothing I Can Do"

Like many poor people who work in low-wage jobs, Carlotta says the biggest deficit in her family's life is medical insurance. "If I had me a medical card, I wouldn't have all these bills and such bad credit," she says.

"It's been thirteen years since I had insurance for the kids, except for the six weeks immediately after Kevin's and Martin's births," she says. She can remember the year with precision because it was the same year Stephen and Orlando, her second- and third-oldest sons, began receiving Social Security survivors' benefits because of their father's death. "With the benefits on top of my laundry wages, suddenly we were making $2 a month too much to get Medicaid," Carlotta recalls.

The sad irony is that according to Kentucky's published income eligibility guidelines for Medicaid coverage, Carlotta's three youngest children should qualify for Medicaid now. The January 1998 eligibility tables indicate that children six and older who were born after September 30, 1983, as Carlotta's youngest two were, are eligible for medical assistance as long as their family's income is below $1,791 a month.

The plight of the Saylor children isn't uncommon. According to a study by the General Accounting Office, about one-third of uninsured children in 1994 qualified for Medicaid but were not receiving it, because of their parents' lack of awareness of their eligibility, their fear of having their children stigmatized, or concerns about the difficulty of applying.[1]

"Knock on Wood"

The loss of medical coverage for the boys thirteen years ago plunged the family into a spiraling nightmare of debt from which they seem unable to emerge. Stephen has chronic asthma, and through much of his early childhood he had to be hospitalized nearly every month. "He had his first attack when he was four months old, and he ended up in Kosair Children's Hospital with pneumonia," Carlotta recalls. "For the next eight years, he'd be in the hospital anywhere from three or four days to seven to twelve days once a month."

The attacks mysteriously stopped when he was eight but resumed when he was eleven, though with less frequency. In each of the next three years, he was hospitalized about twice a year, for seven to twelve days at a time. (Numerous studies have found that poor children are twice as likely as nonpoor children to spend time in a hospital in a given year. Asthma is the leading single cause of hospitalization during childhood.)

Fortunately, Stephen hasn't had an attack in the last two years. "Knock on wood," Carlotta says, rapping her knuckles on her end table.

He finally received a Medicaid card a year ago when he was awarded SSI disability benefits, years after he'd applied. Though his asthma has stabilized and he hasn't had to be hospitalized lately, the medical coverage has still been a godsend, since it pays for his medication, which costs more than $150 a month.

But Stephen's Medicaid card doesn't take care of the thousands of dollars in medical bills that have piled up over the years. "The hospital has been understanding," Carlotta says. "When they call me about the bills, I say, 'What can I do? I've got to pay my rent and feed my children.' They know there ain't nothing I can do."

As Carlotta is talking about Stephen's medical problems, her oldest son, Freddy, comes into the living room and, in a thick voice, complains that his throat hurts. Carlotta gets a thermometer from the bathroom and takes his temperature. It's 101.5 degrees.

"Probably strep," she says, with the certainty of a mother who's seen many childhood illnesses. "My boys get a lot of strep." That means a trip to the clinic tomorrow and another medical bill. With any luck, no one else in the family will come down with it. Carlotta raps her knuckles on the end table again.

A sore throat isn't Freddy's only problem. In clinical terms, Freddy is morbidly obese. The last time he stepped on a scale, he weighed 310 pounds. For medical reasons, he's excused from physical education classes at school. With a family history of diabetes on both sides, Carlotta knows that Freddy is a health problem waiting to happen. "I worry about him being so heavy," she says.

The youngest two boys also have health problems. At age ten, Kevin suffers from chronic sinusitis. His breathing is so labored that it can be heard from another room. "He gets lots of ear infections, too," Carlotta says.

And Martin, now eight, was born with a congenital heart problem that requires regular monitoring. Every year, he must undergo several costly tests—an ultrasound, a stress test, an EKG, and an echocardiogram. He may require surgery in the future, Carlotta's been told.

Carlotta herself suffers from episodic depression, arthritis, and chronic kidney infections. "The doctor says someday my kidneys are going to go south," she says.

Not the least of her problems is that she lost her glasses a few years back and hasn't been able to afford a new pair, so she has to squint to make out objects across the room. She's also plagued by dental problems; most of her molars have been pulled because of decay.

"The last time I went to the dentist with a toothache, she told me she didn't know which tooth was the problem, since they all looked bad, and she had a pulling good time," Carlotta says. Buying a partial bridge to replace the missing teeth is well down on Carlotta's priority list.

Orlando: "Not Like Other Kids"

But it's Orlando who has had the most serious medical problems, with apparently permanent effects on his cognitive abilities. Although he is personable, talkative, and exceedingly polite, his speech is difficult to understand, and he doesn't even know how to spell the name of his school. Carlotta believes his problems are due to the two episodes in his life when his brain was deprived of oxygen.

The first incident occurred during his birth. Carlotta had arrived at a hospital in the final stage of labor. Her doctor wasn't there yet, and as she screamed in pain, she says six nurses held her down, with two pressing her legs together to keep the baby from emerging. Though she can't prove it, she suspects that her doctor told the nurses by phone to try to delay the delivery until he got there so he could be sure to collect his fee from Medicaid. "I kept telling them that the baby was trying to come out, and they told me I was crazy," she says.

Eventually, another doctor heard the shouting and came into the room.

"She put on gloves, and checked me, and said his head was already coming out," Carlotta says. "She said to the nurses, 'What are you trying to do, kill this baby?'"

"By the time he was born, he was all blue."

Carlotta says that the doctor who intervened filed a formal complaint over the treatment Carlotta had received. The two nurses who held her legs together were fired, two others were suspended, and the other two were transferred, Carlotta says she was told. The president of the hospital came to her hospital room to apologize to her personally, she says.

But the damage was done. "They told me before I left the hospital that Orlando would be slow, but they didn't know how slow," she said.

Orlando's second medical crisis occurred when he was a toddler. Carlotta blames the inflexible authorization rules of Kentucky's first managed care program for Medicaid recipients for his near-death that time.

Orlando had come home from child care with a fever and labored breathing. Because Carlotta had had a bad experience with the managed care program just the week before, when its "gatekeeper" refused to authorize a doctor's visit for Orlando, she didn't call. Instead, she carried Orlando to the nearest doctor's office. It was apparent to everyone there that Orlando was very sick, Carlotta says.

"The doctor was way down the hall, and he yelled out, 'Who's breathing like that?'" she recalls. He rushed down to check Orlando and told Carlotta he needed to go to a hospital immediately. Carlotta told the doctor that he needed to call the state program to get authorization first.

"He called and told them, 'This child is having trouble breathing. He needs to go to the hospital,'" Carlotta says. "But they refused to send an ambulance. They told him, 'Give the mom a quarter and put her on a bus.'"

The doctor called an ambulance anyway. (Carlotta later found out that he paid the bill himself.) "The ambulance pulled away like a shot, with sirens blaring and red lights flashing," Carlotta says. At Norton Hospital, several emergency room physicians worked on Orlando while Carlotta tried to keep herself calm.

"I remember one doctor in particular coming up to me and saying, 'I'm going to tell you point-blank, your baby's very sick. We're going to have to take him into surgery and put a tube into his throat so he can breathe. If we don't, he's going to die, because his throat is closing.'"

While Orlando was being intubated, his lungs collapsed. He underwent surgery for two hours and was in intensive care for five days. "They told me he was without oxygen for longer than they wanted him to be," Carlotta says.

It turned out that Orlando had an upper respiratory infection caused by *hemophilus influenzae* type b (Hib), which caused his epiglottis to swell, closing off his airway. Until a vaccine became available in the late 1980s, untreated Hib infections were sometimes fatal in children under age five, with death occurring within a few hours of onset.

Whether or not oxygen deprivation during birth or during his later medical crisis contributed to Orlando's cognitive problems is hard to say. What's certain is that life will always be a struggle for him. Not a day goes by without frequent reminders of his problems.

"He's not like the other kids," Carlotta says. "He's special. It's not that he can't learn. It's that he can't keep what he learns in his memory.

"When he was twelve, I had him tested through the University of Louisville. They said he would never be able to live alone. He might turn the stove on and forget about it and cause a fire, or he might be easily led astray.

"I tell him he is physically disabled. That is the label we use in this house. It is nothing for him to be ashamed of."

Orlando has been in special education since first grade. He did fairly well at school until the current school year, his first in high school. "He was mainstreamed, with very poor results," Carlotta says. The classes were much larger than he was used to, and he didn't get the special help he needed.

His problems are both academic and social. "Most of my problems are because of other kids," he says. "They talk about me being slow, being stupid, not talking right. They call me dirty when I know I'm clean. They make fun of my clothes, because we can't afford the cool stuff."

Midway through the school year, Carlotta insisted that school officials place Orlando in a special education resource room where he could get more individual attention than in a regular classroom. But the switch may have come too late to save the school year. First semester, he got three Ds, a C, and a U (equivalent to an F) on his report card.

"I think I'm going to fail the year," Orlando says sadly.

Freddy: Struggling to Finish High School

School has always been a struggle for Freddy, who, at twenty-one, is probably the oldest senior in his school's history. That he's still in school testifies to Carlotta's willingness to fight school officials over what she believes is best for her children, and Freddy's willingness to persevere in the face of taunts from his peers.

Because he has a December birthday, Freddy was already older than most of his peers when he began kindergarten. Then he had to repeat the first grade. "He just wouldn't do his work," his mother says. "He's smart, and he doesn't have any learning disabilities. But he just doesn't like to study."

When Freddy was required to repeat tenth grade, he started talking about dropping out of school. "I told him, 'You drop out, you can move out,'" Carlotta recalls. He stayed in school.

In eleventh grade, he again talked about dropping out, telling his mother that other kids were making fun of him both for his size and for being so old—he was twenty by this time—and still in high school. "I told him, 'They aren't going to buy your clothes and put a roof over your head for the rest of your life,'" she says. "'The only way you're going to be able to do that is to finish school.'"

At the beginning of his senior year, Freddy again wanted to drop out, and school officials told Carlotta they wanted to transfer him to an alternative high school. Carlotta said no to both ideas.

"I told Freddy he was almost there, and there was no sense quitting now," she says. "And I felt that if I let him go to the alternative school, where it's pretty much independent study, there'd be no hope of his graduating. In a regular school, there's a pace they have to maintain."

Freddy doesn't know what he'll do after he graduates. Sometimes he talks about following his three uncles into the Marines, but with his weight problem, it's clear he couldn't pass the physical. Sometimes he talks about going to college and then to law school, but it's February of his senior year, and he hasn't yet taken the ACT or the SAT, which most college-bound students take when they're juniors. Recently, Carlotta says, he's been talking about "just knocking around for a year and working."

"I don't know what he'll end up doing," she says. "I've never been able to get him interested in anything besides TV and food. That's all he cares about."

Stephen: No Fights This Year

Stephen, the second-oldest child, is guarded around a visitor—and, his mother says, around most adults. Whatever he's thinking, he keeps to himself. He answers questions with as few words as possible, usually "Yes, ma'am" or "No, ma'am." His mother attributes his stocky and muscular build to the steroids he takes to control his asthma. On this Saturday afternoon, he's just come home from a wrestling tournament, where he's won third place in the 189-pound class. It's left him with a nasty black eye.

"Mom, can I go to the store?" he asks his mother.

"What you want there?" she answers. "You ain't got no money."

"Yeah, I do," he says. "I've got $1.50. I want to get something to eat."

"We'll see," she says.

In an aside, she explains, "One of my house rules is if they don't have no money, they can't go to the store."

An hour or so later, Stephen emerges from his room and heads toward the stairs. He's wearing a knitted stocking cap, and the waistband of his sweatpants is pulled way down below his hips, allowing his boxers to show. There's no more discussion about whether he's going out or not; apparently, he's interpreted his mother's "we'll see" as an assent. Still, his mother asserts her authority once more as he heads out. "Pull your pants up, please," his mother says. "You got your gloves?"

"Yes, ma'am," he answers as he pulls up his pants and heads out to the store.

As the door closes behind him, Carlotta says, "I used to hate when the phone would ring while Stephen was in school, because it would always be the school, calling about him. This year, he's doing a lot better. He hasn't been suspended once, knock on wood, and he's only been in one fight. He's changed a lot. He's really into football and wrestling. Even his grades are good."

Carlotta runs a tight household, with each boy responsible for specific chores. She has strict rules about whom they can socialize with, and where. "The house rule is that they can't start dating until they turn sixteen," she says. "And I very seldom let them go to other people's houses. That's the way I was raised, so that's the way I've raised my kids. If they want to have company here, they have to sit on the front porch. Sometimes I'll let them come in and play Sega, but not often, because this is such a small place."

Like many other mothers of young black men in America's urban areas, Carlotta is well aware of the risks her boys face in the outside world. Teen pregnancy is a big problem in her neighborhood, so Carlotta has drilled into her boys the necessity of using condoms if they're going to have sex, which she also tells them she hopes they won't. She wishes there were some way she could protect them from the other risks: African American youths are almost ten times more likely than white youths to be arrested, and many times more likely to be victims of violent crimes.

"I worry about what if they're in a football game and somebody starts shooting," she says. "I worry about things getting out of hand and them being in the way. I tell them all the time, 'Bullets don't have eyes.'"

In 1997 Louisville experienced one of the worst increases in its homicide rate of any city in the United States, and the Saylors' housing complex was the site of several murders. The Saylor family knew six of the victims personally, including the boys' basketball coach and another man the boys regarded as their mentor. Gangs were a factor in Louisville's high homicide rate in 1997, police say, and they're present here. Practically every family in this complex has a member who's been harmed by crack cocaine, including the Saylors. One of Carlotta's sisters is addicted, and her daughter is being raised by another sister.

"I'm not going to say drugs and gangs ain't a concern," Carlotta says. "They are. But I meddle so much in my boys' business that the gangs don't want them. They know I'll come looking for them."

Martin and Kevin: Staying Busy with Dancing

With little income to spare for entertainment, Carlotta's boys take advantage of what's nearby and nearly free. Both younger boys attend a dance school at the housing project's recreation center. Almost two hundred children are enrolled.

The dance classes provide a real community-building focus for the housing complex. They're run with the help of volunteers—including Carlotta, who takes care of the paperwork—so residents have to pay just $15 per month per child, which goes mainly to cover the costs of costumes.

The program emphasizes a dance form called dance-stepping. "It's a combination of tap, ballet, step, African dance, and gymnastics," Carlotta explains. The sound of dozens of feet pounding a stage floor simultaneously resembles that of African drums.

For entertainment at home, Martin and Kevin often insert the videotape of the club's 1995 Father's Day show into the family's battered VCR to watch themselves and their friends dance. "Look at me pimping there," Martin says as he watches himself come on stage for his starring role in a show called "Puttin' on the Glitz."

"The great thing about the dance school is that it keeps them occupied," Carlotta says. They go once a week after school for a couple of hours, and every Saturday. Unfortunately, few boys participate. "It's hard once boys get older to keep them involved, especially living in the environment we do," Carlotta says.

Working for Neighborhood Improvement

It's Tuesday night, time for the third in a twelve-week series of classes that Carlotta is taking on "neighborhood building." The classes are sponsored by the city of Louisville's Neighborhood Institute, and Carlotta loves them. They're being held in Louisville's Memorial Auditorium, a grand old granite structure on the edge of downtown.

Carlotta arrives a few minutes early so she can snare a seat right in front of the instructor. About four dozen other people trickle in, in twos and threes. Most are white. Some live in the Louisville suburbs that are just across the state line in Indiana. A few are students in a master's program in public administration at the University of Louisville.

From the questions, it's clear that the problems in these other people's neighborhoods are a little different from the problems in Carlotta's. Several of the participants complain about how little regard the "renters" in their neighborhoods have for property values. Their comments suggest that they have no idea that there's anyone in the class who lives in a public housing project.

If Carlotta is offended by their comments, she doesn't show it, nor does she try to hide who she is. During a presentation about how to handle community trash problems, Carlotta raises her hand and explains that she lives in a public housing project whose dumpsters are bedeviled by flies and odors in the summer. She wants to know whether the city requires garbage workers to spray the dumpsters with insecticide and deodorizer after they empty them. Told that they are, she writes down the answer, and the name of the man who provided it, leaving no doubt that heads will roll the next time the garbage workers fail to spray.

The next subject on the agenda—how to get a grant to finance a community betterment project—is the one she's been waiting for. Several experts in grant-making are doling out free advice about how to get money from foundations. Carlotta raises her hand.

"If your project is dealing with children, would it be good to take pictures of the kids you're hoping to get help for?" she asks. In the back of her mind, she's thinking about putting together a proposal to buy tap and ballet shoes for the children's dance school.

The facilitator nods. "That's a great idea. Anytime you can put a personal face on a proposal, it works better," she tells Carlotta.

"Then I'm going to do that, just as soon as I get some money together for film," Carlotta says.

Later the class gets some homework to work on over the next two weeks. They're supposed to assemble in small groups to devise a pitch for a grant of up to $10,000 for a hypothetical project. Carlotta's hand flies up again. "Can my project be for real?" she asks.

"I Want to Buy Me a House"

Carlotta finally has the W-2 and K-2 tax forms she needs to file her income tax returns for 1997. She's expecting a large Earned Income Tax Credit this year, maybe $2,000. But first she has to scrape together $75 to pay someone to fill out her returns for her, since there's no free tax help available at her community center this year, and the forms confuse her. "I don't have it this week," she says. "Maybe next week."

The Earned Income Tax Credit is designed to reduce the federal tax burden on the working poor. For many families, it provides a cash transfer large enough to lift the family out of poverty. The Earned Income Tax Credit elevated about 2.5 million children out of poverty in 1997, according to analyses conducted by the National Center for Children in Poverty.

But Carlotta's experience with the Earned Income Tax Credit is instructive. The EITC has been around since 1975 and was vastly expanded in 1993, but Carlotta never even heard of it until 1996. So she didn't benefit from it until years after she could have.

"Last year was the first time I claimed it," she says, speaking of the 1996 tax year. "When I worked at the laundromat, I didn't earn enough to owe anything, so I didn't see any point in filing a tax return. When I think now about all those years I could have been getting the EITC and I didn't know about it! Ignorance is really terrible."

Last year, Carlotta used most of her $2,000 tax credit to pay off bills. "And I bought a washer and paid cash for it," she says. "It was the first time I ever paid cash for anything. I got a washer that was brand-new. Nobody had ever used it before us. It felt really good.

"Then I went to the grocery store and made a big purchase. And I took each of the kids shopping and got them new school clothes and supplies."

The highlight for the kids was a movie and dinner at Ryan's Steak House, one of the few times they had a restaurant meal all year.

This year, Carlotta is going to try to bank most of her tax credit. "I want to buy me a house," she explains. "It doesn't have to be anything grand—just a little house, with four bedrooms and a basement, so the kids have some place to play when it's cold. Just a little $20,000 house in a nice neighborhood, with nobody living above me and nobody living below me. A house of my own, so if I want to paint my walls blue, I can."

When Carlotta allows herself to daydream about living in her own house, what she sees in her mind's eye is the whole family sitting down to eat together at a nicely set table, as she and her siblings used to do at her grandmother's house when she was a child.

"They're always talking on TV about how important it is to eat family dinners together," she says. "Here, we don't have room for a table. It'd be nice to all sit down together at a table someday."

6

BASALT, COLORADO

Isabella, Carlos, and Andrew Gonzalez live in a setting that couldn't be more pleasant.

Hummingbirds buzz from flower to flower in their front yard, and cottonwood trees shelter their trailer from the hot summer sun. A creek meanders along the back border of the one-acre property, and they have breathtaking views of the Elk Range of the Colorado Rockies any way they look. They're just twenty minutes from the ski slopes of Aspen, which has the third-highest per capita income in the United States.

Yet in the short time each of the Gonzalez children has been alive, their family has ricocheted from near-poor to poor and back again several times. In 1997, with an income of under $15,000, the Gonzalez family was officially poor. In 1998, with their combined incomes projected at about $33,000, they were likely to move into the category of near-poor, which is defined as an income under 185 percent of the federal poverty threshold.

The Gonzalez children's situation begs the question: is it easier or harder to grow up poor in a place that's among the most beautiful and prosperous on earth?

A Service Economy

Juan Gonzalez, twenty-seven, and Maria Gonzalez, twenty-five, are among the legions of service workers who make vacationing in places like Aspen possible. They cook the food, make up the beds, gas up the cars, and operate the lifts that take vacationers to the top of the mountains. Juan has been a cook at five different restaurants in Aspen over the last nine years and at the moment cooks at a fancy Asian fusion restaurant there. Maria has worked at a convenience store for nearly five years, rising to assistant manager.

Two of their children were fathered by Maria's previous boyfriend: Isabella, a shy, dimpled seven-year-old who's just finished second grade, and Carlos, an exuberant four-and-a-half-year-old who'll enter kindergarten in the fall. Four months ago, Maria gave birth to Juan's child, a fat-cheeked, bright-eyed baby called Andrew.

The family lives outside Basalt, a former mining and railroad town just about midway between Glenwood Springs and Aspen. Today the town is pretty much a bedroom community for Aspen. But it's also becoming increasingly popular among rich out-of-state residents as a slightly less expensive place than Aspen to build their vacation and retirement homes, a development that is raising the cost of housing for everyone. Town officials estimate that the population grew from 1,359 in 1990 to 2,200 in 1998, an increase of 62 percent.

How to make the area affordable for low-wage service workers like Juan and Maria is a source of contentious debate in the Roaring Fork Valley, which stretches from Glenwood Springs to Aspen. In 1995 the median household income in Pitkin County, where the Gonzalezes live, was $45,254. Although wages in the area are much higher than in most other places in the United States—a novice server at the Aspen McDonald's makes $8 an hour—the cost of living is so steep that many people have to work two or three jobs to support their families. (Maria has done this several times in her life.)

It's not unusual for families to spend more than half of their income on rent. Doubling and even tripling up in trailers and small apartments is common, especially among Latinos, and homelessness has begun to be a problem. So many families were setting up quasi-permanent campsites on public lands in the area that in June 1998 the Bureau of Land Management moved to limit camping stays to fourteen days. Meanwhile, about one-half of the houses sold in Aspen are used as vacation homes—and so are occupied just a few weeks or months a year.

Maria and Juan make numerous concessions in their personal lives to try to keep their household budget balanced. Nothing is bought new. Nearly every Saturday morning, they scout the yard sales in the neighborhood for other people's usable discards. Such sales have been the source of their refrigerator, their washer, their couch, and much of their kitchenware. They dug their vacuum cleaner out of someone else's trash.

Another way they save is by forgoing health insurance for Juan and the children. Maria says it would cost about $193 a month *each* to add them to the policy her employer provides for her, and they'd still have to pay for annual checkups and inoculations, as they do now. Though Maria knows she should add the family to the policy because of the potential costs of a catastrophic illness, she doesn't feel they can afford to just yet.

Most significantly, the couple purposely work two different shifts so that they don't have to pay for child care, which at the nearest child-care center would cost $27.50 per day per child. Maria worries that working different shifts, which leaves them little time with each other, is taking a toll on their marriage. "If day care was cheaper, we'd be able to work the same schedules, and we could have more of a family life," Maria says.

Here's how their budget looks this month, without accounting for incidentals or unusual expenses, such as the two doctor's appointments already scheduled (it costs $65 just to walk in the door) and car repairs. And starting in September, the family will have to pay $150 a month for the second half of the full-day public kindergarten that Carlos will be attending. (As in many school districts where full-day kindergarten is optional, only the first half is free.)

INCOME

Juan	$2,300
Maria	920
Total	$3,220

EXPENSES

Rent	$950
Telephone	31
Primestar TV	33
Electricity (some heat)	128
Natural gas (heat)	200
Gasoline	80

Old hospital bill	50
Car insurance	138
Groceries	360
Diapers	36
Repayment of debt to Juan's brother	500
Support for Juan's parents	200
Total	$2,706

While it looks on paper as though the family has a cushion of more than $500 a month in their budget, Maria is surprised when it's pointed out to her. She must be leaving out some expenses, she thinks. At the moment, she says, the family has just $94 in its checking account. "We live from paycheck to paycheck," Maria says. Juan's income, especially, has been unpredictable over the last few years. The Aspen restaurant scene is so volatile that restaurants have been known to close without warning. Last year, he was out of work for four months—at just about the same time that Maria was on an unpaid four-month sick leave because of pregnancy-related problems.

Over the next few months, Maria plans to put every penny she can into savings because lurking around the next corner, eight months from now, is the prospect of homelessness. The family's rented three-bedroom trailer is to be demolished to make way for a new subdivision of $400,000-plus homes, and the Gonzalezes have little hope of finding another place for the money they have to spend. "It's very possible we'll be homeless," says Maria.

Earlier this month, the family took two boarders into their three-bedroom trailer to help pay the rent while they save up for the costs of their anticipated move. "It's okay, because we never see them," Maria says of the boarders. "They work all the time."

Although $950 a month seems a huge amount to pay for a nineteen-year-old trailer, Maria says it's a bargain for this area, and the "Housing Available" advertisements in the local newspapers confirm her view. Inside, the trailer is comfortable, with lots of homey touches, including dozens of bouquets of dried roses, scavenged by Maria's mother from the trash at the fancy hotel at which she works and hung up by Maria to dry. Maria's housekeeping is impeccable. "My mom taught me even if you're poor, you can keep your house clean," Maria says.

Even with boarders occupying the master bedroom, the trailer offers more room than the family could hope for in an apartment. A deck built onto the front makes the trailer look bigger than it is. There's a large living room, an eat-in kitchen, and two bathrooms. (One is reserved for the boarders.) A small lean-to has been converted into a third bedroom, which the two oldest children share. It's largely because of this uninsulated room that utility bills can run $400 a month in the winter.

Not a day goes by that Maria doesn't worry about what the family will do when they have to move next winter. With two-bedroom apartments in Basalt renting for $1,200 a month, Maria doesn't see how they'll be able to afford to stay in the area. Just changing the lease on their trailer from Maria's mother's name to their name last spring cost them $3,400—first and last month's rent, plus a large security deposit. Doubling up in her mother and stepfather's trailer isn't possible because a brother and his pregnant wife and two children recently moved into the third bedroom, and the fourth bedroom is rented to two boarders.

Five Hours of Sleep

It's three-thirty in the morning when the alarm goes off in Maria and Juan's tiny bedroom. (Their double bed and the baby's crib consume most of the floor space.) Maria's had less than five hours of sleep, and the last thing she feels like doing is getting up in the dark. But she's due at work in an hour, and she's got to get up now to give Andrew a bottle so that he'll go back to sleep long enough for Juan to get a full night's rest.

Maria usually tries to wait up for Juan each night, since they see so little of each other, but last night she was too tired. She left him a note apologizing for not cooking him dinner and went to bed around 10:30 P.M. He got home from work just after 11:00 P.M. and came to bed about midnight, so Maria knows he'd like to sleep until 8:00 A.M. He takes care of the children while Maria works, and it's important for him to be well rested.

By 4:00 A.M., Andrew has been lulled back to sleep by a bottle of formula, and Maria puts him back into his crib. She dresses in her work uniform—black pants, sneakers, and a Hawaiian-style shirt—and heads out to her 1989 Toyota Camry. The convenience store where she works is only about a mile from her home, and usually she walks there, but Juan doesn't need the car this morning. There will be plenty of times she'll have to walk after school gets started again, since he needs the car to take the children to school.

For the next eight and a half hours, Maria never gets a chance to sit down. The store is a busy place: vacationers stop to gas up before they reach Aspen, where gas costs twenty cents more a gallon, and locals come in for a newspaper, a gallon of milk, a cup of coffee or lunch. Throughout her shift, Maria works the cash register, bakes pizzas, puts prices on canned goods, stocks the shelves, and continually tidies up, all the while greeting the customers she knows by name. Several times, she reminds a new stock boy whom she's training that it's his responsibility to take out the trash. When she sees a pile of flattened cardboard boxes in an aisle after he's left for the day, she takes them out herself. "That's what being a manager is all about," she explains. "I have to make sure that this gets done and that gets done."

By the time she finally leaves, fifteen minutes after her shift was supposed to end, she knows she's going to be late for her baby's 2:00 P.M. appointment at the WIC clinic in Aspen. She recently found out from her minister's wife that Andrew might be eligible for free formula through the government's WIC (Women, Infant, Children) supplemental food program, and she's going to check it out. Maria has always hesitated to ask for government help, but Andrew's formula is costing more than $40 a month, about the same as his diapers, and her budget is being stretched.

WIC is one of the federal government's most widely lauded programs for poor and near-poor children. Besides providing vouchers for formula, cereal, and, at the appropriate age, commodities like milk, eggs, beans, and cheese, enrollment in WIC would mean that Andrew's growth would be closely monitored, and Maria would get regular advice about nutrition and health, for free.

When Maria gets home, Juan is watching a World Cup soccer match with Andrew sleeping by his side on the couch. The other two children, eating leftover pizza at the kitchen table, jump up to give her hugs when she comes in. Maria doesn't take time to eat. She rushes into her bedroom to change out of her work clothes and pack up a diaper bag. She and Juan barely have time to exchange information about how the children have spent the morning before it's time to leave for Aspen. Maria's going to drop Juan at work before she goes to the clinic, and he'll catch a bus home tonight.

"You're a Nobody"

At the WIC clinic, Maria rushes up the stairs to the second floor, carrying Andrew in his infant seat and shouting, "Hola! Hola!" as she approaches the landing. "Sorry I'm late!" she tells the receptionist breathlessly.

The WIC eligibility worker has good news. Because the couple's income this year is projected to be below 185 percent of the poverty threshold (which is $35,853 for a family of five), Andrew qualifies for WIC, at least for now.

A WIC nurse takes Maria and Andrew into an examining room to get him signed up and explains to Maria how the program works. One of the best things about WIC, she tells Maria, is that someone will always be available to answer her questions about baby care.

Maria has a question she's been waiting to ask someone: can she start feeding Andrew baby foods? "Not yet," the nurse advises. "Just cereal for now, and at five months you can give him juices in a cup, but not a bottle. Anything you give him that's sweet, give it to him in a cup. Otherwise, his teeth will start decaying, even his permanent teeth. Never give him anything but formula and water in a bottle." The nurse has already noticed that Maria's two older children both show the residual symptoms of "bottle baby" syndrome—rotting baby teeth.

Maria leaves the clinic with vouchers for several cases of formula and a few boxes of baby cereal—which should save her about $100 over the three months for which Andrew's been certified. WIC is only a *supplemental* food program, so Maria knows she'll still have to buy some formula. "But every little bit helps," she says.

Before she leaves the clinic, her attention is directed to a display of brochures about a new low-cost health insurance program for children of the working poor in Colorado. Maria hasn't heard anything about it, but it appears from the income guidelines that her children should qualify. Like many other states, Colorado in 1998 took advantage of a new federal initiative called CHIP (Children's Health Insurance Program) to offer low-cost health insurance to tens of thousands of uninsured children. By the year 2000, Colorado expects to insure 23,000 children whose family incomes are below 185 percent of the federal poverty threshold.

Maria wishes she had known about the program before Andrew was born. Although her own health insurance covered all but $950 of childbirth-related expenses, it hasn't covered any of the numerous "well baby" visits and inoculations required during Andrew's first few months of life. So far, his health care since birth has cost her $600, and he hasn't even been sick.

The two older children have been well behaved during the visit to WIC, so Maria rewards them with a rare trip to McDonald's after her visitor offers to treat. The kids have been hearing about the new Beanie Babies promotion on TV commercials, and they can't wait to see which Beanie Baby they receive with their Happy Meals. (It's a kitty cat.) They're too busy playing with their Beanie Babies to finish their meals, so Maria carefully wraps them up to take home. "With the leftovers, we're already halfway to a dinner," she says. (She'll end up supplementing the leftovers with a can of Campbell's chicken and rice soup.)

Walking back to the car, Maria runs into a half-dozen people she knows and exchanges family news. Aspen may be a favored destination of the international jet set, but underneath the glamorous trappings, it's still a small town.

"I've been around here a long time, so I know all the regular people," Maria says. "Not many Anglos, though, because they don't mix. If you live here and you have dark skin and a Mexican name, you're a nobody."

Maria likes the small-town feel of Aspen, but in its heart she believes it's a sick town. "It's a beautiful town, but there's so much self-destruction going on," she says. "So many people use drugs. Because there's such a demand from the rich people, the young Hispanics look at it as an easy way to make money. But they're the ones who end up getting caught and going to jail, not the rich people." Two of Maria's brothers—and the former boyfriend who fathered Isabella and Carlos—have been arrested for drug-related crimes.

Maria detours to show a visitor the slopeside housing complex where she spent her early teen years. Her parents were among the workers at the old Grand Aspen Hotel who were lucky enough to be offered employer-subsidized housing; though decrepit, it was affordable.

"It's pretty nice now, but it was really a dump when we lived here," Maria says. If these were vacation condos, their location at the base of Ajax Mountain would command top dollar. But what vacationers would regard as ski in–ski out convenience was lost on the families of the service workers. For most of them, including Maria, skiing was something that other people did.

Maria: Abused as a Child

Whenever Maria starts worrying about all the problems in her life, she cheers herself up by placing them in the context of her past. The life she's leading now is so much more secure than the one she led growing up that even at the worst of times over the last few years—and there have been some bad ones—she's had trouble thinking of herself as poor.

Maria was the second of six children born to a peasant couple in the Mexican village of El Colorado, on the outskirts of Puerto Vallarta. Her mother was fourteen when she gave birth to her first child, seventeen when she gave birth to Maria, and thirty when she gave birth to her sixth and last child, who's now twelve. Throughout her early childhood, Maria's parents were only an occasional presence in her life, since they went back and forth to the United States several times each year to work the crops, living in migrant labor camps and sending money home when they could.

Maria remembers life in her village as unremittingly poor. "There were many times we didn't have enough to eat, or clothes to wear to school," Maria recalls. "There wasn't enough of anything. All through my childhood, I never had a toy. I used to pretend that sticks were dolls."

In 1980 Maria's father found stable employment as a maintenance worker at the Grand Aspen Hotel in Aspen, and in 1982 his wife joined him there and got a job as a maid. Maria was sent to live with an aunt in Mexico City, and her younger brothers stayed behind on the ranch with their grandfather. When the parents finally got an apartment in employee housing in 1985, they sent for the four children who were still in Mexico. (Their youngest two were born in the United States.)

With the help of a *coyote*—a paid guide skilled in evading U.S. border patrol agents—the children and their grandfather walked twelve hours, mostly in the dark, across the hills that form the border between Mexico and the United States near San Ysidro, California. They then crowded into the trunk of a car for a two-hour drive to a motel, where the children's father picked them up. Maria was thirteen.

"It was very, very scary," she remembers of the experience. "There were border patrolmen chasing us, and we had to run a lot."

At first, Maria was elated to be reunited with her family. "It was like, 'Wow, we're going to be a family again,'" she says. Then reality set in. Her father wasn't used to having children around and often lost his temper. "I was the one he picked on," Maria says. Her mother was working twelve to fifteen hours a day and had no time for housework, so it fell to Maria, as the oldest daughter, to keep house. Both parents drank heavily, and the children came to dread their arrival home.

Meanwhile, at Aspen Middle School, Maria found it difficult to make friends because she was the only Spanish-speaking student. There were no bilingual classes, and the teachers didn't quite know what to do with her, she says. "It was really hard, and for a long time I didn't understand anything," Maria recalls. She spent the first year carrying around a dictionary and looking up nearly every word that was spoken to her. There was no help at home, since neither parent spoke English, and both had dropped out of school in Mexico after third grade.

But Maria threw herself into her studies, and gradually she caught on. "I worked all the time," she says. "I didn't even take breaks. I just studied and studied and studied." At her eighth-grade graduation, she received awards for most improved in English, most improved in reading, and most improved in math, as well as a special achievement award for courage. She began to dream about becoming a policewoman.

By then, though, things were going really poorly at home. A few weeks before her graduation from eighth grade, her father had beaten her badly. When she was changing clothes for gym class, another student noticed her bruises and alerted a teacher. County child-abuse investigators were called, and Maria was removed from her home and placed in foster care. Eventually, her father was convicted of abusing her and served sixty days in jail.

Maria spent the rest of the school year, the summer, and the whole next school year, her freshman year at Aspen High School, living with a foster family in their trailer in nearby Aspen Village. She missed her siblings desperately and suffered from nightmares and sleeplessness. The child protection agency sent her to counseling, but it didn't help.

"I couldn't explain to the counselor how I felt inside," she says. "I would have had to put my heart inside her for her to really understand. It hurt too much to talk about it."

Just before the start of her sophomore year, she was riding her bicycle one day on a country road outside Carbondale when her father drove by in his pickup truck. When he noticed her, he backed the truck down the road, stopped, and threatened to kill her, she says. Maria managed to get away and go to the police.

Child protection authorities decided that it was no longer safe for her to stay in the area, even though she was in foster care. "They were afraid for me," she says. "They said this place wasn't big enough for him and me." Authorities sent Maria to live with an aunt in Los Angeles.

Maria says the aunt was mean and didn't really want her living there. Maria didn't want to be there either. She stayed for two weeks and then ran away. She lived on the streets of Los Angeles for a week and a half, sleeping under dumpsters and raiding garbage cans outside restaurants to feed herself.

"I didn't have any shoes, or even a change of clothes," Maria recalls. "It was really a tough time." By panhandling, she got enough change together to call her boyfriend, Jose, back home. He arranged for her to stay at his sister's house in Los Angeles, and a month later he joined her. They lived with his sister for a while and then moved into a room at the lumberyard where he'd found work. (It was actually a converted storage shed.) Soon Maria became pregnant. She was seventeen.

Maria remembers her year in Los Angeles as terribly lonely. Jose worked a lot, and she had no friends. She spent her time walking around the area picking up cans and bottles to trade for money to buy groceries. She was so afraid of being arrested for being a runaway that she never saw a doctor for prenatal care.

Isabella was born in mid-September 1990, two weeks before Maria's eighteenth birthday. She weighed nine pounds, thirteen ounces—an enormous amount for a first child, especially for a girl—and the birth nearly killed Maria. She was kept in the hospital for ten days because of uncontrollable hemorrhaging. Maria remembers

little of what the doctors said about the cause of the problem—
"something about me being so young and the baby being so big."

When Maria was finally well enough to leave the hospital, she and
the baby went home to the little room she shared with Jose. She was
very depressed. "I just cried and cried and cried, because I didn't
know what to do," she recalls. "I had no idea how to take care of a
baby, and Jose didn't know anything either."

Two weeks after Maria turned eighteen, she and Jose and their
one-month-old baby rode a Greyhound bus from Los Angeles to
Colorado. Maria was now legally an adult and couldn't be forced
back into foster care. And with Jose by her side, she felt protected
from her father. The couple moved in with friends, and Jose got a
job, cooking and washing dishes at a fast-food restaurant. Maria
stayed home to take care of Isabella.

Over the next two years, Jose became more and more possessive,
and the relationship went from bad to worse. He wouldn't allow
Maria to wear makeup when she went out, and she had to seek his
permission to talk to anyone, even on the phone. "I couldn't even
take the garbage out unless he said it was okay," she recalls.

He also became physically abusive. "I guess I'm lucky that I didn't
get any bad injuries," she says. "There were a few slaps, and a few
black eyes, and a lot of nosebleeds, but no broken bones."

Finally, Maria built up the courage to tell Jose to leave. "It broke
my heart, because he was my first love, but I couldn't take it anymore," she says. "After a lot of years thinking about this, I know
now that what I felt for Jose wasn't love. It was the need for protection. He helped me get away from my father."

Within weeks of Jose leaving, Maria found out she was three
months pregnant with their second child. She had no money, so she
sold the belongings Jose had left behind and lived off the proceeds
for a few months. The county gave her emergency food stamps and
a small cash grant (all of which she later paid back, for fear of jeopardizing her immigration status). By then, her father had returned
to Mexico, and her mother had bought a second-hand trailer in
Basalt. She let Maria and Isabella move in with her and her
youngest daughter.

A month after Carlos was born, Maria got a job as a clerk at a
convenience store. By the time Carlos was four months old, she was
working two other jobs as well—as a cook at a hamburger stand

and as a night cleaner in an office building. "I was working about one hundred hours a week," she says. "I gave one check to my mother as rent, and one check to the baby-sitter, and used the third one for everything else. It was crazy. I never saw my kids."

Juan's Story

Juan came into Maria's life when Carlos was about seven months old and Isabella was going on three years. A shy young man with beautiful almond-shaped eyes, a pencil-thin mustache, and a mouthful of perfect white teeth, he at first just exchanged pleasantries with Maria whenever he came into the convenience store. Then one weekend, Maria's aunt persuaded her to take a cousin who was visiting from Mexico to a dance. Juan was there and asked Maria to dance. That was the beginning of the relationship, which Maria says she entered reluctantly.

"Because of what happened between me and my father and me and my first love, I didn't trust men," she says. "Juan had to earn my trust. I was afraid that if we got married he would change, that he would keep me under his thumb, that he wouldn't let me go anywhere without him, because that's how my previous boyfriend was."

Maria made it clear from the start that if Juan wanted a relationship with her, it would have to include her children. "I told Juan if he wanted to be in my heart, he had to love my kids," she says. "My kids are my life, my everything. They make my heart strong."

In August 1995, the couple married in a civil ceremony in front of Maria's mother's trailer, and after a one-night honeymoon in nearby Glenwood Springs, Juan moved in. Maria says she married Juan mostly for her children's sake. "I wanted my kids to have someone to call Daddy, to be able to say to someone, 'Daddy, I love you,' and to be loved by him in return," she says. "I gave them all the love I could, but I knew they needed more."

With Juan's income coming into the household, Maria quit two of her jobs so that she could spend more time with her family. For the next two and a half years, they shared the trailer with Maria's mother and sister.

Juan had also grown up on a ranch in rural Mexico, in his case in the state of Michoacan. He speaks little English, so Maria translates as he tells how he came to America.

Juan was the youngest of eight children. All four of his older brothers came to the United States in their teens. Because they all sent money home to Mexico, his childhood was more comfortable than theirs had been, he says. With money from their sons, his parents were able to add on to their one-room concrete-block house. "My family was not rich, but not poor either," he says. "We always had enough to eat."

Juan attended school through ninth grade, the customary endpoint in rural Mexico for all but the children of the well-to-do. Soon afterward, he rode thirty-six hours by bus from his parents' home to Tijuana, where one of his brothers had settled by then. He lived with him, earning tips by boxing groceries for customers at a bodega.

All the while, though, he dreamed of going to the United States. "Every time my brothers came home to visit, I would see how well they were dressed, and how much money they had in their pockets," he says. "I wanted to be like them."

Eventually, Juan started crossing the border to find day work, as thousands of other Mexicans do every day. Then, in 1989, when he was nineteen, he took a bus to Colorado, where another brother lived. He moved into a trailer in Basalt with his brother's family and four adult boarders. He became one of the estimated five million undocumented workers in the United States.

"My first jobs were as a dishwasher and a laundry worker at a hotel," he says. "I worked a double shift and made lots of money." A year later, he got his first job as a cook. "I never went to school to learn to cook," he says. "I learned by watching the other cooks. At first, I was just making cheap Mexican food, enchiladas and tacos and burritos. Then I worked in a French restaurant, an Italian restaurant, and an American restaurant, and I learned other kinds of cooking, too."

The job he has now—at a fancy Asian restaurant—is the best he's had, though it requires him to work ten or twelve hours a day, six days a week. He started at $8.50 an hour and now earns a flat salary of $2,300 a month. But his income is not as good as it sounds, since the restaurant often closes for weeks at a time, "when it's too cold to golf and there's not enough snow to ski," as Maria puts it, and his income stops. Last year, Juan was unemployed for four months while the restaurant was being remodeled.

And who knows if the restaurant will still be operating next year? The restaurant business in Aspen is notoriously volatile. This year's hot restaurant can mysteriously become next year's bomb. Ominously, on a Friday night in June 1998, when thousands of people have descended on Aspen for its annual Food and Wine Festival, Juan's restaurant has only five tables of people eating, whereas the restaurants on either side of it are jammed.

Juan has turned out to be a wonderful father, Maria says. Both older children think of him as their father, not their stepfather, and his manner with them is loving and easy. But it took him a while to get comfortable around the baby, Maria says. "At first, when the baby came home, he was scared to hold him," Maria recalls. "He was afraid he was going to break. I said, 'No, you have to hold him, even if you're scared. He'll know that it's his daddy holding him, not his mommy, and it'll be okay.' Now he holds him more than I do."

The only thing Maria faults Juan for is being a little more traditional—"a little more Mexican," as she puts it—than she would like. He would prefer that she not work outside the home, even if it meant that he had to work two jobs. But so far Maria has managed to persuade him that such an arrangement would give them even less time together than they have now.

"Andrew rolled for the first time this morning," Juan suddenly says in Spanish, interrupting her discussion of his machismo problem.

"Well, if you were working two jobs, you wouldn't have been here to see that," she teases him in Spanish.

"Mommy, You're Never Home"

Isabella, like so many other Latino children, is growing up in a way that should ensure that she's comfortable in two worlds, the Spanish-speaking one at home and the English-speaking one that predominates in the Roaring Fork Valley. With a visitor, she speaks in English, in carefully constructed sentences.

"I like Winnie the Pooh," she says, in answer to a question about who her favorite cartoon character is. "My brother likes the Power Rangers. And I think my little brother is going to like Mickey Mouse, because he's got a Mickey Mouse in his crib."

"She's a really good kid," Maria says of Isabella. On her final report card for second grade, she has the primary school equivalent of As and Bs—Os (for Outstanding) and Ss (for Satisfactory.) In her comments, the bilingual teacher has written in Spanish, which Maria translates: "Isabella is doing really well in school. I like that she's reading much better and that she now often chooses to read in English. She does have problems finishing her work."

Isabella had a hard time of it during her first few years of life. When Maria broke up with her father, she was traumatized. "At first, she'd keep saying, 'Papa, Papa, where's Papa?'" Maria recalls. "But then after a while, she just stopped talking altogether. She would just make animal-type noises." Maria took her to a counselor for almost a year, and eventually Isabella started talking again. Today her biological father has no contact with her and doesn't pay child support. Maria believes he may be in jail.

While it had to have been difficult for Isabella to live in a household wracked by domestic violence, Isabella was just a toddler then and probably not fully aware of the problems her parents had, Maria tells herself. She thinks that the years when she worked three jobs and hardly ever saw Isabella might have been more damaging. "One day, she came up to me when I was rushing around at home trying to get ready for work and said, 'Mommy, you're never home. When can you play with me?'" Maria recalls, her eyes tearing up as she recounts the incident.

That memory is one reason Maria now tries to hold her work hours to about thirty-four a week, even though the family could use the income from a full-time schedule. She feels she owes it to her two older children to make up for the two years when she worked nearly around the clock.

"I regret so many things I've done in my life," she says. "I sometimes think about how I might have turned out differently if I had had somebody to guide me when I was a young girl. I really raised my self. But even though I have problems, every day I thank God that he let me survive the rough times, that I'm still alive. I know he was with me through it all, or I wouldn't still be breathing."

Isabella says she wants to be a nurse or a teacher when she grows up. "I hope she follows her dreams," Maria says. "I tell her all the time, 'Honey, follow through, because I never did.'"

A Waiting List for Preschool

Carlos is a cute little boy who rarely sits still. Maria worries about his aggressive behavior around other children and puzzles over the cause.

"He's a wild little thing," Maria says. "If he's not fighting with Isabella, he's throwing papers all over the living room. And when I take him over to my mother's, he's always chasing and punching his cousins, who are a lot smaller than he is." Maria has tried restricting his intake of sugar, which she believes may be the cause of his hyperactivity, but still he doesn't calm down.

During the last school year, Carlos attended a public preschool program at the Basalt elementary school. Maria had found it by accident and still can't believe her good luck. Since there is no Head Start in Pitkin County, she hadn't thought there were any affordable preschool options.

"I took Isabella to school one day and saw all these little kids there," Maria recalls. "I said to her teacher, 'How can those tiny kids be in kindergarten?' She said, 'Oh, no, they're not in a kindergarten. We have a preschool here.'

"Right away, I tried to sign Carlos up. But there was a waiting list, and he had to wait for a spot. He was the twelfth kid on the waiting list, and every Monday and Friday I would go in and bug them about whether he had moved up. Finally, three weeks after school started, they let him in."

Carlos's teacher kept Maria well informed about his progress during the year, and she's reassured Maria that Carlos's behavior is normal for a child his age. "She says he just has a lot of energy, and I shouldn't worry," Maria says. This summer, Maria is spending a lot of time drilling Carlos on numbers and colors, since he's had trouble learning them in two languages. And she's taking him and Isabella to a weekly enrichment program for Spanish-speaking children at the Basalt regional library. "I worry about them losing ground over the summer," she says.

A Third Child

Juan wanted Maria to get pregnant right after they married, but Maria stalled. "I didn't want to have a baby right away, because I wanted to be sure Juan was a good daddy," she says. "It's one thing to be boyfriend and girlfriend, and it's another thing to live together."

Andrew was born in March 1997, two and a half years after the couple married. He's a happy, healthy baby, totally in love with the world around him. Now four months old, he's in that phase of babyhood in which he smiles with his whole body, curling his toes and wiggling his hips in response to baby talk. He's clearly got everyone in his family under his spell.

There was a time when Maria wasn't sure Andrew would make it into this world. "I had so much trouble with my pregnancy that they thought I was going to lose the baby," she says. During the pregnancy, she suffered from blinding headaches, nosebleeds, and several bouts of dehydration serious enough to require hospitalization so that she could be hydrated intravenously.

It surely didn't help that her pregnancy coincided with serious financial problems. "For a while, everything seemed to go wrong," Maria recalls. "Juan's restaurant cut his hours, and he wasn't making as much then as he is now anyway. We got way backed up in our bills, and it seemed like we could never catch up. I had to take a second job cleaning the post office on weekends.

"Then the restaurant he was working for closed, and because it was the off-season, he couldn't find any other work. He tried so many places, but there wasn't any work. It was really hard on our relationship, because I couldn't understand why he couldn't find a job. He'd come home from looking, and I'd say, 'What's wrong with you? There must be work out there.'

"There were days then when we didn't even have enough to eat. A few months before the baby was born, we borrowed $5,000 from his brother so we could catch up with our bills."

Because of her health, Maria had to stop working when she was five months pregnant. (She wasn't paid during these four months.) For the last two months of the pregnancy, she was confined to her bed because she was at risk of going into premature labor. But she managed to carry Andrew nearly to term, and he was born weighing seven pounds, ten ounces. Fortunately, the birth itself was much easier than either of her first two; she and the baby came home after twelve hours in the hospital. (They left so quickly partly to keep down the cost of the birth.)

Two weeks later, she went back to work part-time, taking Andrew with her in an infant carrier. "We couldn't afford for me to stay home any longer," she says.

Maria doesn't want to have any more children, though Juan does. "After I had Andrew, I went to the doctor and got an IUD that's supposed to prevent pregnancy for ten years," she says. "I told them that when the ten years was up, I'd be back for another one."

An Uncertain Future

The front page of this morning's *Aspen Daily News* contains an article that makes Maria wild. "Twenty-two Illegals Found in Van Near Silt," the headline reads. "The illegal immigrants will be deported to Mexico," says the subhead.

> In an incident that has become increasingly familiar, 22 illegal immigrants were found packed into a van just east of Silt on Wednesday.
>
> The van was pulled over by the Colorado State Patrol for weaving, and, upon contacting the driver, the troopers discovered the vehicle's passengers. The stop, which occurred at 1:43 P.M., was the second of its type this year. On March 6, 23 illegal immigrants loaded into a van rear-ended a truck on Interstate 70, near Rifle.
>
> Wednesday's stop did not involve an accident. However, the fate of the passengers in this incident and the one in March appears to be the same. The Immigration and Naturalization Service arrived at the scene to transport the passengers to Denver for processing. After being processed, they will be taken back to Mexico.

"They talk about us like we're from a different planet," Maria says of local residents' attitudes toward Mexican immigrants. "Sometimes they even call us aliens. They look at our color instead of our hearts.

"Well, we're not from a different planet. We're the same color as a lot of Americans, and we have the same feelings, the same hearts. We're human beings. We're not aliens."

Incidents like the one reported in today's newspaper drive home the tenuousness of Maria's own immigration status. Although her parents qualified for permanent resident status under the amnesty Congress granted to undocumented residents in 1986, they didn't take the steps necessary to change formally the status of the four children, including Maria, who had been born in Mexico.

"My parents were fighting at that time, and neither wanted to take the responsibility," Maria says. "My mother said it was my father who was head of the family, so he should do it, and he just didn't."

For the last two years, Maria has been paying a lawyer in southern California to represent her in her "adjustment-of-status" petition to the Immigration and Naturalization Service (INS). So far, she's sent the lawyer $1,000 for his fee, plus another $1,600 in INS fees and fines. (The last $1,000 she sent to the INS was a fine required of undocumented immigrants in 1997 if they wanted to avoid having to return to their home countries while their applications for status adjustments were pending.)

Maria is worried because the last time she tried to call the lawyer, his number had been disconnected. She has no idea how to find him or whether he has actually filed the paperwork to adjust her status. (The couple couldn't afford to file an adjustment-of-status petition for Juan at the same time as Maria, so the plan is for Maria to sponsor Juan for permanent residency once her papers are in order.)

The cloud hanging over the couple's immigration status affects nearly every aspect of their lives. For one thing, Maria has had to abandon her girlhood dream of becoming a police officer. "I often helped the police department when they needed somebody to translate for them, and they kept telling me I should get my GED and they'll send me to the police academy," Maria says. "They don't know about my immigration status, I guess.

"Being a policewoman is always going to be a dream I carry in my heart, but I know in my head that I'm not going to realize it. Carlos wants to be a policeman, and maybe he will live my dream for me."

Another problem is that because the couple is working without proper papers, they can't file income tax returns. Both are overpaying federal and state taxes; they would be entitled to sizable refunds—and in some years even an Earned Income Tax Credit—if they filed returns. "We just let them take the money out and never ask for anything back," Maria explains.

In addition, although the couple would like to buy a trailer of their own, they can't qualify for a loan without proper immigration documents.

Worst of all, the couple knows their lives could come crashing down at any moment if, for instance, one of them is stopped in a routine traffic check or if the INS decides to crack down on workers in the area. "Our lives could change just like that," Maria says, snapping her fingers.

For these reasons more than any others, Maria is not optimistic about her family's future. "We can't make any plans," she says. "I take things a day at a time. I don't like to think ahead, because life has taught me that whenever you make plans, they fall through. It seems like every time I've planned a way for us to get ahead in life, something bad has happened."

She wonders constantly about what would happen to her three children if she or Juan were sent back to Mexico. Her children are all American citizens, growing up with American aspirations and dreams. Maria herself has spent more of her life in the United States than in Mexico, speaks English with hardly any accent, and "passes" for American every day.

"I've cried and cried over all this, but there's nothing I can do. God has seen me through a lot of rough times, and he's supposed to be working on this for me now. All I can think is that maybe he doesn't think it's time yet."

"In Mexico I still have my grandpa and one brother, but I don't have no life," she says. "My life is here, with my children."

7

WESTCHESTER
COUNTY, NEW YORK

The four Scarpato children are among the poorest of the poor. At the moment, they don't even have a home to call their own, since their family lives in a homeless shelter. They're just one parental misstep away from living on the street.

Like 2.5 million young children in America, Jessica, Louis Jr., Jeremy, and Maggie Scarpato fall into the income category of "extremely poor" because their family's income amounts to less than half the poverty threshold for families of their size. (In 1997 the Scarpato family had $2,859 in earned income plus about $4,000 in welfare benefits.)

The Scarpato children have some other things in common with many other extremely poor children—poor school attendance and performance, chronic health problems, and periodic referrals to the child protection system. Jessica, nine, missed ninety-six days of school last year. Louis Jr. and Jeremy, six-year-old twins, didn't even know the alphabet when they began kindergarten. Maggie, four, battles chronic ringworm infections.

Paradoxically, suburban Westchester County, New York, where the Scarpato children live, is one of the richest counties in America, with a per capita income of more than twice the national figure. Child poverty is far from the minds of the suburbanites who shop at the Westchester Mall, just a few blocks from the Scarpato children's temporary abode: a homeless shelter in White Plains, New York.

Not a Pleasant Place to Live

As homeless shelters go, the Coachman Hotel is a good one. It's owned by the county's Department of Social Services and operated by Westhab, a nonprofit, community-based agency. Residents don't just get a bed and a cup of coffee in the morning. They're offered a host of programs designed to prepare them for independent living, including drug or alcohol treatment if they have such problems. Numerous recreation and educational enrichment programs keep children busy after school and on weekends.

Though the social services seem excellent, it's not a very pleasant place to live. As the Scarpato children head out to school every day, they walk by a security post from which two guards monitor all who come and go from behind shatterproof glass. No visitors, not even relatives, can visit the families' living quarters. (The county's Department of Social Services gave special permission for one of the coauthors to visit the Scarpatos in their rooms.) Families can receive telephone calls in their rooms, but not make them.

With almost four hundred residents, more than half of them children, the noise level in the shelter's public rooms is often deafening. Police are called to the shelter, for one reason or another, nearly every day. The small playground is the scene of running domestic arguments; it's not unusual for a beer bottle to come flying through the air as children play on the jungle gym. By late afternoon, it seems as though every other word uttered by an adult is an expletive.

Every family has a different reason for ending up at the Coachman, but drug or alcohol abuse lurks in many of their backgrounds, as it does in that of the Scarpatos.

From Romania to the Bronx

The children's mother, Elise Scarpato, is a petite, pretty thirty-one-year-old who pays careful attention to her appearance, as you'd expect of someone who's been trained as a beautician. She wears long acrylic nails painted magenta and studded with "nail jewelry"—a diamond-bedecked "L" (for Louis, her husband) on one fingernail, and the word "Spoiled" in tiny gold-plated script on another. Because of her tawny skin and hard-to-place accent, she's frequently mistaken for Puerto Rican.

Elise came to the United States from Romania with her parents and older brother in 1981, when she was fourteen. Their sponsor was her older sister, who had married a Romanian American and immigrated years before.

During their first year in New York City, Elise's family crowded into her sister's two-bedroom apartment while they saved up enough money to rent their own place. They all worked, even the children. Both Elise's father and her seventeen-year-old brother worked at a commercial bakery, and her mother became the housekeeper for the bakery's owner. Throughout high school, Elise worked as a cashier in a discount store and later as a manicurist in a beauty parlor. Still, she managed to graduate from high school in 1985 with good grades.

The children's father, Louis Scarpato, thirty-four, is good-looking in a street-tough kind of way, sort of a cross between a young John Travolta and a young Jerry Seinfeld. He walks with a swagger, wears a gold chain and high-heeled boots, and talks with a pronounced Bronx accent. Within minutes of meeting Louis, it's clear that he has to be firmly in control of every conversation, to the extent that he answers all questions put to his wife. And wherever he goes, he must be center stage. Sometimes that requires creating a scene; often he can manage it with charm alone. When he takes the visitor on a tour of the shelter, he tells everyone they run into that she's here to write the story of his life.

Louis was born into a large Sicilian American family that filled six apartments in a building in the Bronx, then the domain of first- and second-generation Italian American and Irish American families. His father made his living by driving an eighteen-wheeler back and forth to Miami and rarely stopped in at home. "If we saw my father four times a year, it was a lot," Louis recalls.

His mother, a barmaid with a drinking problem, moved in with another man when Louis was five, leaving the children with relatives. For the next seven years, Louis and his younger sister lived in various foster homes, and later with his father's second wife, who had six children of her own. "She was a stepmom from hell," Louis says. "She beat the shit out of us." By seventh grade, Louis had attended about a dozen schools.

When Louis was twelve, his paternal grandparents, then in their sixties, finally obtained permanent custody after years of opposition from the children's father. Louis's grandfather ran a card club in the Bronx and was part owner of a scrap-metal business; his grandmother worked for a bank. They adopted him and his sister and brought some stability to their lives for the first time. "To me, they're my real mother and father," Louis says.

Living in a supportive environment for the first time in his life, Louis got himself a paper route, getting up at 4:00 A.M. daily to deliver the *Daily News* to his neighbors, and became an altar boy at the local Catholic church. But he also began hanging out with small-time hoodlums and was out of control at school. He fought with anyone who looked at him—or his sister—the wrong way. Because he was smaller than his peers and suffered from both a wandering eye and a stutter, "kids would make fun of me," he says. He was kicked out of three different high schools before he graduated from a Catholic high school in Westchester County in 1982.

Soon afterward, his grandfather threw him out of the house for talking back to his grandmother. For several months, Louis slept in the backseats of the luxury sedans that made up the fleet of a family friend's car service. During the day, the car service owner let him hang around with the mechanics, and Louis, a quick study, eventually got hired on as both a driver and a mechanic. He worked for the car service off and on until 1989. During much of this time, he also sold and used drugs.

Louis and Elise met on Orchard Beach, one of the Bronx's beaches on Long Island Sound, in 1986. Elise was attending beauty school and working full-time at a salon frequented by Romanian immigrants. The couple married in 1988 and moved into an apartment in the same building in which most of Louis's extended family lived. Elise became pregnant within a month. Jessica, their first child, was born in February 1989. "I worked right up until the day she was born, from 8:00 A.M. to 8:00 P.M., doing nails," Elise remembers.

Louis: Hitting Bottom

A few months after Jessica's birth, some family friends found Louis in a bar, strung out on cocaine and barely recognizable. "I had hit bottom," he says. The next thing he remembers is waking up in an inpatient treatment center in Carmel, New York, a small upstate community. He stayed for a month and, by his account, emerged clean and determined to get free of his old associations. He joined Narcotics Anonymous and has not, he says, used drugs since.

Elise says she hadn't even known he used drugs, let alone sold them. Believing that it would be easier for Louis to stay away from drugs if he stayed away from the Bronx, she moved up to Carmel with Jessica. The couple rented an apartment on the second floor of a two-family house, and Louis and Elise each got jobs on the custodial staff at Putnam Hospital. He worked the day shift, and she worked the night shift so that one of them could always be with Jessica. "It was good money," he recalls. Their 1992 tax return shows a gross income of $18,756, well over the poverty line at the time for a family of three.

Their fraternal twins, Louis Jr. and Jeremy, were born in early 1992, and Elise quit her job to stay home with the three children. A year later, Louis decided he could make better money as a mechanic in the New York City metropolitan area than he was making at the rural hospital. Through family connections, he got a night-shift job doing maintenance work on buses for $500 a week. The long commute to the city meant that he left home at three in the afternoon and didn't get back until three in the morning.

The couple's fourth child, Maggie, was born in January 1994. Not long afterward, Elise began using cocaine. "Not too long ago, my brother and sister-in-law asked me why I used it, and I didn't have a good answer for them then, and I don't have one now," Elise says. "How it happened was that the lady who was living downstairs from us was using, and she offered me some. I was really lonely because Louis was gone all the time. I had four little kids, all under five, and I was stuck in the house without a car. Every time I got lonely, the neighbor lady and I would get together and use.

"I'm ashamed to say it now, but we'd sit outside and watch the kids play in the yard while we smoked crack. When I was high, I didn't want to be bothered with the kids, and they knew it. They could see the changes in my eyes, and how I was talking. It wasn't a nice experience for them."

Elise says Louis never suspected that she was using cocaine. "I'd be asleep by the time he got home," she explains.

Eventually, the engine in Louis's car gave out, and without the money to replace it, he was forced to give up the mechanic's job. He took a series of low-paying jobs in fast-food restaurants in Carmel and nearby Brewster, four in 1995 alone. His income that year to-taled $4,282, putting the family, for the first time, in the category of extremely poor. They qualified for food stamps and a partial welfare stipend. They also came to the attention of the county's child protec-tion system, since Jessica was missing school for days at a time and the police were getting regular calls from neighbors about Louis's frequent rages against Elise. "We argued all the time—we still do—but there was only one time he was ever physically abusive," Elise says. "As far as I'm concerned, he can yell at me all he wants as long as he doesn't touch me."

In late 1996 the couple moved to Yonkers, a Westchester County suburb just across the New York city line. Louis believed he could find a better job there than he'd been able to get upstate. Plus, the couple wanted to be closer to Elise's family, who still lived in the Bronx, because her father had recently had a stroke. They also admit to wanting to escape supervision by Putnam County's child protec-tion system, which neither believed was justified.

Louis's job prospects didn't pan out. For one thing, he had sold his mechanic's tools and couldn't raise the $1,500 it would have cost to replace them. In addition, mechanics were increasingly using com-puterized equipment, which Louis wasn't familiar with. Instead, he took a job as a manager at a neighborhood Burger King, making a dollar or two an hour above minimum wage, about the same as he'd made in Putnam County. Financially, they were no better off.

A few months after they moved to Yonkers, Elise's drug use peaked, and she stopped caring about hiding it from Louis or any-one else. "Every little thing that went wrong in my life triggered me," she says. "Mainly, it was because Louis couldn't keep a job. If somebody gave him a hard time at work, he would blow up and quit, and then he'd come home and blow up at me. And the first chance I got I'd go out and score some cocaine."

Elise's drug use caused a rift with her parents and siblings that has yet to heal. They were already upset with her for marrying Louis, whom they disapproved of. "The only time Louis ever hit me, my brother's wife was there," Elise says. "He smacked me and scratched my face, and no one in my family could understand why I stayed with him."

Late in June 1997, a tense relationship with their landlord in Yonkers escalated into an eviction proceeding. The landlord alleged that the couple wasn't paying its share of the rent. The rent was $1,221 a month, and the federal Section 8 program paid all but $88 of it, which the Scarpatos were supposed to pay. The Scarpatos countered that the landlord wouldn't accept their rent payment because she wanted to evict them to avoid making the repairs the Section 8 program was requiring of her. The couple tried unsuccessfully to get help from their city councilwoman and the governor's office, but the case went to court.

The judge sided with the landlord. County sheriffs evicted the family on July 17, 1997. That night, all but Elise moved into the Coachman Hotel. Louis told shelter officials that his wife was a crack user, and they wouldn't allow her to move in until she enrolled in a drug rehabilitation program. After signing up with a program, she rejoined the family a day later.

"Sorry, Honey"

From day one, Louis was scornful of most of the other residents of the Coachman. "I don't like this lifestyle," he says. "There are people at the Coachman who like it here, who want to live on aid. Not me. If I could get myself a set of mechanic's tools, I'd be back at work tomorrow."

Although the Coachman has a rule against drug use by residents, the policy isn't universally effective. Louis says he frequently smells crack cocaine or marijuana smoke wafting out from beneath closed doors. But Elise says the shelter's policy helped make her stop. Every weekday for her first seven months there, starting with the day after she moved in, she took a public bus to her treatment program in Yonkers. "I got clean," she said. "They didn't require it, but I took a urine test every day just to prove I was clean."

For the first three months, the Scarpatos all shared one small room, approximately fifteen by fifteen feet in size. Louis and Elise slept in one twin bed, and the four children in two others. There were no cooking facilities, so they ate their meals in the group dining hall downstairs. Mealtimes were bedlam, with babies crying, parents shouting at toddlers to sit still, and plates and glasses often crashing to the floor.

"At first, I thought we'd just be here a few weeks, but when I mentioned that to the counselors, they laughed at me," Louis says. The counselors were right. Ten months have passed since the family moved in.

When it became clear that the Coachman was going to be their home for a while, Louis decided to try to make the best of it. He got himself appointed to the residents' council and formed a cleanup committee. He and a few other residents picked up trash, wiped down walls, and waxed floors. Louis also organized some activities for the shelter's children. "We used to have slumber parties for all the kids, and whenever we got our welfare payment, I'd go out and buy a case of ice cream sandwiches," he says.

To make himself more employable, Louis tried to enroll in a training program that provides computer skills to mechanics. But not enough people signed up to justify offering the course, so it was canceled. Instead, he enrolled in a building maintenance course. "There's a big need for people who know how to keep boilers running, so maybe it will lead to a job," he says optimistically.

Louis also took it upon himself to try to rid the Coachman of drugs, complaining to management every time he smelled crack or marijuana being smoked. He became almost a one-man vigilante squad. "I'm not afraid to tell people what's on my mind," he says. "A lot of people don't like that because they don't want to hear the truth."

When a larger apartment became vacant in the fall of 1997, the shelter managers let the Scarpatos move in. It consists of a combination living room and kitchen, a bedroom, and two bathrooms. Although it has more than twice as much space as the room they'd been living in, it's still very cramped. Bags and boxes filled with clothes and other possessions line the walls. The refrigerator is barely large enough to store a day's worth of perishables. The stove has just two burners, and there's no oven.

But with cooking facilities, however minimal, the Scarpatos could at least begin to build a semblance of family life. Louis started working again, as a cook in a restaurant at nearby Westchester Mall. Elise continued attending her outpatient program. And all of the children attended school regularly, for the first time in their lives.

Elise says she met all of the drug treatment program's requirements but failed to be "graduated" in January 1998, as expected, because of her counselor's concerns about the potential for domestic violence in the household. She disagreed with her counselor's assessment and tried to persuade her that Louis was all bluff. But the counselor stuck to her position and told Elise she'd have to continue to attend the treatment program or risk losing her children to foster care. Elise was devastated.

"All I wanted to do was get out of the program, get a job, and begin to have a normal life again," she says. "We've never before been in the position of waiting for welfare twice a month, or needing other people to give us clothes. I wanted to move on. I wanted to be able to spend time at my kids' school instead of going to program every day."

A few weeks later, the family got more bad news. They'd been expecting an Earned Income Tax Credit of $1,150, based on their previous year's earnings of $2,859. But the money was diverted by the Internal Revenue Service to the federal student loan program and applied to Elise's debt for her beauty school loan.

Just as before, when every minor setback in the day sent her out in search of cocaine, Elise responded to her failure to "graduate" and the loss of the EITC by giving in to her craving for drugs. On Valentine's Day 1998, while the rest of the family was sleeping, she took $100 in savings, left a note saying "Sorry, honey," and boarded a train, and then a bus, to Fremont Avenue in the Bronx, where she knew she could buy drugs.

She returned to the Coachman two days later, exhausted and contrite. She and Louis argued. A neighbor called Children's Protective Services, fearing that the children were in danger, and an investigator came to the apartment. "They asked me if I wanted to go, or I wanted the kids to go," Elise says. She left the shelter, spent the night in a motel, and checked herself into an inpatient rehabilitation program in Yonkers the next day. She spent five days under sedation while the cocaine worked its way out of her system. "The only time they woke me up was to eat and go to the bathroom," she says. "I was in such a daze from the sedatives that I didn't even remember what the nurses looked like."

Once she'd been detoxified, she began the task of trying to understand why she keeps craving cocaine. An addiction to crack cocaine is notoriously hard to overcome, especially for women. There's no pharmaceutical treatment, as there is for heroin, and multiple relapses are common before an addict can finally claim success. Even then, stress often triggers cravings, sometimes for life. So rehabilitation programs usually focus on helping addicts understand what sets off the cravings, and how to cope with stress in less destructive ways.

Elise *loved* the rehabilitation program. "You could talk about anything, and nobody put you down," she says. "They helped you with whatever you needed help with. I felt really good being there."

But she missed her children desperately. Louis brought them to visit every weekend and made sure that Elise had enough pocket change to call them once a day. To his credit, he came regularly to participate in family therapy sessions with her. "I want my family to stay together," Louis says. "My mom left me when I was five, and I refuse to let that happen to my children."

After thirty days, Elise was discharged to an outpatient program. That was two months ago, and she's still clean.

"I regret so much what I put my children through," she says. "I hate myself for it. I don't ever want to put myself or my kids through it again."

Louis interjects. "You ought to hate yourself for it," he tells her. "You're lucky I don't hate you for it. Any other husband would have left you long ago."

In an aside, he adds: "I feel like I'm involved in a daily battle to keep my family together. And the reason I keep fighting is that I love my wife, and I love my kids."

A Monitor in Their Midst

After the child abuse investigator came to the family's apartment following Elise's relapse, the Westchester County Department of Social Services opened a new protective services case on the family. (As the Scarpatos had hoped, moving away from Putnam County had indeed permitted them to escape supervision, at least for a while.) The agency's top priority was helping keep the family together, since there was no evidence that either Louis or Elise were physically abusing the children. The department provided a paid homemaker so that Louis could continue to work while Elise was hospitalized. Mary, a Ghanaian immigrant who appears to be in her late forties, came early to get the children ready for school and stayed late to get them ready for bed. "When Elise was away in the hospital, she was a great help," Louis says. "She did everything for us. She really helped me hold things together."

When Elise came back from inpatient treatment, Mary's hours were cut to five hours a day, five days a week. She's supposed to be modeling healthy adult-child interactions and teaching Elise and Louis how to manage a home and work out their domestic problems amicably. But it seems that she spends most afternoons lying on one of the children's beds watching soap operas, yelling at the children when they become too noisy, and shooing them out of the bedroom when they squabble. "I hate Mary," a tearful Maggie says after Mary pushes her out of the bedroom one afternoon while a visitor is talking with Louis and Elise at the kitchen table.

The Scarpatos have come to resent her presence. "We don't need Mary in our lives now, even if she was doing her job," Louis says. "It causes a kind of codependence. My wife and I can do all this stuff she's supposed to be doing ourselves."

But the Scarpatos are afraid to complain too vigorously for fear that Mary will say something about them that could cost them their children. Since she's assigned to the family by Child Protective Services, Mary is what's called a "mandated reporter," obligated to report any suspicions of abuse to the child abuse hotline. The Scarpatos are so fearful of retaliation that they frequently sign her time sheet indicating that she worked a full shift even if she left an hour or two early.

At Last, Some Good News

Today's mail has brought official confirmation of some long-awaited news. The Scarpatos had challenged their eviction and the revocation of their Section 8 status and were told informally a few weeks ago that they'd won Section 8 back on appeal. A letter today confirms it. With their Section 8 certificate restored, they should be able to move out of the Coachman within a month. Under the Section 8 program, they'll have to pay about one-third of their income as rent, and the government will make up the difference between their payment and the market rate. As their income rises, so will their required payment.

In anticipation of the news, the Scarpatos have been checking out apartments for the last few weeks. At first, they concentrated on finding housing in White Plains so that the children wouldn't have to change schools again. But they had no luck. "As soon as a landlord hears 'Section 8,' he says the apartment's taken," Louis says. "They don't want poor people living in this town."

It's been hard searching for housing without a car. Every time they hear of a vacant apartment and a landlord willing to consider a Section 8 tenant, they have to figure out how to get there to see it. They've made few friends among the other residents at the Coachman, so they don't feel comfortable asking any of them for rides. Usually, they've ended up loading the whole family onto a bus to go on scouting missions, even though they worry about what a landlord thinks when he sees a family of six on his doorstep.

Last week, they found a three-bedroom apartment in Yonkers that seems to meet their needs. The landlord told them he had no problem with Section 8 tenants, and he's been holding it for them while they awaited confirmation of their subsidy. The market-rate rent is $1,400 a month, and Louis believes the monthly contribution required of them will be about $170 until they leave the welfare rolls and get jobs, when it will go up.

"I really don't like the area," Louis says. "I'd like to keep looking in White Plains, but we don't have that much time to find a place. I'm afraid if we lose our certificate again, we'll never get it back. But at least, with this place, I'll be close to public transportation, so I can get to work. The next thing is to find me a decent job that's going to pay me the money so when we come off of welfare we don't ever have to go back on."

Maggie: A Health Scare

It's a beautiful May morning, the first sunny morning in three weeks, which is lucky because Maggie's Head Start classroom is going on a field trip to Muscoot Farm, a working farm operated by Westchester County as a park. Elise is taking the day off from her rehab program to chaperone. "We're going to see ducks and cows and chickens and bunny rabbits," Elise tells Maggie as she dresses her this morning in a long-sleeved shirt and pants, as she's been instructed. "Mommy and Maggie are going to have fun."

Louis would like to be going, too, but he's got to attend the Department of Social Services' "Power" program in nearby New Rochelle to learn job-seeking skills. He skipped his class yesterday to help Maggie's Head Start class bake cakes, and he can't chance another absence this week for fear the family's welfare benefits will be cut off as a sanction. But he doesn't have to catch the bus to the program until around noon, so he goes along to the Head Start program to eat breakfast with Maggie and her classmates. The Scarpatos' three other children have already left by bus for elementary school.

Maggie attends the St. Bernard's Head Start program, which is unique in the area. All but a handful of the eighty children who attend classes there live in homeless shelters. With the help of psychologists from the Center for Preventive Psychiatry, a community mental health center in White Plains, the center's curriculum was crafted to take into account the special problems that homeless children bring with them to group settings, whether an inordinate need for attention or a tendency to withdraw. (A self-contained therapeutic classroom provides one-on-one attention to the most troubled children.) For many children, the four-hour period they spend here every weekday is the most structured part of their day.

Louis and Elise are popular with the staff here because they're always volunteering to help with special projects, and they obviously dote on Maggie. "I see them as parents who are really attendant to their kids," says Mary McGovern, the center's social worker. "When Elise fell off her program, Louis was there to hold the family together. They've got a strong sense of pride and work ethic. At the moment, they're really fighting a battle, with multiple agencies involved in their lives, but I think they're coping well under the pressure, given that they really want to be making their own decisions about their lives without all of us knowing about them."

As two dozen four-year-olds eat their breakfasts of Cheerios and bananas, the school nurse comes in to make sure they're all well enough for the field trip. There have been a lot of illnesses lately— primarily strep throat—and the day is going to be longer than usual, so the children have to be in top form. Elise asks the nurse to take a look at Maggie's face, which has been marred for the last month by a nasty silver-dollar-sized ringworm infection. It covers her left cheekbone, and Elise is afraid that she's got a few new spots on her scalp. "That's the thing I hate most about the shelter," Elise says. "There are so many things the kids can catch. Last week there was a girl playing on the swings with chicken pox."

Elise sounds worried as she talks to the nurse. "I've been taking her to the doctor for this for more than a month, and it's not getting any better," Elise tells her. "And last night I noticed that she wouldn't eat. She said her mouth hurt, and she was really crabby."

The nurse examines the ringworm infection, but she's more alarmed by what she sees on Maggie's neck and, when she investigates further, on her chest, inside her elbows, and behind her knees. She's got a raw red rash in all those places. When the nurse looks in Maggie's mouth, she sees something else she doesn't like—a swollen, strawberry-red, bumpy tongue. She goes into her office and comes back with an excerpt from a pediatric health book.

"I think she's got scarlet fever," the nurse tells Elise and Louis. The written description of the symptoms of scarlet fever seems to match Maggie's symptoms. Elise's face blanches when she hears the tentative diagnosis, because she knows that scarlet fever was until recently a killer in her home country, where antibiotics have been scarce.

"She really has to be seen by a doctor," the nurse says. "I feel terrible that she can't go on the field trip, but this is nothing to fool around with."

Elise calls the clinic in White Plains that treats residents of the homeless shelter, but it turns out to be closed on Fridays. The emergency room in White Plains is an option, but the family's insurer, a Medicaid health maintenance organization, won't cover an emergency room visit during normal office hours. (Louis and Elise haven't been pleased with the care their children have gotten there anyway. Only two days ago, Elise had taken Maggie in with a fever of 103 degrees and a bad sore throat. The emergency room doctor hadn't even done a strep test before giving them a prescription for penicillin.)

Louis and Elise decide that their best bet is to go to Yonkers, fifteen miles away, to the Valentine Family Practice, the clinic they used before they became homeless. It's run by Montefiore Medical Center and provides top-notch care to a largely low-income clientele. But how to get there? Normally, they'd take a bus to Yonkers, an hour-long ride, at a fare of $3 each round trip. But they spent the last of their semimonthly welfare stipend the previous Sunday and don't even have pocket change left. (Money has been particularly tight this month because the family's welfare benefits have recently been cut. They had been receiving $700 a month but will be getting only $564 a month from now on because the state says it erroneously overpaid them $1,520 in the previous few months, and they have to pay it back. Because of a paperwork error, they had continued receiving a "restaurant allowance" after they moved into a unit with a kitchen.)

It seems to make sense for the family's visitor to drive them, and we set out at 10:00 A.M. Maggie is excited to be in the subcompact rental car. It's the first time in a long time that she's traveled in any vehicle besides a bus.

A Different Diagnosis

We arrive at the Valentine Family Practice at 10:30 A.M. It's on the second floor of a corner storefront just up the street from the apartment that the Scarpatos were evicted from almost a year ago. The waiting room is filled with mothers and children talking to each other in numerous languages other than English. The educational posters on the walls make it clear that doctors here treat a clientele at high risk of contracting infectious diseases; the messages deal mainly with HIV and AIDS and teen pregnancy prevention. But the facilities are as nice as those found in a suburban family practice anywhere, and the staff is pleasant to all.

A nurse weighs and measures Maggie. She's small for four and a half—just thirty-two pounds and three feet, three inches tall—but not alarmingly so. The nurse warns that there's a long wait until the doctor can examine Maggie, since she didn't have an appointment. Maggie passes the time in the examining room by opening drawers, playing with a blood pressure cuff, and looking into her parents' ears, over and over again, with a lighted otoscope.

"I want a soda," she begs after an hour, but her parents don't even have three quarters to put into a vending machine. By 12:45 P.M., when the doctor finally comes in to look at her, her parents' patience is exhausted. Maggie begins whimpering the moment she sees him. "No shot, no shot," she pleads.

Elise explains why they're there. To her relief, the doctor quickly rules out scarlet fever.

"That's a rash from an allergy, not scarlet fever," he says. "It's classic eczema. But the rash on her scalp, now, that's a different story. That could very well be ringworm of the scalp. That's much more serious than the ringworm on her face."

The doctor takes a scraping of the rash on Maggie's scalp so he can examine the cells under a microscope. He returns a few minutes later and confirms that she has ringworm of the scalp. There's no ointment that's effective on scalp ringworm, he tells Maggie's parents. The only effective treatment is an oral medication. But it can have serious side effects—liver dysfunction and blood problems—so he can't prescribe it unless blood tests show that Maggie's system is up to it. "We have to be very careful with this," he says.

As for the sore throat, the doctor shakes his head disapprovingly when he hears that the emergency room doctor failed to perform a strep test before he gave them a penicillin prescription a few days ago. "We'll do one now, but it won't tell us if she had a strep throat three days ago, only if there's still strep present now," he says. In his view, it's likely that Maggie's sore throat wasn't caused by strep at all, but by the Coxsackie virus (named after the town in upstate New York in which it was first recognized). If it's Coxsackie, it won't respond to penicillin. So Maggie's probably been on penicillin for three days for no good reason, and as a result, its effectiveness is likely to be compromised the next time she needs it for a bacterial infection.

Maggie becomes hysterical as the doctor puts an elongated cotton swab down her throat for the strep test. Her parents have to hold her down. The exertion causes the rash on her body to redden further. Her hysteria mounts when a lab technician comes to draw blood for the tests needed to determine whether her liver can tolerate the medication for scalp ringworm. Because of the raw eczema rash, the technician can't even cleanse her arm with alcohol before drawing blood. Maggie screams as the needle punctures her vein. "It hurts," she whimpers. "I want a Band-Aid."

When the technician is finished, Maggie throws her arms around Louis's neck and buries her face in his chest. "Daddy'll make you feel better," Louis tells her as he lavishes her with kisses.

At 2:00 P.M., three and a half hours after they arrived, the family finally leaves the clinic. They have two prescriptions to fill—one for the ringworm on Maggie's face, the other for the eczema. Treatment of the ringworm on her scalp will have to wait until the results of the blood work are in, five days from now.

Fighting Women, Flying Beer Bottles

By the time they arrive back at the shelter, it's after 3:00 P.M. Six police cars, lights flashing, have blocked the street next to the shelter, and uniformed officers are everywhere. One is interviewing the shelter's director, who appears shaken. Shelter residents are standing around in clusters waiting to see what will happen next.

In the midst of the commotion, two school buses pull up and start disgorging the elementary school children who live at the shelter. They pour into the shelter's small playground. They're excited by the presence of so many police officers, and instead of rushing to the climbing structure, as usual, most of them crowd around to watch what's happening.

A few minutes later, several police officers escort two female shelter residents out of the shelter's security office, their hands cuffed behind them. It turns out that the two had gotten into a fight on the playground, and the shelter's director had tried to intervene and been shoved aside. Inside the shelter office, the paperwork is already being prepared to evict the women and their children from the shelter.

Jeremy and Louis: "Off the Wall"

Not long afterward, Annie Caldecott, the teacher's aide in Louis Jr.'s kindergarten classroom, drops by to visit the family and present them with a photo album that she's put together to chronicle Louis's progress over the last year. Since visitors aren't allowed in the family quarters, she sits with them on a bench on the playground while they examine the scrapbook. It's filled with pictures of Louis in the classroom and on the many weekend outings she's taken him on.

Annie has bonded more strongly with Louis Jr. than with any of the thirty-seven other children in the morning and afternoon classes in which she helps out. When she watches him climbing on the jungle gym, her eyes shine with love.

"I guess I like him because he's so resilient," she explains. "When he first came to school last fall, he had no idea how school worked. He was all over the place, completely off the wall. He wouldn't follow directions or stick to routines, because he didn't know that that's how school works. When we gave him a crayon and asked him to do a self-portrait, he just produced scribble.

"I still remember the first day he drew his first figure—a cat. In the last three months, I'd say, he's learned how to sit and do work. His drawing has gotten really good. He can draw all sorts of figures now. And he just loves playing with blocks, building things."

Last fall, the Scarpato twins were among just a handful of kindergartners entering the White Plains kindergarten classes without any previous group learning experience, such as nursery school, child care, or Head Start. In most suburbs and cities in the United States today, many children have their first group learning experience at the age of three, and by the time they start kindergarten at age five, almost all know their ABCs and colors, and many can count to 100. Not Louis and Jeremy. Even though they'd watched *Sesame Street* on television for hours on end, they appeared to have learned nothing from it beyond the characters' names.

"Even now, after almost nine months of kindergarten, Louis still has problems with basic things," Annie said. Although he appears quite normal in a social setting, he has problems retaining information, she says.

Jeremy has serious fine- and gross-motor problems, possibly because of a neurological injury at birth. Louis, the firstborn, was born without incident. But Jeremy got stuck in the birth canal for what his mother says was thirty minutes. Doctors performed an emergency caesarean section, but it seems likely that he was deprived of oxygen long enough to impair his cognitive abilities permanently. He's seriously delayed developmentally, in almost every respect. Ominously, his eyes lack the sparkle that animates Louis's, and he speaks much less intelligibly.

"He gives his teacher real problems," Annie says of Jeremy. "His behavior is really erratic and unpredictable. He doesn't listen to instructions."

For the last few months, both Louis and Jeremy have been receiving special education services at their school. They attend special education classes all morning and regular kindergarten classes in the afternoon. Annie says they were clearly in need of such assistance from the beginning of the school year, but Louis and Elise refused to cooperate with the process of screening them.

"We pushed for a long time, but the parents wouldn't come in to talk to us," Annie says. "They're in serious denial. They've told the school that there's nothing wrong with their kids. They just think that they're a little behind because of what they've been through in the past two years. I'm sure that's part of it, but I think there's much more to it, too."

Annie thinks both boys would probably benefit from repeating kindergarten next year, but it's very rare in this district, she says, for children not to be advanced to first grade. She believes that, at the very least, both boys will need special education services throughout their school careers.

Jessica: Ninety-six Absences from School

The Scarpato firstborn, Jessica, is an immensely appealing nine-year-old with an endearing smile. But she, too, has educational problems. In the 1996–1997 school year, during which she was repeating first grade, she missed ninety-six days of school. "I was still using cocaine, and there were a lot of times when I just didn't feel like getting out of bed and walking her to the bus," Elise admits. "I made excuses, like I didn't feel good, or she didn't feel good. But a couple of times she was really sick."

Louis adds: "I was working at Burger King, so I didn't know she wasn't going to school. When letters came about the absences, Elise would rip them up."

This year, Jessica is in second grade and attending school regularly for the first time in her life. The bus picks her up right at the shelter and drops her back there at the end of the day.

Annie has taken an interest in Jessica's social and educational development, too. She's collected bags full of nice hand-me-downs for her so that Jessica can fit in better in her school, where most of the children come from affluent families. When Jessica's second-grade class celebrated her ninth birthday a few months ago, Annie provided a cake and came to the party. She says it broke her heart when several children asked Jessica why she was turning nine and most of them weren't yet seven.

"Jessica looked like she wanted to disappear into the floor," Annie recalls. "She was incredibly embarrassed. Fortunately, the teacher stepped in and said something really nice. She told them that when they were in the first grade learning to read, Jessica's family was moving, and she didn't get to go to school very much and learn to read."

Now, one month short of the end of second grade, Jessica has finally started reading simple books. "She has a lot of trouble with multi-syllabic words, but she really tries," Annie says. "She really wants to be reading chapter books like the other girls in her grade."

"Go the Other Way"

After watching the children play for a while on the shelter's play-ground, Elise decides to go out and try to get Maggie's two prescriptions filled. Louis won't let her go alone. He tells Mary, the home-making aide, to go with her. "You see trouble, you go the other way," he instructs Elise sternly. "Any arguments, any fights, walk away. Do you understand me?"

Since Elise returned from the inpatient treatment program two months ago, Louis has barely allowed her out of his sight, except to attend her outpatient program. He won't keep any money in the apartment for fear that she'll take it and buy drugs.

Naturally, all the children want to go to the drugstore, too. Only Jessica decides to stay behind to tend to a caterpillar she found in her schoolyard and brought home on the bus. She's determined to keep it as a pet. Elise and her entourage troop across the street to one pharmacy, only to learn that it's out of one of the skin creams. They pick up the one that is in stock (Medicaid pays) and walk three blocks to another pharmacy. It doesn't have the second drug in stock either. The displays of candy in the drugstores trigger a clamor from the children for a treat, but Elise doesn't have a quarter to her name. Luckily, a kind clerk witnesses the scene and gives each of the children a souvenir keychain, which thrills them. They happily begin walking the three blocks back to the shelter.

While they've been gone, Louis has gone inside the shelter to pick up the day's mail. He comes out of the mailroom waving a sheet of paper over his head, his jaw clenched and his eyes clouded with rage. He's holding a hand-delivered letter, dated that day, informing Elise that she's been dropped from her rehabilitation program because of "sporadic attendance." As he's ranting about it to Annie, Elise and Mary and the children arrive back at the shelter.

"You've been kicked out of the program," Louis tells Elise. It turns out she had missed three days this past week, which is auto-matic grounds for expulsion. Never mind that she had good reasons for missing each of the days—Maggie's medical problems and volun-teer work at Maggie's Head Start. Rules are rules. She didn't clear the absences in advance.

Elise looks momentarily troubled and then shrugs her shoulders nonchalantly. "I'm not worried about it," she tells her husband, trying to calm him down. "I'll go to the other program. I'd rather go there anyway. Don't worry about it. It's no big deal."

But to Louis, it *is* a big deal, another example of a bureaucrat trying to screw up his life, and his wife letting him down. "What I'm worried about is that they're going to go to court and tell them that we're not in compliance with the order to you to be in drug treatment, and that they'll try to take the children away," he says.

"Don't worry," Elise says again, trying to calm him. "I'll go in on Monday with the letter, and tell the worker I want to go to the other program, and that'll be it."

Maggie's rash has gotten even more pronounced from the exertion of walking to the two drugstores and back, and she's scratched it so hard it's started to bleed. Elise wants to keep looking for the second cream. There's another pharmacy eight blocks away. Sensing an opportunity to talk to her alone, the visitor offers to drive her.

The third pharmacy has the drug in stock, but there's a pile of other prescriptions waiting to be filled, so it will be an hour until Maggie's is ready. After ordering a soft drink at a sidewalk café, the next hour is passed sharing common experiences as parents and talking about Elise's prospects for staying off drugs. "I think this is the first time I've sat at a sidewalk café since we left Romania twelve years ago," Elise says, leaning back in her chair and looking relaxed for the first time in days.

Elise firmly believes she's beaten her addiction to cocaine. "The most important thing in my life is my family, and I realize now that I can't keep my family together if I do drugs," she says. But she acknowledges that she thought so once before, not too long ago.

"I learned to never say never, because I know now that I've got a lifetime disease," she says. "But you can kick it if you really want to, and I want to."

"Think About Your Kids, Man"

When Elise returns to the pharmacy an hour later to pick up the prescription, a clerk tells her that her husband had been there looking for her. "He seemed real mad," the clerk says.

Back at the shelter, Elise can't get into the corridor that leads to their apartment because the family has only one key, and Louis has it with him. She pounds on the door at the end of the corridor, hoping he will hear her. She's been gone longer than expected, but at least she's gotten the second drug that Maggie needs. She hopes an end to her daughter's itching is near.

As she's starting to pound again, Louis comes raging down the hall. "Where the f—— have you been?" he shouts, jabbing his index finger into her chest as she cowers against the wall. "You picked up those drugs an hour ago. Your daughter is in the room crying because she thinks her mother's left her. What kind of mother are you?"

Louis is in such a state that the veins in his forehead are engorged and spittle is flying out of his mouth. A man in a neighboring apartment opens his door to see what the shouting is about. "Hey, man, I don't want to get into your business, but think about your kids, man," he tells Louis. "That's their mother you're talking to."

"Get the f—— out of my business," Louis shouts at the neighbor, who closes his door and locks it.

Elise tries to explain that the pharmacy took an hour to fill the prescription, and the visitor tries to assume the blame for not bringing Elise back to the shelter to wait. But Louis won't listen to either.

"You're a lying bitch," he tells Elise. "I went to the pharmacy, and they told me you picked it up an hour ago."

Elise tries to show Louis the cash register receipt, which is stamped with the time she picked up the drug—about ten minutes ago. The visitor again tries to intercede, telling Louis it had been the visitor's idea to get an iced tea while waiting for the prescription to be filled. That seems to make him even more angry.

"Where do you get off thinking you can go have a drink while we're waiting for you here at home?" he shouts at Elise.

The argument by this time has moved into the apartment, where Mary, the homemaking aide, is frying vegetables, Maggie is napping on her parents' bed, and Jessica is staring, wide-eyed and scared, at her parents. The boys are in the bedroom, watching TV.

Louis won't listen to any explanations from anyone. Is it that he thinks his wife was off somewhere using drugs? Not likely, given that she had no money and was in the company of a journalist. Are his nerves rattled from the stress of Maggie's clinic visit and Elise's dismissal from her rehab program? Maybe. Is it that he can't stand the thought of her talking about their life together, without him there to censor her story? Possibly. Whatever the reason, as the seconds pass, he's getting more and more angry instead of calming down.

Finally, he makes an announcement. "We're going right back to that pharmacy, and we're going to find out when you picked up the cream," he tells Elise. "If you've been lying, I'm going to beat you up right there. And if it's that bitch clerk who's lying, I'm going to beat her up."

A few minutes later, Louis and Elise fly out of the shelter and head down East Post Road, on their way back to the pharmacy, more than a mile away. Louis is striding five paces ahead of Elise. Seven inches shorter, she's running to keep up. And she's still trying to explain.

Five Months Later

The visit with the Scarpatos ended abruptly. Five months later, Annie Caldecott, the teacher's aide who'd taken a special interest in the children, provided an update on how the family was doing.

Louis and Elise had told her about the altercation they were involved in on that afternoon in May, Annie says, and had blamed it on the stress of Maggie's illness and the sweltering heat. "If you remember, it was unbearably hot and humid," she says. "The kids really acted up after Elise left for the pharmacy. They were hungry and thirsty, and Louis was getting stressed out because Mary, the aide, wasn't doing anything."

Since then, Annie reports, the family has had some ups and downs.

They moved out of the homeless shelter soon after the school year ended and into the three-bedroom apartment in Yonkers. They retrieved their furniture from storage, but it doesn't begin to fill the apartment. They've got beds for everybody, but no furniture at all in the living room. "It's barren-looking and feels very temporary," Annie says. "It's not very homey."

The family is happy to be out of the homeless shelter, but just getting a place of their own again didn't turn out to be the answer to their problems, Annie says. "The shelter was a horrible place to be, and they hated every minute of it. They had big dreams and high expectations about how their lives would be once they left. But now they find they're in a place that isn't much better. The bathroom's falling apart, the neighbors are loud, and there's drinking all the time in the street below their windows."

For a while, Louis worked a part-time job in the Bronx as a mechanic. But he wasn't being given enough hours, so he recently quit to take a $7-an-hour job as a stock clerk in a supermarket in his neighborhood, Annie says.

Elise relapsed over the summer but immediately admitted herself to the inpatient treatment program that had helped her before. She was detoxified and released after one week, and since then has been attending a new outpatient treatment program. "If I want to keep my children, I have to stay clean," she's told Annie. Recently, she's been working at a beauty salon two days a week, for $30 a day, but she doesn't think she'll be able to continue much longer because the hours overlap with Louis's and they have no one to watch the children. Instead, she's trying to get a part-time job, during school hours, at the supermarket where Louis works.

The children are all attending school regularly in Yonkers. The three oldest also attend an after-school program that provides them with recreational opportunities and homework help until 5:30 P.M. every schoolday. The boys' special education records didn't arrive at their new district before school started, so they were placed in regular first-grade classes, without special education services. A month into the school year, the new district sent Louis and Elise a letter suggesting that the boys would benefit from special education, but the parents didn't act on it. "They don't need special ed," Annie says Elise told her. "There's nothing wrong with my boys."

Annie has since persuaded the parents to accept the district's recommendation. But by late October 1998, they still weren't receiving any special help. "I'm really worried about them," Annie says. "They're in classrooms where they're being set up for failure, and it will be just one more blow to their self-esteem."

Jessica was promoted to third grade. Elise has told Annie that Jessica's doing well in school this year, but Annie worries that she won't be able to pass the competency test that all New York third-graders have to take in the spring of 1999. Though she's still a pleasant girl, Annie is beginning to see signs of strain in Jessica's face. "She's never really gotten to be a little girl, because she has to be a mom to her little brothers and sister so much of the time," Annie says. "Because of everything the family's been through, I think she feels like she needs to take care of them."

Maggie is attending a public preschool program at the same elementary school her siblings attend. Her ringworm infections are under control. But her first month of preschool was marred by a frightening bus accident. Annie says she fell out of the emergency door of her school bus, while it was moving, and sustained an eye injury. Fortunately, there appears to be no permanent damage.

Because of Elise's relapse over the summer, the county's family court has required Child Protective Services to continue to supervise the family for at least another year. So Mary, the homemaking aide, still comes to help with the children five days a week, and another aide comes for several hours each weekend. Annie doesn't believe either aide is helping Louis and Elise improve their parenting skills, as they're supposed to. Annie would like to intervene but doesn't know who to call. "They need help, but I don't know how to make it happen," she says.

On one of those brilliant Indian summer days that help fortify everyone against the winter weather that's coming, Annie picked up the Scarpato children and took them to Oakland Beach in nearby Rye. The water was surprisingly warm for mid-October, and the children raced into the waves as soon as they arrived. For two hours, they chased waves, built sandcastles, and collected shells.

"I wish you could have been there," Annie says. "They were so happy during those two hours that you would never have guessed there was a thing wrong in their lives."

8

SUBURBAN ST. LOUIS

The third heat wave of the summer of 1998 has settled over the Mississippi Valley, and the temperature in suburban St. Louis is 95 degrees, with 98 percent humidity. The inside of the Peterson family's tiny brick home feels like an oven.

The three Peterson children—Alexander, eight, Erica, six, and Claire, almost three—are trying to shake a few drops of water out of a bone-dry water hose so they can play in their wading pool. All three have stripped down to their underwear—in Claire's case, a urine-soaked disposable diaper—and are clamoring to swim.

Their parents, Ken and Laura Peterson, have been trying to fix a water pipe in the basement so that they can hook up the hose to fill the kids' pool. The parents are no strangers to plumbing problems—their kitchen sink hasn't had hot water or a functioning drain for a year, and their bathroom sink has no water at all. Neither of those problems has responded to their repair attempts, but they're hopeful that this one will. Still, they've been at it for four hours now, with no apparent success.

Suddenly, the familiar melody of an ice cream truck can be heard coming up the street. As luck would have it, the driver stops right in front of the Petersons' house while he waits for the neighborhood children to win the battle over their households' spare change. A half-dozen other children come running out of nearby houses, clutching quarters or dollar bills in their hands.

"Mommy, Mommy, the ice cream man's here!" Erica yells excitedly through the basement door.

"Not today," Laura responds. "You know I don't have any money. If you're hungry, go inside and get some chips."

Fortuitously, Ken finishes fixing the water pipe a few minutes later, and water comes gushing out of the hose. The kids are ecstatic, their disappointment over having to forgo ice cream quickly forgotten. The day has been redeemed.

Behind the Miniblinds

Their friends and relatives don't know it, but the Peterson family is on the verge of financial collapse.

They're more than $4,000 in debt—to the phone company, the electric company, the sewer company, and several banks. The $900 that Ken Peterson brings home from work each month doesn't begin to cover their bills.

Neither their air conditioner nor their furnace has worked for fifteen months, a potentially life-threatening problem in a climate of extremes. Their phone service was cut off last week.

A month ago, Laura Peterson, the family's only driver, had her license and her car's plates confiscated, the result of being caught driving without insurance. Because Laura can no longer drive him to work, Ken Peterson has been staying with his sister in another county so that he can be sure of getting to work. An already fragile marriage is being subjected to additional strain.

Perhaps worst of all, the mortgage company that financed their $52,000 home is threatening to foreclose because the couple owes four months' worth of payments.

Any day now, Laura and Ken expect to be out on the street, along with their three young children. At the moment, they have no idea where they'll go. Before they moved into this house two and a half years ago, they seemed to have exhausted the hospitality of their relatives by camping out with them whenever things went wrong.

The Peterson children are among the 1.9 million poor young children who live in America's suburbs. The suburban poor are the fastest-growing geographic subset of poor families with young children. The Petersons live in St. Louis County, Missouri, a conglomeration of ninety-plus suburbs of St. Louis that range from several with a socioeconomic profile as bad as that of the worst inner-city neighborhood to a few that regularly make the list of the richest suburbs in America. (The Petersons' suburb is somewhere in the middle:

the most recent census found that just over 8 percent of the residents are living in poverty.)

"I Was Young and Dumb"

As in many poor families with young children, this family's problems began with an unplanned out-of-wedlock pregnancy when Laura Peterson was seventeen, and they deepened when she gave birth again just thirteen months later. The birth three years later of a third child with a chronic illness further dimmed the family's prospects for moving out of poverty, since it became virtually impossible for Laura to take a full-time job.

Laura Peterson says it herself. If she hadn't become pregnant during her junior year in high school, her life today would be completely different. "I was on my way to college," says Laura. "The last thing I wanted in my life was a baby." Nationally, the young child poverty rate for children born to teen mothers is about 47 percent, compared with a poverty rate of 21 percent for children born to adult mothers.

Now twenty-three, Laura is tall and slim, with naturally white-blond hair and eyebrows and heavily freckled skin. She's well-spoken, but strangely without affect. It's rare for her to laugh or smile or get outwardly angry. The only emotion she regularly shows the world is nervousness; a leg shakes constantly with nervous energy anytime she sits down. The fact that she bottles up her emotions probably explains why she's been feeling for the last few weeks as though her stomach is tied in knots.

Laura was a 4.0 student at a suburban St. Louis high school and a violinist in the school's orchestra when she realized in the fall of 1991 that she was pregnant. Until a few weeks before, she had been going steady for eighteen months with a boy she had met at the local YMCA, where they both worked as lifeguards. He attended a prestigious Catholic boys' high school across the county, and during the time they went out together they escorted each other to their schools' proms and homecoming dances, the usual content of high school romances.

But he was two years older and graduated from high school the month she finished her sophomore year. When he went off to college that fall, the relationship weakened. The couple had just formally broken up when the telltale symptoms of pregnancy became too consistent for Laura to ignore. Even so, it took her four more months to get up the nerve to tell anyone.

"I was halfway done with the pregnancy by the time I told any-one," she recalls. "I told my best friend and a lady at church, and I made them come with me to tell my mom and dad, because I knew the shit was going to hit the fan. It did, and it flew all over the place for a long time. My dad didn't talk to me for two and a half months. The way we were brought up, that kind of thing didn't happen. You knew what was right and wrong, and getting pregnant before you were married wasn't right."

Within a few days of getting the news, Laura's mother came around. "She was disappointed in me, and hurt, but she bounced back, and she was with me every step of the way," Laura says. "She told all her friends she was going to be a grandma, and she went with me to every doctor's appointment and to Lamaze classes."

At school, Laura's peers were incredulous because they thought she was too smart to get pregnant. "They kept asking me, 'How could this happen to you?'" she says.

"I told them, 'You know how it happens. It doesn't take a rocket scientist to figure it out.' I was young and dumb and didn't know enough about birth control."

Laura's high school didn't offer any special support services for pregnant students beyond a monthly group counseling session. But she managed to stay in school and maintain good grades. Most of her teachers made accommodations for doctor's appointments. To save up for the expenses that would be coming with the birth of a child, she got a part-time night-shift job at the nearby Taco Bell, working right up until she went into labor.

Meanwhile, the father of the baby made it plain that he wanted nothing to do with her or the baby. "He never actually told me that was what he decided," Laura says. "He just let his actions speak for him." His parents, who had seemed to like Laura, told her that they had left it up to their son to decide what to do about the pregnancy and that they would support whatever decision he made.

Alexander was born on Memorial Day 1992, weighing eight pounds, four ounces. Laura took him home to her parents' two-bed-room house, which was already bursting at the rafters because it housed not just her parents but her four younger siblings. Laura stayed home and cared for Alexander for five weeks and then returned to work on the night shift at Taco Bell. Her mother took care of the baby while Laura worked, charging her $35 a week.

When fall came, Laura went back to her high school. "I told myself that just because I was a mother didn't mean I had to give up my education," Laura says. She still aspired to go to college to study accounting or deaf education. But her daily schedule was punishing. She would rise every morning at 6:00 A.M. to get herself and the baby ready for the day. A girlfriend would pick her up at 7:00 A.M., and they'd drop Alexander at his sitter's and head over to school. At 3:00 P.M., the same friend would drive Laura to pick him up, and Laura would take him home, where she'd prop him in his "pumpkin seat" while she did her homework. At 5:30 P.M., her mother came home from her secretarial job and took over his care, and Laura went off to work at Taco Bell. She came home at 11:00 P.M., gave Alexander his bedtime bottle, finished whatever homework was still undone, and went to bed.

By late September, one month into her senior year, Laura was exhausted. She was earning $4.25 an hour at Taco Bell, and using most of her income to pay for Alexander's care. (Besides the $35 she was paying her mother, she was paying his daytime sitter $75 a week.) Her home life was becoming increasingly stressful, with her mother charging her $20 every time she did the baby's laundry and her siblings complaining that there was baby stuff all over the house. Meanwhile, Laura had a new boyfriend, Ken Peterson, who worked with her at Taco Bell. Two years older, he had recently moved to Missouri from Ohio and was living with his sister in another suburb.

Fed up with the situation at home, Laura decided to take Alexander and move in with Ken. She skipped a day of school to pack up their things, wrote a note to her parents saying she'd be in touch, and loaded her belongings into the back of a pickup truck that belonged to a friend of Ken's. They stayed with Ken's sister for a week or two and then moved into a two-bedroom apartment with a coworker from Taco Bell. Laura continued attending high school but gave up her night job, since she didn't want to depend on her mother to baby-sit anymore. For three months, she and the baby collected welfare benefits—$170 a month plus food stamps. The welfare check didn't even cover the cost of Alexander's daytime baby-sitter.

A Second Pregnancy

As it turned out, Laura was just trading one stressful living situation for another. The Taco Bell coworker didn't much like sharing a tiny apartment with a couple and a baby. So just after Christmas, Laura and Ken and the baby moved into the home of one of Ken's sisters in a suburb about twenty miles from the one Laura had grown up in. Because of the distance, she could no longer get to her school. She tried to transfer to a high school near Ken's sister's home, but because the second semester had started two weeks before, the school wouldn't admit her, she says. So midway through her senior year, with her 4.0 average intact, she dropped out. "I was really upset that I couldn't continue," she recalls. "I loved school."

About the same time, Laura found out she was pregnant again, even though she says she was on birth control pills and Ken was also using condoms. (Research has found that teenagers who use birth control pills often fail to take them consistently, which undermines their effectiveness, and condoms have a notoriously high failure rate.) When they learned about the pregnancy, their parents insisted that the couple get married.

"I really didn't want to get married," Laura says. "We'd only been going out for six months, and I didn't think the relationship was strong enough."

Ken was also reluctant to tie the knot. "I wanted to be financially stable before I started a family," he says. "And Laura and I hardly knew each other."

But their parents prevailed. Two weeks later, Ken and Laura were married in a ceremony that Laura recalls as "the worst wedding I've ever been to." (Ken demurs. "It wasn't that bad. We didn't have a whole lot of money to put into it, and it wasn't like I'd always wanted it to be, but it was okay.") They moved into a $300-a-month trailer in Jefferson County, the next county out from St. Louis County. It's one of several formerly rural counties ringing St. Louis that have become suburbanized in the last decade.

Laura's memories of their first year of marriage aren't happy. Ken worked at another Taco Bell for two or three months and then switched to another restaurant chain that offered more opportunities for advancement. But that restaurant was farther away from the trailer park, and without a car or a driver's license, he had continual transportation problems. For a while, he kept trading in one low-paying job for another. "In our first year of marriage, he had thirteen jobs," Laura recalls. "It drove me nuts. My stomach was in knots for a year."

Luckily, Laura had an easy pregnancy, and just as important, she still retained hope that she could get her life back on track. She took the GED test three days after Erica was born and passed with flying colors, even without taking a preparation course. College was still an option in her mind.

But she hadn't realized how much more difficult it would be to take care of two babies than one, and to support a family of four on a single income. "If I hadn't gotten pregnant the second time, I think things would have been a lot different," she says now. "Believe me, I never would have planned to have a second child so soon. Right from the start, I loved being a mom, and I knew I wanted to have more kids, but not that fast."

Soon after Erica's birth, Ken pawned his most valuable possessions—some hunting rifles that had been handed down to him by his father—to pay the rent. The couple realized that they could no longer afford the trailer. So in August 1993, they moved into the basement of Laura's parents' home. A month later, they found a cheap rental house nearby and moved in. But nine months after that, with financial pressures building again and their relationship severely strained, the couple separated. Laura took the two children to an uncle's home in rural Missouri, and Ken moved in with his sister again.

By then, Laura was so angry with Ken for his spotty work record that she filed for divorce. "I was lazy then," Ken admits. "I had been spoiled all my life and hadn't yet faced up to my responsibilities."

Two months after they separated, Ken appeared on the doorstep of Laura's uncle's home and asked for another chance. The couple talked and decided to give their marriage another try. "Basically, he decided to grow up," Laura says. "That's what I'd been trying to get him to do for two years."

Laura's uncle agreed to let the family stay with him for a while and even moved them with him to Leavenworth, Kansas, where he got a job as a prison guard. Ken found a minimum-wage job in a slaughterhouse. But after two months in Kansas, the family wore out its welcome. In October 1993, they returned to the St. Louis area and moved in with Ken's sister again. Two weeks later, Laura found out that she was pregnant with her third child. Ken's sister told them they'd have to start looking for their own place.

"She's really a wonderful person," Laura says. "She hates to see someone in need. But her family needed some time by themselves. They'd had other people living with them off and on for years. And they weren't really in much better shape than we were."

Laura and Ken still had no savings—not even enough for the security deposit on an apartment. None of their relatives were willing to take in a family of four. So they came up with a patchwork, and by no means ideal, solution: the two of them would stay with Ken's brother and his wife and child in their two-bedroom apartment, and their own children would stay with Laura's parents. Laura would go to her parents' house during the day to take care of their children, and at night she'd baby-sit for her six-month-old nephew while his parents worked.

It was stressful for two couples to be living together in such a small place, Laura and Ken say, and this arrangement lasted only two months. Fortunately, a neighbor of Laura's parents offered them temporary sleeping space in his house. The couple spent three weeks there, sleeping on a mattress on the basement floor. Laura's parents finally relented and allowed them to move into their basement. Ken and Laura, by now six months pregnant with her third child, were together with their children again.

"That year, we moved around an awful lot," Ken recalls. "We just didn't usually have the money for a place of our own, and when we did get one, we couldn't afford to keep it. Through it all, we just tried to keep the kids as happy as we could."

Claire: "What's Wrong with Her?"

Laura gave birth to Claire in early June 1995. Though Claire was about two pounds smaller at birth than her siblings, she seemed healthy. However, when she was three weeks old, she became terribly ill.

At first, the only symptom was a nasty rash that appeared on her forehead. "It looked like she'd scraped her body against concrete," Laura recalls. Then the rash turned into large oozing blisters that crusted over and spread from her forehead to her abdomen, scalp, arms, legs, and feet.

The family first sought treatment from a chiropractor, which was their customary practice for health problems. But it soon became clear that Claire needed specialized medical care. She began receiving treatment from a pediatric dermatologist at St. Louis Children's Hospital. At the time, Missouri's Medicaid program covered infants in families with incomes up to 185 percent of the poverty line, so her care was paid for.

Claire's benign-sounding diagnosis—acute eczema—doesn't begin to capture the state of agony that she lived in day and night, or how awful she looked. "Babies with eczema don't sleep," a pediatrician explains. "The itching is so terrible that they can't be consoled. It's like having poison ivy all over their bodies all the time." Luckily, Claire has a pleasant disposition, so between bouts of uncontrollable itching she was a happy child.

Testing determined that Claire was severely allergic to many foods, animal dander, dust, and pollen. Besides eczema, she also had asthma. Giving her daily breathing treatments and eliminating the irritants from her environment did little to relieve her symptoms. So she was put on low doses of antihistamines, partly so that she could sleep without interruption for more than a few hours at a time. When she was eight months old, she had to be hospitalized for three days because of dehydration, a side effect of the antihistamines.

Nothing the doctors suggested for the eczema seemed to help very much. Often she would scratch herself so hard that her lesions would bleed. For almost a year, she got frequent bacterial skin infections from scratching. One was so serious that she had to be hospitalized for IV antibiotic treatment.

When Claire was twenty months old, her doctors decided to try a treatment generally regarded as a last resort for a child this age: a two-week regimen of oral steroids. Unfortunately, they didn't help either, and even worse, they left her with lasting side effects, manifested most vividly in her stunted growth. Now three, Claire weighs just twenty-four pounds and stands less than two and a half feet tall, making her smaller than 95 out of 100 girls her age. She looks like an eighteen-month-old—and babbles like one, too.

"For more than a year, she didn't gain an inch or add a pound, and she stopped trying to speak," Laura says. "Basically, she just shut down completely."

Seeing Claire clad only in a diaper drives home the social ramifications of her illness. Her torso is covered with crusted-over splotches of raw red skin, and there are also spots on her face, her arms, and her legs. With her wispy white-blond hair, she looks like a waif.

"The eczema is really hard for her," Laura says. "It still itches all the time, but the worst thing is when she's around other kids and they ask her, 'What's wrong with you? Why do you look like that?' At the playground, sometimes kids don't want to play with her because they're afraid they'll catch it.

"Her brother and sister are really good about it. In fact, I think they play with her more because of it. They don't want her to feel badly that no one else is playing with her."

In the last few months, Claire has started growing again, and she's beginning to string three words together. But a recent developmental evaluation by the St. Louis County Special School District placed her at the level of an eighteen-month-old for most skills, including speech and fine-motor skills. So in the fall, she'll be given four hours of special education services each week through the Special School District and attend a regular Head Start preschool every afternoon. "My goal is that she'll be caught up by the time she starts kindergarten," Laura says.

Selling Food Stamps and Blood

In November 1995, the Petersons heard that a two-bedroom brick house down the street from Laura's parents was coming on the market. The house cost $52,000, somewhat under the median price for a house in their suburb, and the couple thought that by watching their budget carefully, they would be able to manage the $450-a-month payment.

By this time, Ken had been working as a shift manager at the local Taco Bell for almost two years and was making $7.75 an hour, or a gross income of $1,333 a month. Laura was working there weekends, too. In addition, Laura had finally begun collecting $74 a month in state-ordered child support from Alexander's father, and the state was also giving the family about $250 a month in food stamps. All in all, the family was doing much better financially than ever before. The hitch was that they had only a few hundred dollars in savings, not enough for a down payment, so no bank would give them a loan.

Fortunately, the couple thought then, the seller was determined that they would get her house. "She'd known me since I was a baby, and she liked the idea of me and my family living there," Laura says. The seller lent them $2,000 toward the required down payment of $2,175, and a mortgage company gave them a thirty-year $52,000 loan at 8.5 percent interest, enabling them to immediately pay back the seller's $2,000 loan. The family moved in in January 1996. For the first time in years, they weren't sleeping on somebody else's floor.

In hindsight, Ken and Laura now realize that they couldn't really afford a house given the inevitability of repairs and the relentless upward push of property taxes and homeowners' insurance premiums. Being able to make the initial $450 monthly payment presupposed predictable monthly expenses, an impossibility given the state of the house and their inexperience in running a household. They didn't even realize that the required monthly escrow payment would grow as taxes and insurance premiums went up, as they inevitably do. Currently, their mortgage and escrow payment amount to almost $600 a month—almost $150 more each month than when they first moved in two and a half years ago.

Furthermore, the house turned out to have a lot of problems that they hadn't known about. The sun porch that they'd hoped to convert into a bedroom for Alexander turned out to have both a leaky roof and rotten floorboards. In many spots, a tattered wall-to-wall carpet is all that holds the floor together. As a result, it's used mostly as a storage area, with boxes positioned strategically to prevent children from falling through the floor. The three children share a bedroom.

Throughout the house, the plumbing barely works. The kitchen sink has neither hot water nor a working drain, and the pipes in the bathroom sink are so corroded that they produce no water at all, leaving the bathtub as the only source of hot water in the house. And the heating and cooling systems turned out to be on their last legs when the Petersons moved in. They gave out in the spring of 1997, and more than a year later, the Petersons still don't have the money to replace them.

"Oh, man, it just seemed like everything went downhill," Ken recalls. "I'm not much of a handyman, but I tried to keep things going, and Laura's dad tried, too. But we just couldn't do it ourselves, and we didn't have the money to bring in skilled repairmen."

For the first year and a half, the family managed to stay current with their mortgage payments, even if it meant skimping on food sometimes. "We didn't have anything left over at the end of the month, but we paid everything on time," Laura says. Sometimes Laura traded food stamps for cash so that she could buy such essentials as diapers, toilet paper, and laundry detergent, which can't be purchased with food stamps. She'd get $.75 for a $1 coupon if she was lucky, but $.50 most times. "I know people think that's wrong, but you got to do what you got to do," she says.

Once, with no food stamps left, and no cash or diapers in the house, Laura went to a storefront in downtown St. Louis to donate plasma. "They gave me $20, and I went out and bought four packs of diapers, two for each of the girls," she says. "That got us through the next week." She never told Ken where the money came from.

In late fall 1997, the family's house of cards lost one of its most important footings. Their car, a 1986 Chevrolet Cavalier wagon, failed its state inspection. It needed four new tires, a new exhaust system, a heater core, and a blower motor. "We had to put over $1,000 into it," Laura says. "We didn't have it, so we diverted money from our other bills." They didn't pay the mortgage for two months.

The car problems coincided with the beginning of the winter heating season. With temperatures regularly plummeting into the teens, and sometimes lower, and without a working furnace, they tried to heat the house with two space heaters and their electric oven. As a result, their monthly electric bill soared to $200 from $40.

"In the daytime, we'd put both space heaters in the living room, and just stay in there," Laura says. "When we went into the kitchen, we turned on all the burners and the oven, and left it open so we'd get the heat. And at night, I'd put one space heater in the kids' bedroom and keep the other in the living room, and Ken and I would sleep there. In the rest of the house, it was so cold that when we went into the bathroom in the morning, we could see our breath."

Their problems were still to get worse. On December 22, 1997, Laura was in an automobile accident. Laura says it was the other driver's fault, but she nonetheless got a ticket for driving without insurance, a serious infraction in Missouri. A few months before, when their finances started getting tight, she had ignored the notice to pay the next six-month premium of $320.

"I'd been driving for six years, and it was the first accident I was ever in and the first ticket I ever got," Laura says. It would take six months for the full ramifications of the accident to play themselves out.

With Christmas bearing down on them, and no money for gifts, the couple was in despair. Miraculously, it seemed to them, on Christmas Eve someone from their church arrived with a food basket, and a couple that had "adopted" them for the holidays arrived with four shopping bags filled with gifts. "We got lucky," Laura says. "The people at Head Start had given them a profile of each of the kids—what they needed, what they liked, what sizes they wore. We put the presents under the tree, just as though Santa had brought them, and those were the only presents they got. They ended up with like six presents apiece. When they woke up and came out and saw all the presents under the tree, their eyes popped out of their heads."

Falling Further Behind

Two days after the new year began, Ken started a new job at a better rate of pay. He went to work as a welder at a factory in Jefferson County at $8.50 an hour, and with health insurance for him and Laura, something they had never had before. (The children continued to be covered by Medicaid.) Ken studied welding at a technical high school in Ohio and had been trying for years to get a welding job. A sister worked for the company and helped him get hired. Finally getting a job in the trade in which he was trained gave him hope that eventually he'd land a union job, with a starting wage of $15 an hour.

"I was hoping this new job would be the answer to our problems," Ken says. "It was more money than I had ever made in a job, and I was happy to be welding. All the union jobs require five years of experience, and I looked at this as getting my foot in the door. I thought that five years later, I might be able to get on at one of the auto plants."

The downside of the new job was that the factory was almost forty miles from the Petersons' house, and Ken doesn't drive. (All his life he's suffered from test anxiety; he's afraid he wouldn't pass a driving test.) So every morning, Laura would load the three kids in the car and drive Ken to work, then drive herself and the kids back home again. They left at 7:00 A.M. and usually got home by 9:00 A.M., if traffic wasn't too bad. The reverse trip in the afternoon would take longer because of heavier traffic.

What the couple didn't realize when they began this routine was that although Ken was earning more per hour, all of the increase—

and more—was consumed by the cost of gasoline, which, for their gas guzzler, was costing about $100 a week. In addition, their twelve-year-old car was getting less and less reliable with each trip. "We weren't really better off at all," Ken says.

By February, the couple was $2,160 behind in their mortgage payments and $600 behind in their electric bill. Luckily, their tax refund of nearly $3,000 (including an Earned Income Tax Credit) came just as the bank was threatening foreclosure. They had intended to use the refund to pay the legal fees for Ken to adopt Alexander. Instead, they used it to bring the mortgage up-to-date, pay the electric company enough to forestall a cutoff, and catch up on some other bills.

By the end of the next month, though, they were behind again. The car needed more work, and they had learned from Laura's December accident that they had to keep their insurance current. Because of her accident and ticket, the premiums were much higher, too.

And there were still more delinquent bills. They owed the sewer company $200, since Laura had simply ignored that bill for months because she knew that there was no way the house could be disconnected. "Our bill from them was like only $12 a month, but I would end up taking that $12 and putting it towards the phone or the electric bill, because otherwise they were going to be cut off," Laura says. Two banks had given them credit cards when they became homeowners, and their collection agencies were also baying at the door. Together, the credit card bills came to more than $2,300. Ken borrowed $600 from his boss to make the March mortgage payment.

In April, Laura went to traffic court and pleaded guilty to failing to show proof of insurance. She was ordered to pay $1,420 to the other driver, for damage and loss of use, and told that her license and plates would be suspended for sixty days as soon as the paperwork was processed.

It took two months. The notice arrived June 3, the same day the phone company cut off service for nonpayment of a $230 bill.

The loss of Laura's driver's license and the car's plates precipitated a new crisis. How would Ken get to work? There's no bus service between the couple's suburb and the neighboring county in which he works, so public transportation wasn't an option. And none of his coworkers live anywhere near him, so he couldn't hitch a ride. So the couple decided that for the next two months, Ken would stay with his sister, who would drive him to the factory every day. He would come home on weekends if he could get a ride.

Breakfast: Potato Chips and Egg Whites

It's the end of the fourth week that Laura has been a de facto single mom on weekdays. Fortunately, Ken is home for the weekend. Even so, everybody's on edge. The heat this summer has been relentless, and without air conditioning, the house is virtually uninhabitable. The plumbing problem in the basement is the last straw.

While Ken is cleaning up the mess from the broken water pipe, Laura walks up to her parents' house to use the phone. She's trying to find a ride for herself and the kids down to Branson, about five hours southwest of St. Louis, in Missouri's Ozarks region. Her grandmother and several other relatives live there, and she's been promising the kids for weeks that they'll spend the Fourth of July there.

She calls all the other relatives who she thinks may be heading down, with no luck. Nobody's got room for four more. "The really bad thing is that I promised the kids, and if there's one thing I hate to do, it's break a promise to a kid," she says.

As a consolation prize of sorts, Laura's oldest brother and his wife offer to take her children with them for a few days to visit the wife's parents, who also live in rural Missouri. The kids will be able to play in the Meramec River, a favorite swimming hole for St. Louisans during the dog days of summer. "It's like a vacation from Mom," Laura says. Early Sunday evening, Laura's brother comes for the kids, and Ken's sister comes and gets him to drive him to her house so he'll be able to get to work by 8:00 A.M. Monday.

That night, Laura is alone in her house for the first night since the family moved in. But it doesn't turn out to be a restful experience. "I'm running on three hours of sleep," she says the next morning.

"Last night, I couldn't sleep at all," she says. "I had a lot of things racing through my mind. I was letting everything get to me. I was pushing ideas around, like if I do this, then that will happen, and if I do that, then this will happen. I didn't get to sleep until 4:30 A.M., and then the kids I baby-sit arrived at 7:30, so that was that."

At the moment, Laura is taking care of three other children as a favor to two friends. One is her best friend's ten-year-old daughter, who Laura's been caring for, without charge, three days a week since school let out. (Although the friend doesn't pay her, she's been driving Laura to the grocery and wherever else she needs to go since her license was confiscated.) The other two children are siblings from Kansas, a ten-year-old girl and a six-year-old boy, who are visiting their father for a month. He's Ken's best friend.

"He'd been out of work for two and a half months and just got a job, right before they were arriving," Laura explains. "He didn't know what he'd do with them while he was at work, so I offered to watch them. He told me he couldn't pay me, and I said, 'That's okay. I'm home with my own kids anyway. What's a few more?'"

The kids have been snacking on potato chips all morning and, as noon approaches, are clamoring for something more substantial. All Laura has in the house is a quart of milk and a dozen eggs. She puts the eggs on to boil, apologizing to the children that the pickings are so slim. The children eat only the whites of the eggs, so Laura saves the yellows for her dinner.

With the weather so hot, she's been taking the children to the public swimming pool every weekday. Her brother and several of his friends work the desk there, and usually they let Laura and her crew in for free. After the meager lunch, Laura gathers up a few towels and the pool toys, and they head over, cutting through a neighbor's yard to shorten the walk from three blocks to one.

"The Reason I Get Up"

One of her brother's friends is indeed behind the reception desk at the pool, and Laura nods at him as she breezes in. Without special treatment, she'd have to pay $1.50 for herself and $.75 for each child. "We wouldn't be able to come here if we couldn't get in for free," she says. On the few occasions they've been turned away, the children have gotten really upset, she says. "We're so hot by the time we get over here, and then we have to walk back to our hot house, and it's just too much for them," she says.

Laura lathers her three charges with sunscreen, and they jump in the pool. At the moment, they're the only children here, but several local day camps will be arriving within the hour. Laura reminds the children that they have to stay in the shallow end and positions her chair so that she can watch them.

"I know this doesn't look good to you, sitting by the pool all day, but it's actually really demanding, because I don't let them out of my sight," she says. "Because I was a lifeguard, I know how quickly things can go wrong. I keep my eyes glued to them. I can't relax. By the end of the afternoon, I'm exhausted."

After a while, the lifeguard calls out, "Free swim," which means that the diving boards are off-limits so that children can practice diving from the sides of the pool's deep end. The children come running over to Laura, begging, "Please, Laura, please. You promised." She excuses herself from the conversation so she can go into the pool with them and give them diving lessons. She treads water in the deep end for twenty minutes while they practice diving. In that time, they advance from belly flops to something resembling a dive. "Wait till your mother hears that you can dive!" she says to Jeannie, her friend's child. "She'll be so proud of you."

After she towels off and settles back into her chair, she admits to missing her children. "I feel like my arms have been cut off," she says. "They're the reason I get up in the morning. They're my everything." She gets out her wallet to look at their pictures. There's Alexander in his yellow t-ball uniform, with his bat slung over his shoulder, poised for a hit, and Erica, all smiles, in a formal portrait taken at the Head Start center she's attended for the last two years, and Claire, all dressed up in a holiday portrait at a discount store studio.

"My two older kids are really doing great," Laura says. "Alex is a little bit ahead of where he should be developmentally, and Erica's chugging along at a normal pace. They've both had good health, except for ear problems. Alex has had two sets of tubes inserted in his ears, and Erica's had one."

Laura thinks she and Ken have protected the children from most of the possible ill effects of poverty. "When they were really little and we were moving from place to place every few months, they didn't realize why," she says. "They probably thought it was fun. It's going to be a lot harder on them if we have to move now because they've got friends in the neighborhood and are looking forward to going to school with them."

"Everything Is Day to Day"

At noon the next day, Laura is sitting side by side with Jeannie on a battered and stained old couch. They're playing "Pacman" on a video game system, with two box fans blowing warm air on them from four feet away. The two other children Laura took care of yesterday are at their grandmother's house today, and her own children are still visiting her brother's in-laws.

The living room is a mess, with extension cords crisscrossing the stained carpeting, empty Vienna sausage cans perching on the windowsill, and a set of barbells resting among the dirty dishes, empty soda cans, and wet towels on the floor. Two framed samplers hang on one wall. "A mother holds her children's hands for a while, their hearts forever," one says. "When there is love in the home, there is joy in the heart," says the other. Another wall displays a dozen family photos.

Laura apologizes for the state of the house. "I was going to clean up this morning, but it's already so hot," she says. The temperature outside is 97 degrees, with a heat index of 103.

Laura looks as tired as she did the day before, and her face is sunburned from the afternoon she spent by the side of the pool. It turns out she didn't sleep much again last night, for the second night in a row. It was still 95 degrees in the house when she went to bed, and she couldn't get comfortable.

"And my nerves are acting up," she says. "I haven't been able to eat for the last three days."

Even though it's not yet the hottest part of the day, the house is stifling, and Jeannie begs Laura to take her to the pool again. They gather up their towels and head over. But their luck getting in free has run out. One of Laura's brother's friends sidetracks her as she approaches the counter; the manager is behind the cash register. "Laura, we're going to have to charge you today," he tells her. "We had a staff meeting this morning, and we were told that if we were caught letting anyone in free, we'd lose our jobs, so I can't do it no more. I'm sorry."

Laura answers: "That's okay. I know it's not your fault."

As she turns to leave, her visitor offers to pay, and she accepts, with obvious embarrassment. "Well, Jeannie," she tells her young charge, "you better enjoy yourself today, because this is the last day we'll be able to come for a while."

As she sits by the pool, keeping an eye on Jeannie, she's asked to talk about her hopes for the future. "I don't really have any anymore," she says. "Everything is day to day."

What about getting a part-time job? "I've tried to work off and on since I had kids, but the child care costs eat up everything I earn," she says. "Until they all go to school full-time, I'd just be working to pay for child care."

What about baby-sitting in her home, for pay? She seems to like having other people's children around, so why not try to turn that interest into a home-based business?

"I did it, for almost a year," she says. "I took care of three kids, and I got $4 an hour for all of them. But then the family of one of them moved away, and the mother of the other two didn't need me anymore. I've put the word out that I'm willing to do it, but nobody's asked me. And actually, I have to admit that my house is probably too trashed right now for me to be able to do it."

By next week, though, the family may have their mortgage foreclosed on and be ordered out of the house. Why isn't she experiencing a sense of urgency? What's the plan to keep the house from being seized?

"We don't have a plan, because it's not really in our hands," she says. "We've saved up enough to pay two months of the mortgage, but the mortgage company won't accept it unless we pay the whole amount we owe. I've asked if we could refinance and get a lower rate, since interest rates are about a percentage point and a half lower than when we bought the house. But they say they won't do that with someone who owes money. So it's like a catch-22.

"What we're thinking now is that we'll have to use the $1,000 we've saved up to put a deposit on an apartment and pay the first month's rent. But I'm not sure we can even afford to do that, since two-bedroom apartments around here cost about $550 a month, which is almost as much as our mortgage. And we wouldn't be able to get the electricity switched on at a new place while we still owe Union Electric for the old one."

Laura also worries about the possibility of losing their monthly allotment of $250 in food stamps. Like many other states, Missouri has imposed a two-year lifetime limit on food stamps for some recipients, as part of welfare reform. Laura isn't sure what her family's status is, but a question about it prompts her to express her political views.

"I can understand wanting to keep control of food stamps, but I don't think a lifetime limit of two years is fair to the kids," she says. "Yeah, sure, we've been getting food stamps off and on for six years, ever since Alex was born, but one of us was working all that time, and sometimes both of us. It's not like we weren't trying to support our families. If we didn't have food stamps, I don't know how we'd eat." (In fact, Missouri doesn't plan to restrict food stamps to eligible families with children.)

Is she optimistic about the future, or pessimistic?

"Right now, I have no idea what the future will bring," she says. "Actually, I couldn't even tell you what next week will bring. But it can't get much worse than it already is."

"We Were Always Fighting"

Three months have passed when we call to check up on the family. It turns out that in late July, a few weeks after our visit, the couple had put a $500 down payment on a double-wide trailer at a trailer park in Jefferson County, close to Ken's job. But a few weeks after that, their application for financing was turned down. They continued to live in their house, on borrowed time, as the foreclosure process worked its way through the courts.

Just before school started in September, Laura told Ken that she didn't want to be married anymore. He begged her to try to work things out, but she told him she didn't want to. "When we were together, we were always fighting," she explains. "Finances were a big part of our problems. If we would have had a way to take care of our bills, we wouldn't have taken it out on each other. You don't want to scream at the kids, so you scream at each other. It was hard on everybody."

Ken agrees with Laura's analysis of their problems but thinks that her refusal to try to work things out was also a reaction to having had so much responsibility thrust upon her so early in her life. "I think she likes the freedom she has without the rest of us there, even though she doesn't have any money," Ken says.

By mutual agreement, Ken moved the two girls to his sister's house, where he'd already been living during the week, and Alexander stayed behind with Laura. Ken enrolled Erica in kindergarten at a public school near his sister's house. To his regret, he couldn't get Claire into the Head Start program in the new neighborhood because there was a waiting list. Nor could he arrange transportation for her to attend the Special School District's half-day program for developmentally delayed preschoolers. "I would have liked her to receive that special help, but I just couldn't work it out," he says. Instead, he found a baby-sitter who would care for Claire all day, and for Erica before and after school, for $125 a week. On a monthly basis, that will add up to more than his old mortgage payment.

The foreclosure process concluded in mid-October, and the finance company seized the house. Laura put the family's possessions into storage, and she and Alexander moved in temporarily with her best friend and her daughter. They had only $24 a month in cash income to live off of, since the state had begun diverting $50 a month from Alexander's child support to the driver of the car with which Laura had collided in December 1997. After a two-month job search, she finally found work as a $6.25-an-hour front-desk clerk at an airport hotel.

Until she puts in a few months on the job and saves enough money for a deposit and first and last month's rent, no landlord will even accept an application from her for an apartment. But down the road, she hopes to find an affordable one-bedroom apartment for herself and Alexander. "It should be a lot easier to find a place just for Alexander and me, rather than all five of us," she says.

Ken recently changed jobs. He's given up on welding, at least for now. The promise of a union job three and a half years from now began to seem too elusive. He's gone to work for a franchised service that cleans up after house fires, floods, and violent crimes. He took a $.25-an-hour pay cut—to $8.50 an hour—but believes there's a possibility of becoming a crew leader soon, since the company is growing fast.

"This might be ignorant to say, but having Laura tell me to leave might have been the best thing for me," Ken says. "She was the love of my life, but I'm beginning to understand that we just can't live together, that it wasn't good for us or the kids.

"I'm moving on. There isn't a book out there about how to be a single dad, but I'm learning as I go and just trying to do the best I can. It's a big responsibility, more than I was ever willing to take on before. Quite a few people say to me, 'Why do you want to take on all that responsibility for yourself? Let them live with Laura.' And sometimes it's really hard, especially with Claire's eczema.

"But I'm trying to deal with it as best as I can. The greatest thing is when I come home at the end of the day and have them run up to me and give me a big hug.

"I'm optimistic about the future. For one thing, I'm planning for it, trying to get my driver's license and save up for a car, and our own trailer. I want to create a good environment for me and my kids, instead of depending upon everybody else.

"I guess I'd say that what I really want for us is just to have a normal life."

9

BELZONI, MISSISSIPPI

During their childhoods, the children in the Lyles family have lived in many places. The worst was probably the single room in a boardinghouse that two of the children shared with their mother during their family's darkest days. The dilapidated two-bedroom trailer they later moved into seemed like a palace in comparison.

Finally, the family seems to have it pretty good. The oldest child is on his own, and the three youngest now live with their mother in a three-bedroom, ranch-style apartment in a relatively new public housing complex just off the state highway that runs through Belzoni, Mississippi, the Catfish Capital of the United States.

The family still can't afford a phone, but it splurges on cable TV and a VCR. Medical care is no longer a problem, since the mother's work policy covers them part of the year and Medicaid takes care of the rest. They're hardly ever hungry, and everybody has a bed.

"There's poor, and there's *po'*," the children's mother, Celeste Lyles, explains. "We're just poor."

Even so, there are many poverty-related stressors in this household.

Because Celeste's work is seasonal, there are some months when she makes enough to pay the family's bills, and other months when she doesn't.

Like many of the one-story duplexes on their street, the Lyles family's shelters three generations because of economic necessity. The youngest girl, who's ten, shares a bedroom with her teenage brother, and the oldest girl, who's nineteen, shares a bed with her three-year-old daughter.

There's no adult male in the household, and there rarely has been. Celeste Lyles was pregnant at thirteen, married at fifteen, and a grandmother at thirty-one. Though her second-oldest child was born while she was married to the child's father, the other three children were fathered by men who were simply passing through her life.

The two oldest Lyles children have themselves become parents as unmarried teens, a common fate for children growing up in Humphreys County, which has one of the highest teen pregnancy rates in a state that itself has the highest rate in the nation. Curtis, twenty-two, recently moved into his girlfriend's apartment across town. That Curtis will soon finish a two-year program at the local community college is nothing short of a miracle. He failed ninth grade and for a significant chunk of his early adolescence was virtually the full-time caretaker for his baby brother. To his regret, Curtis lives apart from his own two young children, both born when he was still in high school.

Latoya, nineteen, is a part-time cashier at a dollar store in town and a full-time college freshman at a nearby state university. For a while, it seemed as though Latoya was destined to repeat many of her mother's mistakes. She gave birth to a daughter during the first term of her sophomore year in high school. But unlike her mother, she went on to graduate. After finishing college, she hopes to be a teacher someday.

Celeste's two younger children are Nelson Mandela, fourteen, and Brittany, ten. It's still too early to predict how either will be affected over the long term by their family's poverty. At the moment, though, they represent opposite poles on the continuum of school success. Nelson Mandela is in danger of failing eighth grade. Brittany, on the other hand, is a regular on her school's honor roll.

Jonquil, Latoya's three-year-old daughter, recently began attending a licensed child-care center after spending much of the first few years of her life in what sounds like a substandard child-care home.

Making Ends Meet, One Catfish at a Time

Celeste, the family's matriarch, works as a band-saw operator. That's a pretty benign-sounding job title for what she does—cut the heads off of catfish. One a second. Sixty a minute. Three thousand, six hundred an hour. Twenty eight thousand, eight hundred a day.

"Basically, I work in an indoor field," she says. "A *refrigerated* indoor field."

Celeste, thirty-seven, has been working in the Belzoni plant of Delta Pride Catfish, the nation's largest producer of farm-raised catfish, for about ten years. She makes $6.20 an hour, a total of $10,855 in 1997. (The poverty threshold for a family of five was $19,380 in 1997.)

At the moment, the Lyles family is in a relatively stable period, with the children all attending school, Celeste working a lot of overtime, and most material needs being met. Yet Celeste is deeply in debt—to the tune of $12,000, give or take a few thousand. With creditors baying at the door, she's considering declaring bankruptcy. Her mistake, she says, was saying yes every time she was offered a credit card—Mastercard, Visa, Radio Shack, Discover—and trying to give her children memorable Christmases. "You do what you have to do to make your children happy," she explains. Already she's got two court judgments against her—for a total of $10,304— and a few others are likely.

In the past week, Celeste grossed $311.25, which included $63.62 in overtime pay. Deductions reduced her take-home pay to $235.22. Most of the deductions are for mandatory contributions like Social Security and Medicare and union dues. But a few are discretionary: $2.40 a week for a cancer insurance policy that would pay Celeste $10,000 if she or a child were diagnosed with a serious cancer; $11.40 for a $53,000 term life insurance policy on her and $10,000 policies on each child; and $10 for savings. (No one can tell Celeste, who survived a life-threatening illness, that the cancer insurance is most likely a scam.)

In the four months of each year during which Celeste usually works some overtime, the family lives on about $940 a month, plus $140 worth of food stamps. Here's how they spend her monthly income when the plant is working at capacity, as it is now:

INCOME

Celeste's take-home pay	$940

EXPENSES

Rent	$227
Car payment	150

Car insurance	40
Gasoline	35
Electricity	45
Garbage	15
Cable TV	48
Dryer payment	15
Groceries	240
Total	$815

As anyone can see, in the *best* of months, there's just $125 left over for unanticipated expenses, such as school supplies, clothes, a visit to the doctor, medicine, or a car repair. How does Celeste make it all work? "The Lord blesses me every day, and I thank him for it," she says.

Celeste is nothing if not resourceful. When she runs low on money, she simply figures out how to make more. The first weekend in April, for instance, she set up shop at Belzoni's annual catfish festival, which draws thousands of people from all over the Delta. She figured a lot of people, catfish workers in particular, would want to eat something besides catfish, so she made and sold chicken kabobs. All the children helped out. The family spent $40 on supplies and took in $382. "That's a $342 profit for a day's work!" she exclaims. With the profits, she bought new outfits for each child, stocked the refrigerator with staples, and took them all out to dinner.

But basically the Lyleses live from paycheck to paycheck, and often the week's paycheck goes to pay bills that are already two months overdue. Most of the last paycheck of each month is set aside for the next month's rent, since the housing authority doesn't look kindly on late payments.

Although the family's rent is supposedly subsidized and goes up or down with their household income, the current rent of $227 a month is actually close to the market rate for an apartment of this size in Belzoni. Before the Lyleses moved here five and a half years ago after three years on the housing authority's waiting list, they paid $110 a month to rent a ramshackle two-bedroom trailer across town.

Celeste might be faulted for a few extravagances—her car maybe, or cable TV—but she's got a good reason for each of them. The fact is that a car is a necessity in the Delta. Without a car, there's no going anywhere since there's no public transportation, and taxis cost as much as in cities. Celeste bought the car, a '96 Geo Metro, three years ago, in partnership with her best friend, Teresa, when the transmission on her old car went out. The two women split the cost in half; when one is having a bad month, the other makes her payment.

As for cable TV, it's the only entertainment the children have, so Celeste thinks it's worth the splurge. Plus, she lives for the programs that help her see beyond Belzoni: CNN, documentaries on exotic places and diseases, old movies.

Although Celeste has health insurance through her job, a substantial copayment is required for doctors' visits and prescription drugs. Last month, when she was suffering from asthma, she went to a doctor five times, at $22 a visit. Her asthma medication cost her $200. (She buys it only when her asthma is acting up. "Paying for my drugs is like paying another rent," she says.)

Luckily, she worked a lot of overtime last month. But there's a price to be paid for working overtime. "I get home at nine or ten o'-clock at night and just have time to get to bed before I have to get up again," she points out. "Sometimes my kids wonder if they have a mother."

When the catfish plant cuts back its workers' hours—a virtual certainty from June through December—the family's budget is seriously squeezed. "They don't call it that, but I've really got a seasonal job," Celeste says. During these months, her income falls enough for her two youngest children to qualify for Medicaid. She cuts back on food—less chicken, more potatoes. And she lets the utility bills ride until the utilities threaten to cut off service.

"We haven't had our lights turned off yet," she says, "and we've never gone to the refrigerator and found nothing in it, so I can't complain."

"I Went Wild"

Celeste grew up in southern Ohio in the home of her great-grandmother and her second husband. "My mother was seventeen when she had me, and my great-grandmother thought she was too young to raise me," Celeste says. Celeste never even knew her father's identity until after he died. (Only then did she learn that he had lived less than a mile away, on a street she frequently walked down.)

Celeste's great-grandmother died when Celeste was thirteen, and she was sent to live with an aunt and uncle. It's probably no coincidence that a few months later she became pregnant with her first child. "It was the first time in my life I could breathe without asking, and I went wild," she says.

The baby's father was eight years older than Celeste. The pregnancy caused a falling-out with her aunt, so Celeste and baby Curtis went to live with her mother in Cleveland while she attended ninth grade. At her mother's home, she met a twenty-three-year-old man. They married soon after she turned fifteen—the legal age for consent in Ohio.

When she was a junior in high school, Celeste became pregnant with her second child. Her husband, who made good money at a plating company, urged her to drop out of school so that she could be a full-time wife and mother. "It was the worst mistake of my life," she says now.

The relationship wasn't a happy one, and it grew more strained as Celeste matured. "When we first met, I was young, and it was easy for him to have the upper hand," she explains. "But as I grew older, I grew more independent, and he didn't want that."

When she was twenty-one, and married five years, Celeste had a medical crisis that changed her life in ways she can't fully explain. She had gone to a clinic to have an intrauterine device inserted to prevent another pregnancy. Two weeks later, after her kidneys began to fail, Celeste underwent emergency surgery. It turned out the IUD had perforated her uterus and punctured her large intestine. Her heart stopped on the operating table, and she had to be resuscitated. Doctors removed one ovary, a fallopian tube, and a section of her intestines. When she was discharged from the hospital, she knew she didn't want to go home. "It was over," she says of the marriage.

Celeste and the two children lived with her mother for four months while she recovered. Her husband wanted her back and came by often. But Celeste wanted out of the marriage, and she felt that to extricate herself, she needed to move away. "He said, 'You ain't going nowhere, but if you do, I'm keeping the kids,'" Celeste says. She moved as far away as she could imagine—880 miles—to Ebenezer, Mississippi, to the home of a sister-in-law. She thought her husband would soon grow tired of caring for two young children and call her to come and get them.

As it turned out, it took two years to get Curtis to Mississippi, and another six to get Latoya. The long separation was so painful that Celeste and both children still have trouble talking about it.

By the time Curtis moved to Mississippi, he was ten, and Celeste had had another child, Nelson Mandela, by then four months old. Celeste and the two boys shared a $30-a-week room in a boarding-house in Lexington, Mississippi. Celeste had a job on the night shift at a chicken processing factory in Morton, Mississippi, ninety minutes away. She left home every day at 1:00 P.M. and didn't return until 2:30 A.M. So by the time he was eleven, Curtis was in charge of his baby brother most of the time Celeste was at work. (The boardinghouse operator helped a little, but Curtis was the primary caregiver.) "He was like a daddy to him," Celeste says.

The job at the chicken plant was awful. "They'd hang the live chickens by their feet and shock them to make them lose consciousness," she explains. "The chickens would release their bowels, and you can't imagine the mess. Then a machine would de-feather them. They weren't dead, just numbified. Then there'd be a line of ten or twelve workers who'd do different things to them—cut their throats, remove the bowels, de-wing them, cut them into pieces. By the time the chicken's at the end of the line, all you've got is a carcass."

Trading Chicken for Catfish

Celeste quit her job at the chicken plant just before she gave birth to Brittany. For three months after her birth, the family somehow managed to live on Mississippi's $100-a-month welfare benefit. Then Celeste heard that the catfish industry was hiring in Belzoni, which is only thirty miles from Lexington. She took the job because it meant a less draining commute.

Working at the catfish plant was better than working at the chicken plant, but not much. In 1988 Delta Pride paid its workers minimum wage, and overtime hours were paid as straight time, not time and a half. There were no benefits, not even guaranteed bathroom breaks.

Two years after Celeste started at Delta Pride, discontent over wages and working conditions led to a three-month strike by the Food and Commercial Workers' Union at the company's nearby Indianola plant. The workers won the strike, and wages and working conditions improved at both plants. Celeste's wages went up 20 percent overnight, and the company began paying time and a half for overtime. The workers also became eligible for low-cost health insurance for their families and received guaranteed bathroom breaks.

Still, even with the union-won improvements, Celeste's job is nothing short of grueling. Because of the risk of repetitive strain injuries, she must tape her wrists tightly before taking her place on the line. Then she dons rubber gloves to protect the fish from bacteria, and wire-mesh gloves to protect her fingers from the saw blade. The temperature in the room is kept around sixty degrees, so she wears several layers of clothes to keep warm. To prevent back strain, she also wears a brace, which has the added benefit of serving as further insulation. Still, she says, "it's like working in a refrigerator."

"I hate the job," she continues. "It's hard work, and it's cold work, but it's the best job there is around here, because the other factories are piecework. I have to have a job where I know what I'm going to take home at the end of the day."

Celeste's biggest job-related concern is her health. She's worried that it won't hold up much longer, given the working conditions. She's cut her hand badly three times and lost the tip of one thumb to the saw. "Their goal is to get as many fish processed as possible. Mine is to leave the plant every day with all my body parts," she says, only half joking. In addition, she's convinced that her asthma was caused by her job.

Celeste's great-grandmother died during an asthma attack, and she worries that she'll die that way, too. Her brush with death during the removal of her IUD seems to have made her hypersensitive to her own mortality. She talks frequently with her children about what they need to do if she dies.

"I'm preparing my children for it," she says. "I tell them that it may be that I won't be here for their whole growing-up, but that as brothers and sisters, they have to be responsible for each other."

Curtis: "I Want Better in Life"

It's a Saturday morning, and Curtis has brought his two little boys, ages five and four, to visit their grandmother. Curtis's two boys have different mothers, and Curtis hardly ever gets to see them both at the same time, so it's a rare opportunity for the two to play together. But like many barely grown-up children, Curtis has an ulterior motive for coming over to his mother's house: he wants to use her washer and dryer.

Curtis is a tall, slender young man with a pencil-thin mustache and a well-trimmed goatee. He wears two gold hoops in his left ear, a gold chain, and a Nike baseball cap, with the bill facing back. An amateur tattoo on his forearm reads "TCAT." "I used to have a girl-friend with the initials TC," he explains. "After we broke up, I added AT to it so my new girlfriend wouldn't get mad."

Curtis is asked what he remembers about his childhood, particu-larly his preteen period, when he had to care for Nelson while their mother worked. If he's resentful, he doesn't say so. "I knew what I had to do and what not to do," Curtis says. "My main responsibility was watching Nelson. I had to take Nelson every place I went. The second thing I had to do was keep our place clean.

"At the time, it wasn't much fun. But I think it made me a better person. That's why I'm working and going to school. I want better in life for my kids."

Celeste knows that she robbed Curtis of part of his childhood by forcing so much responsibility on him, and she feels guilty about it. There were some days when she didn't come home at all, she admits, because she had to work a double shift. On those occasions, she'd work her two shifts, catch a few hours' sleep at a friend's house near the plant, and go back to work as soon as she woke up, sometimes working a double shift again. "When you ain't got nothing, you do what you have to do to get what you need," she says.

Celeste is proud of how well Curtis has turned out. Soon after he entered his teens, he started hanging out with what Celeste consid-ered the wrong group of kids. "These kids were what I call 'half-raised,'" she says. "Their parents didn't have any control over them. I could see where they were going, which was nowhere."

Because he spent too much time with these friends and too little time on schoolwork, Curtis flunked the ninth grade. But he never thought of dropping out, as many of his friends did, he says. For one thing, he knew his mother wouldn't have let him. For another, he knew that dropping out would mean a life with no prospects other than working at a catfish plant.

When Curtis was sixteen and in the tenth grade, he became a fa-ther. The child's mother was a casual girlfriend. Curtis didn't tell his mother about the baby until six weeks after he was born. "I wasn't sure it was mine until after he was born," Curtis explains. "I was in denial until I saw the baby face to face. He looked just like me."

The child's mother is now in the military in Texas, and the boy lives with her mother. Curtis sees him occasionally but doesn't pay child support. "His mother makes good money, and she knows I don't, so she doesn't care," he says.

His second child was born his junior year. That child lives with his mother, who works at a catfish plant. Curtis sees him more regularly than his first child, about twice every three weeks. He doesn't pay child support for him either.

"If I could do it over, I wouldn't have had kids so young," Curtis says. "But I'm going to be there for my boys, because my father wasn't there for me."

Curtis is finishing up his second year of general studies at Mississippi Delta Community College, in nearby Morehead. He also works part-time at Belzoni's only grocery. After he finishes school, he hopes to find a job as an air-conditioner technician. A friend who does that makes $250 a week, which Curtis considers "good money." Once he gets a job like that, Curtis says, he can start giving money to the mothers of his children.

Curtis admires his mother for raising her children without any help from their fathers. "She always found a way to get what we needed," he says. "There were times when we struggled, but she always came through."

Celeste interrupts as he's talking. "I did not want my children to end up the way I have," she says. "I wanted them to have a functional family, even if I was the only parent functioning."

Latoya: "I Was Just a Bother"

It's hard to believe that Latoya, nineteen, is her mother's daughter. She seems to go out of her way to dress down—wearing a clean T-shirt and jeans is her idea of dressing up, whereas her mother doesn't leave the house before she's put on her makeup and painted her nails to match her outfit. Unlike her loud and brazen mother, Latoya is quiet and soft-spoken. When Latoya begins talking about her childhood, it's clear she has deep emotional wounds from her mother's disappearance, her father's inattention, and the years of doing without.

"I was so young when my mother left that I couldn't even remember what she looked like," Latoya says. When her school friends asked why she had a stepmother rather than a real mother, "I would tell them that she died," Latoya recalls. "I guess I was ashamed to say she'd moved away from me."

Latoya spent much of her childhood fantasizing about living with her mother. "I wanted to go and live with her, but my father wouldn't let me," she says. "When she'd call, he wouldn't tell me, and when she'd send me things, he wouldn't give them to me. He never talked bad about her. He just wouldn't talk about her at all."

Latoya remembers the first few years with her father fondly, but the later years with deep sadness. "I think he really wanted me with him at first," she says. "We were really close. But once he had women coming into his life, I was just a bother. He was never there for me. He would work all day long, sleep all night, and go fishing on weekends."

Latoya's father had a series of girlfriends, each of whom told Latoya to call her Mom. "The first really tried to treat me like a daughter, but then when she and my father would fight, she'd take it out on me after he left for work," she says. "The last one didn't beat me, but she didn't like me. She acted more like a baby-sitter than a stepmom. She made me stay in my room all the time, even to eat. I couldn't even come into the living room."

The one constant in Latoya's life through her childhood was her paternal grandmother. "Anytime my dad had problems with a girlfriend, we'd move back in with his mother, and I liked that," she says. "But it meant I hardly ever attended one school for a whole year. Between first and sixth grade, I went to four different schools. It made it hard to have friends."

Celeste came and got Latoya after she finished seventh grade. "I had a falling-out with my father's last girlfriend," Latoya explains. "They didn't want me around anymore." Although Latoya had yearned to live with her mother for years, the reality was not as she had imagined.

"The family was living in a two-bedroom trailer," Latoya recalls, "and I arrived in the summer, when it was really hot. There really wasn't no space for me. All four of us kids stayed in one bedroom, two in top bunks, two in the bottoms."

Latoya had trouble making the change from life in a big northern city to life in a small southern town. "People treated me like an outsider, somebody who was stuck up because I was from up north," she says.

She found relations between the races in Mississippi hard to adjust to. She had attended integrated schools in Cleveland, but in Belzoni she was shocked to find that her class was all black and there were fewer than a dozen white students in the whole school. (Most of the town's white children attend a private Christian academy.) In her six years in Belzoni, she's never had a white friend. The only time she comes in contact with white people is at Fred's Dollar Store, where she works part-time.

There were other things about school that she found difficult, too. The rules were stricter and the consequences for violating them included paddling, which had not been permitted in Cleveland. (Nor is it permitted, for that matter, in most states.) She always seemed to be at odds with school officials. Except for her senior year, she was suspended at least once a year.

"I wasn't accustomed to getting whuppings in school, and I didn't like it," Latoya says. "I remember the first time I was suspended, when I was in the eighth grade. I was tardy for study hall, and the principal took me into his office. He yanked me real hard to get me close enough to him to paddle, and I told him he wasn't going to put his mother-f——ing hands on me."

Latoya was in ninth grade when she found out she was pregnant, which was not surprising, given both her chaotic childhood and the community in which she was now living. According to the Centers for Disease Control and Prevention, Mississippi has the highest teen birth rate of any state, with 52 of every 1,000 fifteen- to seventeen-year-olds giving birth in 1996, compared with a national rate of 34. And Humphreys County has one of the highest teen birth rates of any county in Mississippi. According to state records, 27 percent of all births in the county in 1996 were to teens, compared with a state average of 21 percent and a national average of 13 percent. Put another way, one out of every nine black teenage girls in the county had a baby in 1996. There were no births that year to fifteen- to seventeen-year-old whites.

"I took a home pregnancy test, and it was positive, but I didn't want to believe it," Latoya says. "I knew I wasn't ready to be a mother, and I asked my baby's daddy for some money to get an abortion. He wouldn't give it to me, so here we are." As she's discussing her unwanted pregnancy, her daughter is sitting on her lap sucking on a lollipop.

Latoya hid the pregnancy for months. "I was scared to tell my mother, because it seemed like she was always in a bad mood," Latoya explains. "She'd come home from work and be mad at everybody because she'd had a hard day. I finally told her one day when she came home for lunch. She stormed out and slammed the door.

"I thought, 'Well, it went all right. I'm still alive.'"

At this point in Latoya's story, Celeste jumps into the discussion. "I was disappointed in her, given my own background," Celeste says. "I had to speak harshly to her just to make sure she wouldn't get it in her head that she had an exit route from responsibility. I told her that she was going to stay in school if she had to strap this child to her back. I also told her I wasn't going to raise her baby, that I wasn't going to be the one getting up at 2:00 A.M. to feed her when she cried.

"Everybody's got to take responsibility for their own mistakes."

Latoya's boyfriend broke up with her when she was about four months pregnant. Latoya gave birth to Jonquil over Thanksgiving weekend 1994 and missed only a few days of school. She couldn't apply for welfare because she was under eighteen, but she did begin receiving Medicaid coverage and WIC vouchers, which provided formula and, later, cereal, milk, and baby food.

Rather than sap her ambition, as motherhood often does to teens, becoming a mother seemed to motivate Latoya. Later on in tenth grade, she was elected Miss FFA (Future Farmers of America). She began doing better in school, often making the honor roll, and played the French horn in the band.

Still, being a teen mother hasn't been easy. Finding someone to care for Jonquil while she attends school has always been a big problem. Jonquil bounced from one baby-sitter to another for much of her first year of life.

"I finally found a woman in her seventies who took in five or six children, for $25 or $30 a week each," Latoya says. "For the first few months, Jonquil's father paid for it, then all of a sudden he stopped. I couldn't ask the state for help because the lady wasn't re-porting the income and didn't want the state involved. I thought for a while I'd have to drop out. Finally, the lady told me she'd just keep a tab until I could pay. She kept Jonquil without me paying for my whole last year in school. At the end, I owed her more than $1,000. But I've paid most of it back. Now I just owe her about $100."

In her senior year, Latoya started going out with a classmate named Kevin, who is as soft-spoken as she is. Every day after school, he would walk Latoya the mile and a half to the baby-sitter's house to pick up Jonquil, and then walk with her another mile and a half to her home, often carrying Jonquil for her. A year and a half later, Kevin and Latoya are still going out.

In September 1997, Latoya started classes at Mississippi Valley State University in nearby Itta Bena, with the help of a Pell grant and some loans. She wants to be a teacher. Jonquil is now going to a li-censed child-care center, where the quality of care is much better than at her old baby-sitter's. The state pays most of the cost, but La-toya has to pay $120 a month, which consumes about 40 percent of her take-home pay from the dollar store. (The rest goes mostly for school-related expenses. She doesn't earn enough to help her mother with household expenses, except for an occasional purchase of laun-dry detergent or the ingredients for a meal.)

"It's hard going to college full-time and going to work and trying to be a good mother, too," she says. "I really don't have a lot of time with my daughter. All I want out of life now is the best for her. I want to be there for her, because my parents weren't really there for me. I didn't have a mother, and I only had half a father, because when he was home he was asleep."

Since October 1997, after intervention by the state child support collection agency, Latoya has been receiving $118 a month in child support from Jonquil's father, who works at a catfish plant. Al-though Jonquil's father isn't involved in his child's life, her paternal grandmother is. She drives Jonquil to child care every day and often keeps her on weekends so that Latoya can study.

Now that Latoya is a mother herself, she realizes how little nurtur-ing she received as a child, and how much she missed. It's been hard to establish a relationship with her mother, she says. "The mother-daughter feelings, I'm having trouble getting used to that," she says.

She and Celeste are more like friends than mother and daughter, she says.

Latoya misses her father and grandmother and the two half-sisters her father fathered by two different girlfriends. "I've written to him a few times, but all he sends me is a little card every now and then," she says. "He doesn't really tell me anything about his life." She wants to visit her grandmother before she dies so that she can fill in a few holes in her memories of her childhood.

"I had a dream last week that I was going to make a surprise visit, and when I got there everybody was gone, even my grandmother," Latoya says. "It was a nightmare, really, more than a dream."

A Mississippi Miracle

It's Saturday night in the Delta. Latoya and Jonquil are watching a movie on the VCR, side by side with Latoya's boyfriend Kevin. But it seems as though anybody with access to a car is streaming down the highway toward Greenville, the home of three riverboat casinos. The first casino here opened on October 30, 1995, and the city's other two followed in the first half of 1996. Although they're called riverboats, they don't actually sail. They're permanently moored in Lake Ferguson, a backwater of the Mississippi River.

"It's what you do here on Saturday night," Celeste explains. "There sure ain't nothing else to do." Nelson and Brittany are visiting Nelson's paternal grandmother for the weekend, so Celeste doesn't have to feel guilty about leaving them home alone while she gambles.

Since 1992, when the state's first casino opened upriver in Tunico, Mississippi has become the second-largest gaming state in the nation. By early 1998 there were thirty state-regulated casinos operating (not counting those on Indian reservations), with several more under construction.

In 1997 alone, bettors wagered almost $34 billion. Yes, *$34 billion*—ten times the state's annual budget. According to the state, about 31 percent of the 12.8 million patrons a year are Mississippians. (In Greenville the casinos draw 48 percent of their patrons from Mississippi.) If the state's estimates are right, then the average adult Mississippian visits a riverboat three or four times a year. Last year, they left $2 billion behind—$156 per patron—in losses.

Tonight Celeste is in a good mood as she drives the fifty miles to Greenville, past thousands of acres of soon-to-be-planted cotton and soybean fields and scores of catfish ponds teeming with fish that may someday cross her sawblade. Two months ago, she had a three-week winning streak, and it's time for another one, she thinks.

As always, she's planning to wager only $40. She explains her basic rules: "You do not spend your rent. You do not spend your grocery money. You do not spend your light bill money or your gas money. You do not sit and gamble away your children's money, because you work too hard for it. And above all, you don't gamble more than you can afford to lose."

Celeste parks on the stone levee above the Las Vegas Casino, her favorite, and heads into the huge warehouse-sized casino. The walls are painted black but flash with neon signs. White lights twinkle in the black mirrored ceiling, looking like constellations in another universe. You could cut the cigarette smoke with a knife, and the noise of clattering coins makes it hard to have a conversation.

Celeste takes the elevator up one floor to the balcony, the domain of the nickel slot players. Almost all of the women feeding nickels into the machines are African American. The table games downstairs—craps, roulette, and black jack—are more popular with whites, as are the slots that require larger wagers, from a quarter all the way up to a $25 token. Celeste changes her $40 into twenty rolls of nickels and heads for a machine she's had luck on before. "I only play the nickel slots," she says. "I get to sit there for four hours or more on an investment of $40. It's good entertainment."

Celeste has been a confirmed gambler since April 27, 1996, just a few months after the first two Greenville casinos opened. "I can remember the date for several reasons," she explains. "The day before, we got laid off. They called us into the break room one morning and told us they were shutting down. I came home that night and prayed for a miracle. I didn't know what I was going to do.

"At three o'clock in the morning, something told me to wake up and go to the boats. I took $40 from my last paycheck and went over to the boats. I went into the Las Vegas Casino and played $20 in a nickel slot, and it jackpotted for $300. Then I got another jackpot, on the same machine, within an hour. I walked off that boat with $700.

"I went to the boat next door, the Jubilee. I lost $200, and then hit for $275. I said, 'Lord, you're working with me. Move me where you want me to go.' So He put me on another machine, and it jack-potted for $500. I was so scared I didn't know what to do.

"When I came home and counted my money, I had $1,263, off of $40 and a dream."

Those winnings enabled Celeste to pay her rent, keep the refrigerator stocked, and stay current on her utility bills during the three-and-a-half-month layoff. She wouldn't have been able to make it on her $120-a-week unemployment checks alone, she says.

Tonight, though, is another story. Celeste can't find a machine that feels right. She moves from one to another, getting ahead for a while and then falling behind. The clatter of other machines paying off drives her into a dark mood. After three hours, she calls it quits. But she still has $19 of the $40 she came with.

"It's an off night," she says as she leaves.

"Church Sunday"

It's "church Sunday" for Celeste's family—the fourth Sunday of the month. Their 110-year-old Baptist church can afford a preacher only one Sunday a month, and this is it. Celeste and her granddaughter Jonquil dress in their proverbial Sunday best—a purple and gold lamé two-piece dress for Celeste, accented by gold-sequined, rhinestone-bejeweled heels and fingernails painted purple and gold to match the outfit. Jonquil is wearing a dress with a nautical motif and a hoop skirt, along with a matching sailor's cap. Latoya begs off, as usual. Nelson and Brittany would be going, too, but they're still visiting Nelson's grandmother.

Their church is a country church, founded in the 1880s by freed slaves. The oldest legible tombstone in the church's small cemetery marks the demise of a man born in 1868, not long after the Emancipation Proclamation freed the slaves. Some of the graves are marked with hand-lettered tombstones. Some aren't marked at all.

A recent remodeling inside the white cinder-block building has created a comfortable gathering place: the floors are carpeted in crimson, the pews are covered with matching cushions, and a lace curtain hides the baptismal pool. A formal portrait of the elderly pastor occupies a prominent place on the wall behind the pulpit, just above a painting of the Last Supper. The minister is a circuit rider who serves four churches in the Delta.

Four male deacons occupy a bank of pews on one side of the pulpit. The four "church mothers"—members of what the church calls its "Mother Board"—sit in a bank of pews on the other side. Each wears a fancy broad-brimmed hat. Celeste takes her place in the all-women choir, and Jonquil sits beside her grandmother, her legs dangling from the pew. Two dozen people, half of them children, are in the audience.

The minister starts the service with a reading of Corinthians I, chapter 11, immediately raising Celeste's hackles. The message of the passage seems pretty clear to her—women are inferior to men—and she doesn't agree. "A man . . . is the image and glory of God: but the woman is the glory of the man," the minister intones. "For the man is not of the woman; but the woman is of the man. Neither was the man created for the woman; but the woman for the man."

Celeste attends this church mainly out of loyalty to her best friend Teresa, who's recently become the assistant pastor (an unpaid position). After the Bible lesson, Teresa goes behind the pulpit to lead the prayer and the singing. Her powerful contralto voice booms into the microphone while she leads the group in singing "One More Time." Members of the choir sway to the music, many with their eyes closed, while the first of three offerings is taken, this one for the poor.

Celeste puts a dollar bill in the plate. Brother John counts up the total as the choir sings "Have Your Way, Lord," and then announces the take—$27, all in $1 bills and coins. Then another offering is taken, this one for the church's expenses. "We thank God for the sum of $35," Brother John announces. And then there's a third collection: the "Calendar Drive" targets people who have celebrated birthdays or anniversaries this month. Once again, the donations are all in $1 bills and coins. Teresa is now leading the singing of "Lord, I'll Make It Somehow." After the song is finished, Brother John announces: "We thank God for $17.60 for the Calendar Drive."

The minister's sermon—on the subject "What Is Man?"—lasts forty-five minutes. By the end of it, most of the children are sleeping. Jonquil, up in the choir loft, is lying with her head in Celeste's lap. When the time comes for communion, Celeste carefully lays her out on the pew so that she can partake.

After communion, the church secretary reads the names of all the members who have contributed their monthly dues. No one from the Lyles family is among them. The congregation links hands and sings "Reach Out and Touch Somebody's Hand." The service is over, two hours after it began.

As the congregation trickles out, babies are passed from person to person for admiring. "You sure look pretty today," everybody tells Jonquil, who hides behind her grandmother's skirt.

Nelson and Brittany

It's Sunday evening, and Nelson and Brittany have just returned from their weekend with Nelson's grandmother. He's carrying his birthday present, an underwater mask and snorkel, which was a curious gift, since he can't swim. With Teresa and her thirteen-year-old daughter visiting as well, the living room is crowded.

The family's home is much more comfortable than you'd expect for a family on such a tight budget, but then, each piece of furniture, each wall hanging, each knickknack, has a story. For instance, an old boyfriend gave Celeste the dining room set as a housewarming present. She bought her bedroom suite on time: $135 a month for twelve months, at an exorbitant interest rate. The washer was bought over time as well, and she's now renting the dryer for $15 a week, on a rent-to-own basis. The color television and stereo system and the wall-size set of shelves they rest on were bought on time for $40 a week over two years. "It costs me more than twice what it would have cost if I'd have been able to pay cash, maybe twice and a half," Celeste acknowledges.

Celeste is also a habitué of rummage sales and auctions, and she's the type of woman who can easily make a silk purse out of a sow's ear. She recently re-covered the sectional sofa, bought ten years ago on the installment plan, so that it looks as good as new. "I got a whole bolt of fabric for $14 at Wal-Mart," she boasts. To round out the look, she's made puffy valances for the windows and accent pillows for the couch.

Nelson Mandela, named after one of Celeste's heroes, turns fourteen tomorrow. He's having trouble with adolescence and is at risk of failing eighth grade. Celeste thinks most of his problems are due to his short stature, which makes him self-conscious. He's much shorter than his sister, Brittany, even though she's four years younger.

"He's got an inferiority complex because everybody has passed him in size," Celeste says. "He's always trying to fit in, which means he does things contrary to his better judgment, stupid stuff like putting tacks on people's chairs, just to be noticed. And kids push him around because he's small."

Nelson wears a very somber look on his face. He rarely smiles, and his eyes lack the sparkle of his younger sister's. He answers my questions in a monotone, and his answers consist mostly of "Yes, ma'am" and "No, ma'am." When pressed about school, his answers indicate that he regards it as a not very friendly place. Someone in his class gets paddled every day, three to five swats with a wooden paddle, "just for talking or laughing or talking back to a teacher," he says.

On the most recent occasion on which Nelson himself faced a paddling, he believed he was being unfairly punished for someone else's infraction. Since a student is sometimes allowed to choose suspension instead of a paddling, he called Celeste at work and asked her to come to the school and get him. "But she wanted me to take the paddling instead of missing school," Nelson says.

Celeste interjects: "It doesn't make sense to me to send a child home for talking in class. I didn't want him to miss school."

Brittany is absolutely gorgeous, with huge eyes, an impish smile, a cascade of ringlets, and long, slender legs. If she lived anywhere near a big city, she'd probably be recruited to be a child model. She's in classes for the gifted at her elementary school and always makes honor roll. Her academic plaques and trophies fill the display shelves in the living room. She's clearly the apple of Celeste's eye.

Although Brittany likes school, she, too, complains about the paddlings. Just a few days ago, she got paddled, along with everyone else in her class. "We had just come in from recess, and one girl started singing, and then everybody else started singing, and the teacher came in and gave everybody a whack," she says.

Brittany says she wants to be a lawyer. Whether this is her own dream or her mother's dream for her is hard to tell. "I don't expect any less from her, because she has a great mind," Celeste says. "I'm not going to force her to be a lawyer or anything else she doesn't want to be, as long as she doesn't end up working in the fishhouse. I expect great things from her. She's been way ahead of her age ever since she was a baby."

"We Want to Be Entrepreneurs"

As twilight falls, the family sits around the television watching a documentary on professional wrestling. Hulk Hogan dominates the screen. Celeste and Teresa are talking about the bad old days in Mississippi, when children chopped cotton in the fields for $3 a day, Teresa included, and most everybody had an outhouse in their yard. Both know older women who gave birth in the fields and then resumed picking cotton, their newborns strapped to their backs.

"We've come a long way, but there's still a long ways to go," says Teresa, who has a job teaching computer skills to mothers who are trying to get off welfare. "Now we have women losing welfare benefits because they can't get jobs because they can't read."

As they do almost every time they're together, Celeste and Teresa talk about their mutual dream of opening a dress shop that would cater to African American women. "It's 73 percent black here in this county, and all the stores are geared to what conservative white women want to wear," Celeste says. "I have to go to Greenville to buy my clothes." The two women have gone so far as to take some courses at the community college, draw up a business plan, and have business cards printed up.

"Teresa and me, we want to be entrepreneurs," Celeste says. "We're tired of working for other people and not having a quarter to our names. We want to be our own bosses."

They know it may be hard to rent space in Belzoni's small, faded business district. Celeste says that only one business there is owned by a black person, and she isn't sure the other business owners would welcome her. After all, in front of the blond brick Humphreys County courthouse is a Civil War memorial "to the men who wore the gray and were faithful to the end."

So Teresa and Celeste have decided to start small and continue for a few more years in their current jobs. They plan to put a hitch on their Geo Metro, hook a used trailer to it, fill it with stylish clothes, and set up shop at the flea markets that dot the Mississippi roadsides on weekends.

With the profits from the enterprise, Celeste eventually wants to buy her own home. She figures she and Teresa can go in on it, as they did on their car, with each buying half of a duplex.

"Everybody wants to leave their children something," she says. "They want their children to be able to say, 'My mommy left me this. I know this belongs to me.'

"That's something I can't say myself, but it's something I want my children to be able to say."

10

GRAND RAPIDS,
MICHIGAN

Someday sixteen-month-old Tyrone Washington is going to ask his mother who the other people are in the photograph that shows him blowing out the candle on his first birthday cake.

"Those are some nice church ladies who helped make sure you celebrated your first birthday," his mother, Sylvia Washington, may tell him. "They baked you that cake, and they sang 'Happy Birthday' to you. They even brought you some presents."

If he's old enough to understand, Sylvia may tell him more.

She may tell him about the series of crises that propelled her family from a nice suburban duplex to a homeless shelter.

About almost losing him during her pregnancy because of complications.

About having to leave him alone all night with his teenage sisters because she couldn't find a baby-sitter while she worked her nightshift job.

And about opening her front door one morning to a deputy sheriff bearing an eviction order.

"A lot of things happened to us that I feel were beyond my control," Sylvia will tell him. "Things just kept coming up, and we were living from paycheck to paycheck, and I didn't have any sort of cushion."

By then, Sylvia will almost certainly be able to tell her son about her successful struggle to raise her family out of poverty, because by the time Tyrone is old enough to ask about the photograph of his first birthday party, the hard times should all be a distant memory.

Sylvia has big plans for herself and her three children—Letisha, sixteen, Laura, fourteen, and Tyrone. She's determined that when the final chapter of her family's history is written, this period of extreme poverty will stand out as an aberration.

"I don't know if we'll ever be middle-class again, but I don't see us spending much time being poor," she says.

A Split-Shift Marriage

Sylvia grew up in poverty, first in Marvel, Arkansas, where her parents were cotton and soybean sharecroppers, and later in Grand Rapids, Michigan, where her mother moved the children in search of a better life after she was divorced. True to the American dream, most of the nine children in the family have done better financially than their parents ever did, with four attending college and all but Sylvia currently employed.

While in high school in Grand Rapids, Sylvia was editor of her school newspaper and captain of the pompon squad. She got her first job at age sixteen, through the federally subsidized CETA work experience program. She got a taste of office work by answering phones, typing letters, and filing reports in her high school's attendance office.

After her 1978 graduation, Sylvia worked for a year, holding down part-time jobs in her family's church and at a Sears store. By the next summer, she had saved enough to afford her own apartment and begin attending Grand Rapids Community College part-time. She also worked a full-time job as a housekeeper in a hospital emergency room, on the 4:00 P.M. to 12:30 A.M. shift.

In November 1980, at the age of twenty-one, Sylvia married a young man who'd been born in Clarksdale, Mississippi, and then moved north with his parents as a baby. They'd had similar childhoods. He, too, had been raised by a single mother, since his father died a few years after the move.

Sylvia was forced to leave college when their first child, Letisha, was born ten months after the couple married. She took only a few months off from her hospital job then, and again in August 1983, when her second child, Laura, was born. "My husband worked nights and I worked days, so one of us was always with the kids," she says. "We did that so we wouldn't have to worry about baby-sitters."

After a few years of the split-shift marriage, the couple decided that Sylvia should give up her full-time job and stay home with the girls. They planned for her to take temporary work whenever the household budget needed a boost. But in 1985, their finances fell apart when her husband was laid off. The couple ended up going on welfare and moving in with her husband's mother. A personal tragedy compounded their problems. "I was pregnant with my third child when I got the chicken pox," Sylvia recalls. "I was really sick, and I lost the baby. It took me a long time to recover. I couldn't really hold a job, and my husband couldn't hold things together himself."

But with well-paying industrial jobs plentiful in the Grand Rapids area in the mid-1980s, the couple bounced back financially within a year. Sylvia's husband got a steady job with a factory that made packaging materials. The couple rented a nice duplex in Kentwood, a comfortable suburb of Grand Rapids, where they lived for the rest of their marriage. "It was a great neighborhood, with great schools," Sylvia says.

This predominantly white suburb near the Grand Rapids airport is populated largely by people who work in the city's manufacturing industries, many as managers or skilled machine operators. Most of the families have two parents present in the home. Four of five housing units are occupied by their owners. Fewer than one out of ten young children live in families with incomes below the poverty line, and those that do were all in female-headed households when the last census was taken.

Over the years, Sylvia's husband received regular promotions and raises, eventually becoming a supervisor at the office furniture company he'd switched to a few years after they moved to Kentwood. Meanwhile, Sylvia put aside her hopes for a career in communications to focus on raising her girls. "I tried to work mostly temp jobs so I'd have the flexibility to be home for my kids," she says. "Somebody has to be there for the children."

The marriage foundered for years before Sylvia and her husband officially separated in 1993. "My husband and I didn't spend enough time together," Sylvia says. "He got to the point where he wasn't happy, and I wasn't happy."

Their divorce was finalized in early February 1996. Looking back, Sylvia sees the separation as the beginning of her family's downhill economic slide.

Sylvia and the children stayed in the duplex for about a year, until it was sold to new owners who wanted to live there themselves. When Sylvia looked for a new place, she found she couldn't afford the suburbs anymore. So she moved into Grand Rapids, where housing was cheaper.

Moving from the suburbs to the city was "a big change for the kids," she says. "The quality of their education has changed dramatically. Before, they were in a smaller school where they got more attention. In the city, the classes are much larger."

The only jobs Sylvia could find were on the night shift, and she didn't want to leave her two teenage girls home alone at night in a neighborhood she considered dangerous. As an alternative, she began taking care of other people's children in her home.

Finalizing the divorce eased the financial pressures a little, because Sylvia was awarded a portion of her husband's 401(k) retirement plan. She set aside some of it to help pay her rent over the next year and used the rest to buy an '88 Chrysler New Yorker. "If you live in Grand Rapids, you've got to have a reliable car, because the buses stop running at 6:00 P.M.," she explains.

With income of about $800 a month from baby-sitting and $240 a month in child support, she put together a bare-bones budget—$455 a month for rent, $80 for car insurance, $100 for utilities, and about $400 for everything else—food, gasoline, school supplies and fees, clothing. It was a big change from the final year of her marriage, when she and her husband had a combined income of more than $50,000.

An Unplanned Pregnancy

It's a Saturday night in early March. The family is spending the evening at home, hoping for a call from the video store that will alert them that *Eve's Bayou,* a movie they've been wanting to see, can be picked up.

Sylvia's teenage daughters are devoting the evening to self-improvement. A friend is helping Letisha give Laura a hair relaxation treatment at the kitchen sink. Sylvia is sitting at her glass-topped dining room table putting pictures of Tyrone in a scrapbook titled "Our Baby, Heaven's Gift of Love."

First come a half-dozen pictures taken even before he was born, via ultrasound. Then come snapshots of the baby shower that

Sylvia's sisters threw for her. And then there's Tyrone as a newborn, looking plump and healthy at seven pounds, seven ounces, a happy surprise given how difficult the pregnancy was.

Seeing these pictures again causes Sylvia to reflect back on how she ended up with a third child.

Newly divorced after a long separation, Sylvia had been seeing a disabled gospel singer named Horace and had even been considering marrying him. But she had concluded that their lifestyles weren't compatible and had broken off the relationship.

A few weeks later, Sylvia went for her annual physical. The doctor performed a sonogram because he suspected she had fibroid tumors. The sonogram confirmed the suspected diagnosis, and another unexpected one: a pregnancy.

"I was in shock, because I had been on birth control pills," Sylvia says. "But a few weeks before I had gone on antibiotics for a tonsil infection, and the gynecologist later told me that sometimes antibiotics can make birth control pills less effective. And that's how Tyrone got to be here."

From the start, the pregnancy was touch and go. Nourished by pregnancy-stimulated hormones, the fibroids grew faster than the fetus did. "They didn't think I could make it through the twentieth week," Sylvia says. "They didn't think there'd be room for the baby to grow."

Fortunately, there was, though with the fibroids sharing the womb with a baby, Sylvia got so big that everyone thought she was pregnant with twins. She managed to keep baby-sitting into the seventh month of her pregnancy, when her doctor ordered her to stop. Her amniotic sac had begun leaking fluid, and she needed to rest so that the pregnancy could continue as long as possible.

Unable to work, her only alternative was to go on welfare. She applied reluctantly, since she's not the type of person to want to sit home and wait for a check. Michigan's Family Independence Agency began sending her a check for $474 and a voucher for $334 in food stamps each month. (Michigan, like every other state, keeps its welfare benefits well below the poverty threshold. In 1997, 36 percent of all the nation's poor young children were in families that received public assistance.)

On November 20, 1996, a few weeks before the baby's due date, the doctor decided it was time to induce labor because there was too little amniotic fluid left to sustain a healthy baby. After nine hours of hard labor, Sylvia's cervix was ready to deliver a baby, but the baby wouldn't come out. "They tried to pull him out with forceps, because they could see his head in the birth canal, but then they realized that the cord was wrapped around his neck," she says. "I had to have an emergency C-section. They had to pull him back up into the uterus from the birth canal. It was a terrible experience. My doctor said it was the most difficult delivery he had ever done."

Sylvia's baby was healthy, but she wasn't. First, she had to go on hormone therapy for almost three months to shrink the fibroids. At the end of February, she had to have a hysterectomy.

Back to Work

Even before she was fully recovered, the Family Independence Agency sent her a notice ordering her to look for work. "The rule is that when your baby's three months old, you have to go to work," Sylvia says. "I took the first job that came along, without thinking about whether it was the right one for me or not."

It couldn't have been much worse. Sylvia's job was on the overnight shift at a factory that made plastic molds. She worked from 10:45 P.M. to 7:15 A.M., earning $7.40 an hour—which, on an annual basis, would have provided an income below the poverty threshold for a family of four. The hours meant that she had to leave her three children home alone at night, and one of her daughters had to get up in the middle of the night to feed Tyrone. To make matters worse, Sylvia couldn't get home before it was time for the girls to leave for school. "They were missing their first-period classes because they were staying home with Tyrone," Sylvia says. "The school was sending me notes about truancy."

Even if she hadn't had child-care problems, the job wasn't right for a woman who was still recovering from major surgery. "It was really too soon after my surgery for me to be standing on my feet for ten hours at a time," Sylvia says. And then there was the issue of sleep. "I had trouble sleeping during the day because I had to take care of Tyrone." Everyone who saw her thought she looked exhausted.

After about a month, Sylvia quit, even though she feared that she wouldn't be certified for welfare again. Fortunately, her caseworker authorized another month of benefits while Sylvia looked for something else.

This time, Sylvia found that the only available factory jobs were on the second shift—basically, 2:45 P.M. to 10:45 P.M. Finding a baby-sitter for Tyrone during those hours proved impossible, and she couldn't rely on her daughters because of their school activities. "So I started baby-sitting kids in my home again, charging $50 per week per kid, or $200 a week total," she says. "It wasn't a whole lot. But it was better than welfare, and we got by."

In September 1997, Sylvia finally found a day-shift job, as an $8.40-an-hour inspector at a plastics company, and she found someone to take care of Tyrone. She felt she was finally beginning to get back on her feet, both physically and financially.

Meanwhile, though, a dispute with her landlord was escalating into a full-fledged court fight.

For months, she says, she had been after her landlord to fix a leaky pipe behind the bathtub. He had hemmed and hawed, until the floor around the tub started feeling spongy and the plaster on the bathroom wall started crumbling. When Sylvia received a quarterly water bill for more than $600—more than ten times the usual amount—she asked him to pay it, since she believed the steep bill was due to his negligence in not repairing the leak. While the two were arguing over who would pay, the water company turned off the water.

"We couldn't live without water," Sylvia says. "Tyrone was still on a bottle, and I needed to be able to make his formula, and the girls needed to be able to bathe so they could go to school." So instead of paying her rent in September, Sylvia used the money to pay most of the water bill. The Family Independence Agency gave her an emergency grant of $160 to pay the balance.

The landlord took her to court over the withheld rent, and Sylvia filed a countersuit. Eventually, the judge ordered that the landlord was responsible for $100 of the bill, and Sylvia for the rest. He gave her ten days—until October 1—to pay the September rent. Sylvia had no savings, and she wouldn't get her next paycheck from her new job until October 2, so she had no hope of meeting the deadline.

At 9:00 A.M. on October 1, a deputy sheriff knocked on the door of the apartment and handed Sylvia a notice ordering the family to vacate the premises by noon. Sylvia spent the rest of the morning renting a storage locker for her furniture and a truck to move it.

"Nobody Shed a Tear"

Then she called First Call for Help, a local hotline for families in crisis. Sylvia felt that the homeless shelter system was her only alternative. There was no one in her family she felt comfortable turning to, she says. "Like me, most of them were one missed paycheck away from disaster," she says. "I figured I got myself into this situation, and I could get myself out. When you're a responsible adult, you don't go around crying about things that happen to you. You do what you can to fix things."

None of the city's homeless shelters had room that night, but First Call arranged for Sylvia and her children to spend two nights at a motel. On the third night, First Call referred the family to the Interfaith Hospitality Network, a partnership of fourteen Grand Rapids churches that turn their Sunday School classrooms into sleeping rooms for five or six homeless families for a week at a time.

Sylvia displays no emotion as she discusses the family's period of homelessness. She didn't while she was living through it either, she says.

"I was pretty calm," she says. "I told the girls that it would work out somehow, to just be patient. Nobody shed a tear, not one. They just asked me, 'Mom, what are we going to do?' At the time, I didn't have a clue as to what we were going to do, but I didn't let them know that."

At first, Sylvia thought they'd be in the shelter system for two weeks at the most. She continued to go to work every day, getting up at 4:00 A.M. so she could drop Tyrone at his sitter's house and punch the time clock by 6:00 A.M. The girls went to school every morning as usual. Sylvia advised them to tell no one about their plight.

When Sylvia sat down for the first time with a counselor at the day shelter, she outlined her plan—to save her next two paychecks for a deposit on another apartment, sign a lease, and move in.

"The counselor looked me in the eyes and said, 'Ms. Washington, you've got to be realistic,'" Sylvia recalls. "'It's going to take a lot longer than a month. For what rents cost and what you're making, it's probably going to take you two or three.'

"I sat there thinking, 'I'm going to prove you wrong.'" She didn't want Tyrone to spend his first birthday—November 21—in a homeless shelter.

But three weeks after the family entered the shelter system, Sylvia's car was broadsided by a taxicab. The car was totaled, and Sylvia's left leg was banged up. She missed three days of work because of her injuries. When she returned to work, she was fired for the absences. Because she was still on probation, she didn't have sick leave.

"That was that," she says. "I was back to the ground floor. I felt like everything in my life was going wrong."

For two and a half months, Sylvia and the three children slept on cots in church basements and kept their clothes in plastic bags. "The church ladies brought us dinner, and we cleaned up," Sylvia says. "We had to go to bed at 9:00 P.M., which was hard on the girls." Every week, they had to move to a different church, since each church opened its doors to the homeless only for a week at a time.

And since the host church was off-limits to families during the day, anyone who wasn't in school or working had to trek to a day shelter in another church across town.

Back on Welfare Again

With her job gone, Sylvia went back on welfare. The family began receiving $578 a month in welfare benefits, plus $50 in child support. (As is customary for families on welfare, Sylvia's ex-husband pays child support directly to the state, which uses it to offset the cost of the children's welfare benefits. The state gives the custodial parent $50 a month for cooperating in the collection of support.) The family also began getting $334 a month in food stamps, and Tyrone received food vouchers from the federal WIC supplemental food program.

With the help of counselors at the day shelter and, later, at the YWCA's Women's Resource Center, Sylvia began to realize that she needed to come up with a long-term plan for financial stability, not just a job.

She scaled back her expectations for getting out of the shelter system quickly and applied for a spot in Project FIT (Families in Transition), a new program for homeless families. Sylvia was among the first ten parents to be accepted into the program, which provides subsidized housing and child care for up to two years, along with job-readiness training and counseling, for homeless families. In return, participants agree to have every aspect of their lives scrutinized, right down to the contents of their refrigerators (no liquor allowed), the state of their housekeeping, and their relationships with men. They must also enroll in job-training and self-improvement classes that will lead to stable employment and housing.

"I had to go through three different assessments with three different people and take a drug test before they accepted me," Sylvia says. "I had to prove that I was the kind of person they wanted to help, somebody who was trying.

"Some people might consider all this an invasion of privacy, but it's nothing I can't live with. When your life falls apart, you need to impose some structure, and I don't mind getting some help with that. Once I got into counseling, I could see our future ahead of us."

In early December 1997, the Washingtons moved into a two-story blue frame duplex on a residential street on the south side of Grand Rapids. It's one of twenty-four houses that Community Rebuilders has bought and rehabbed for rental, at subsidized rates, to formerly homeless families. Although Tyrone celebrated his first birthday in the homeless shelter, he and his sisters had Christmas in a real home.

The Washingtons are the first tenants to live in the three-bedroom house since it was rehabbed, so the carpets and linoleum floors are brand-new and the walls freshly painted. Sylvia has hung dark green miniblinds at the front windows, to match the wall-to-wall carpet, and family photographs on the walls. The furniture she salvaged from her marriage fits nicely into the spacious living/dining room. Each of the girls has her own bedroom, and Tyrone sleeps in a crib in Sylvia's room.

All in all, it's a very nice house for $96 a month—Sylvia's current rent, based on her income from welfare. Utilities are included, except for telephone and trash pickup. As she moves into the workforce and her income goes up, her rent will, too, to a maximum of 30 percent of her monthly earnings.

Sylvia is happy with the house but wishes it were in a better neighborhood. In this neighborhood, more than twice as many young children live *below* the poverty line as above it. The median household income is less than half that of her old neighborhood's in Kentwood.

"This was a drug house before Community Rebuilders bought it and cleaned it up," Sylvia says. "I still get people at my door in the middle of the night looking to buy drugs. People come and go at all hours of the night."

As if to prove her point, three days after Christmas, someone smashed in the window of the back door while the family was making a sympathy call on a bereaved friend. The burglar stole most of the family's Christmas presents, plus Tyrone's piggy bank and Letisha's leather jacket.

"I Want More for My Family"

Although she's not yet employed, Sylvia's weekly schedule is so busy that she carries a leather-bound planner to keep track of her appointments. As part of its new welfare system, Michigan requires most welfare recipients to devote twenty hours a week to community service or self-improvement efforts. The week coming up for Sylvia is typical.

Monday morning, she's got to start looking for child care for Tyrone, since she's starting a full-time class in office skills in three weeks. She's put off the search for child care as long as she could, because she's deeply conflicted over it. "I don't like the idea of leaving him with strangers all day, but since I have to, I'd think I'd be more comfortable leaving him in a day care center than a private home," she says.

At 12:30 P.M., she's due at the YWCA's Women's Resource Center for her weekly meeting with her employment counselor. Each week, she and the counselor review Sylvia's accomplishments the previous week and fill out a form itemizing her objectives for the coming week. This past week, Sylvia accomplished three of five goals. Finding child care is one of the two goals she's carrying over to next week, along with practicing her typing, and she's already got a plan for meeting that goal: she'll spend a few hours typing after meeting with her employment counselor. Sylvia is pleased with herself for satisfying her other goals: undergoing an assessment for the Michigan Works! job placement program and signing up for two workshops, "Bridges and Boundaries," about office communications, and "Mirror, Mirror, on the Wall," where she hopes to learn how to dress for office work.

At 10:30 A.M. Tuesday, another YWCA caseworker is coming to the house for a weekly counseling session. She and Sylvia usually talk about housekeeping and parenting issues. Then from noon to 1:30 P.M., Sylvia's got to go to a meeting of the board of Community Rebuilders, which she's been invited to join as a client representative. She feels honored by the invitation, but a little nervous. Tuesday night, she's got the first of her twice-weekly keyboarding classes, from 6:00 P.M. to 9:00 P.M. The girls will watch Tyrone for her.

Nothing's scheduled yet for Wednesday during the day, but from 6:00 P.M. to 8:00 P.M. she always goes to Bible class at the Institute of Divine Metaphysical Research, a religious organization to which she's belonged for seventeen years. Sylvia devotes six hours a week to these classes and draws considerable strength from them. "To me, it's therapeutic," she says. "The last year has been really trying, and the Bible class takes my mind off of things. It helps me to keep from getting depressed. I just think to myself every day that God wouldn't give me more than I could handle."

On Thursday, from 10:00 A.M. to noon, she's signed up for a workshop on self-esteem at the Women's Resource Center. She plans to spend the rest of the afternoon in the computer lab there, teaching herself how to use the Internet. "Only a small percentage of the jobs that are available are advertised in newspapers," she explains. "A lot of companies list openings on the Internet, so I want to learn how to use it. Maybe I can help my kids with their homework, too." Thursday night, she's got her keyboarding class again.

Friday daytime is still open for unexpected appointments and more typing practice. Friday night is reserved for another Bible class.

Although some welfare recipients chafe at the requirement that they attend so many self-improvement workshops, Sylvia loves them. "She wants to do every piece of it for her own good," says her employment counselor, Deanna Rolffs-Elzinga.

Sylvia ticks off what she's learned from each of the last few. "Career Exploration" helped her decide that she wanted an office job. "It's better to find out before you go into a career whether you're cut out for it," she says. "Effective Communication Skills" taught her how to communicate with coworkers. "If I'm going to go into an office environment, that's something I need to know," she says. In "How to Dress Like a Million Bucks," the presenter performed a "color analysis" on each participant, confirming Sylvia's view that the color she looks best in is blue.

"Most of these I'm doing because I want to," she says. "It's all stuff I need to know. A lot of the other women who are in these workshops are there because they have to be, but I like them. I'm not happy with my situation, and I want to do everything I can to get out of it, quickly."

Three weeks from now, Sylvia is scheduled to start attending an office skills class from 9:00 A.M. to 3:00 P.M. every day at Goodwill Industries. After that, she hopes, she'll find an office job. One of the reasons Sylvia is determined to switch from factory to office work is so that she has a better chance of working a day shift. "In this particular neighborhood, I wouldn't feel right about going off at night and leaving my kids alone," she says. "I want to be at work while they're at school so I can come home and be there for them at night.

"And I want a job with benefits. I could get a temporary job now with the skills I have, but I want more for my family. The research I've done has made me understand that I need to shoot for something better. That's why I want to learn computer skills. That's what you need to be competitive in today's market.

"Eventually, my goal is to go back to college and get a degree. But right now, I've got to think about earning income to support these kids."

Trying to "Keep Things Normal"

Sylvia is making Sunday dinner when Letisha dances into the kitchen. She's in the mood to talk. As all parents of teenagers know, you cherish whatever crumbs of attention your teenager throws you.

"Mom, I have to start saving for the prom," Letisha says. "I need to get a job."

"I agree," Sylvia answers as she pours bottled French dressing over salad greens. "Get a job. That'll be less money you'll be begging me for."

Letisha is the kind of daughter anyone would be proud to have— bright, attractive, and personable. She's a standout athlete and leader in the student government at her school, Central High School, which, she brags, is "one of the oldest schools on the western side of the state. Booker T. Washington spoke in our auditorium. Betty Ford went there. It's really historic."

Sylvia petitioned the school board to keep Letisha and Laura at Central when the family moved into the Community Rebuilders house, which is in the enrollment area for another high school. "I have tried really hard not to let my kids be affected by our situation," she says. "I have tried to keep things as normal as possible." Even when money is tight, she makes sure the girls have the fees they need to play school sports or be on the cheerleading squad.

Letisha, a high school junior, wants to attend Ferris State University after high school. At the moment, she wants to be a neurosurgeon. "I'm just fascinated by the brain," she says. "It controls everything in the body. Did you know we only use a little part of it?"

Letisha's interest in science is no passing fancy, her mother says. "When she was in second grade, she used to draw pictures of herself dressed in a white lab coat and surrounded by bottles," she recalls. "Her goal then was to discover a cure for AIDS. She's been very consistent all her life about what she wants to do. I wish I could say my younger daughter was as focused."

Laura, who's almost exactly two years younger than Letisha, has spent the weekend in pursuit of beauty. Besides the hair relaxation treatment, she's given herself a facial, covering her cheeks with a blue masque treatment that keeps her from talking, because she's afraid she'll crack it. Like fourteen-year-old girls everywhere, she spends much of her free time on the phone. At school, she's a cheerleader.

Sylvia is proud of the way her children behaved while they were living in the shelter system. "Many of the volunteers complimented me about them," she says. "A lot of the other kids in the shelter acted out, but not mine. I feel like I've got really well-adjusted kids, considering what they've been through."

Even though Sylvia wanted her to keep the family's troubles to themselves, Letisha says she confided in several of her friends that the family was homeless. "My best friends knew what I was going through," she says. For her, the worst thing about living in the shelter system was being cut off from friends, she says. "They couldn't call me, and it was hard for me to call them," she says. "I had to be back there every day at six, and in bed at nine. I read a lot of books."

Laura took the experience much harder than Letisha, Letisha and her mother agree, though she doesn't want to talk about it. "She was really stressed out," Letisha says.

As for Tyrone, he was too young to form memories of the shelter system. With luck, he'll suffer no ill effects from being born into poverty. Research shows that about one-third of all American children are poor for at least a year of their childhoods. But two-thirds of these children spend less than five years in poverty, with far fewer adverse effects on their well-being than on children who grow up in chronic poverty, researchers say.[1]

Dirty Dishes and Gloomy Thoughts

It snowed all night long, and by Monday morning, Grand Rapids is paralyzed. The wind chill factor is two degrees Fahrenheit, and the snow that fell overnight is blowing into drifts. On radio and TV, police are advising people to stay home. All schools are closed. Abandoned cars litter the streets. Sylvia's painstakingly planned schedule will have to be revised.

To top it off, both she and Tyrone are sick. He's got a drippy nose and a cough. And she's got a temperature of 102 degrees and a terrible cough.

When she answers the door at 2:00 P.M., still in her nightgown, there are a few cracks visible in the calm and collected persona she usually presents to the world. She's cranky and within a few minutes launches into a litany of complaints about her case manager, who's coming tomorrow.

During her last visit to the house, the case manager had chided Sylvia for keeping the thermostat in the house too high and for failing to rake the leaves out of the gutter. Somehow, remembering this makes Sylvia start thinking about how little her ex-husband pays in child support, which, in turn, makes her start thinking about everything she's got to do in the next few weeks to make herself employable. As she talks, she's standing at her kitchen sink tackling a weekend's worth of dirty dishes.

"When you're a single parent and you're sick, you have to do things whether you feel like it or not," she says as she rinses off a plate encrusted with Sunday's lasagna. "Especially when you have someone coming into your house to inspect every two weeks, you have to keep up with things. I'd like to be able to let things go a little bit and wait till I feel more like doing them. I really need to be in bed, but I can't afford to be."

The more she thinks about how little her ex-husband is paying in child support, the madder she makes herself. He pays the state just $110 a week for the two girls—$5,720 a year—even though he earns more than $40,000 a year. And because she's on welfare, Sylvia collects only $50 a month—$600 a year—of the support he pays. Once she's off welfare and entitled to all the support, she thinks then she'll try to go back to court to get it raised. "It's really bad when a mother has to resort to legal measures to get a father to support his kids," she says. "You'd think that since they're his kids he would want to do more for them."

As for Tyrone's father, Sylvia has no hope of ever collecting much child support from him. He's on disability because of serious health problems, and his monthly check is barely enough for him to live on, she says. He periodically picks up some under-the-table cash by removing asbestos and lead paint from condemned houses in Detroit, and when he does, he usually brings over a box of diapers or a couple of baby outfits. "But long-term support? No, not from him," Sylvia says, though without bitterness.

Sylvia's beginning to despair, too, of ever having enough income to satisfy one of the requirements of Project FIT—to save something each month toward permanent housing. Although she received a $3,200 settlement from the insurance company after her car was totaled, she used it to purchase and license another car, an '88 Chevy Celebrity with 80,000 miles on it. To her dismay, the Chevy hasn't turned out to be as reliable as the car that was totaled, and her maintenance bills are mounting.

"Since I've bought it, I've had to replace the alternator, which cost over $200, and two of the tires," she says. "I still need two more tires, but I'm trying to get by for a while. And the tie rods on the front end are going bad. That's a $275 job, which is a lot of money when you're living on $628 a month."

While she's talking, Tyrone starts pulling at her bathrobe, trying to get her to pick him up. There's still a pile of dishes to be washed, so she ignores him, and he pulls harder. Finally, he begins whimpering. She picks him up and kisses him on the forehead. "You happy now?" she asks him.

"I feel like I have a two-foot-tall shadow," she says.

"It Could Have Been Worse"

On Tuesday, Sylvia feels better. The streets have been plowed, and the sun is out. Her girls have been able to get to school. The Monday appointments that had to be canceled have been rescheduled. Everything is back on track. Sylvia is once again looking at her cup of tea as half full rather than half empty.

The worst part about her current situation, Sylvia confides, is that she senses that people regard her differently than they did before, when she was married and living in a nice suburban neighborhood.

"When you become homeless, the first thing people assume is that you have a drug problem," she says. "It really makes me mad, because I've never touched a drug in my life."

But spending two and a half months in the shelter system helped Sylvia put her own problems in perspective. "Being homeless is nothing to be ashamed of," she says. "What happened to me could happen to anybody. Illness, an accident, downsizing at the factory—these things happen to more people than you realize.

"Everybody at the shelter was there for different reasons. One lost everything in a fire. Another was being beat up by her boyfriend and had to escape. We were all there for different reasons, yet we were all in the same boat.

"I thought I had it bad, but from some of the other stories I heard, it could have been much worse."

Five years from now, Sylvia expects to be working full-time, in an office job with benefits, and attending college part-time. She hopes both girls will be in college—Letisha pursuing her dream of becoming a neurosurgeon, and Laura studying computers. Tyrone, by then, will be in first grade.

One of the positive things she's learned from the last year is how much support her community provides to families like hers.

"They've got a lot of good resources for women that a lot of people don't know about," she says. "The harder you try, the more they support you. And I can't imagine why anyone in my situation shouldn't be willing to help themselves."

PART TWO

THE STORIES IN CONTEXT

11

THE DEMOGRAPHICS
OF YOUNG CHILD
POVERTY IN THE
UNITED STATES

Putting the Families in Perspective

It's difficult to imagine, but true: the United States, a nation of remarkable wealth, has the dubious distinction of having the highest young child poverty rate (YCPR) in the Western industrialized world.[1] One out of every five children under the age of six in the United States lives in poverty.[2] (Updated information on child povert statistics and strategies to prevent child poverty are available at www.nccp.org, the web site of the National Center for Children in Poverty, at Columbia University's Mailman School of Public Health.) The runner-up in this race to the bottom is the United Kingdom, with a rate of 19 percent in the early 1990s. After Canada, where 14 percent of young children fell into this category, the figures fall off precipitously. In some nations, such as Finland and Denmark, the rates are so low (2 and 4 percent, respectively) that it is rare to encounter a poor child.[3]

However high the U.S. YCPR may be, this statistic obscures much of the great variation that exists in this country when it comes to who is poor and who is not. By no means are we all equally likely or unlikely to be poor. Although some groups are actually more likely than not to be poor, others are considerably less prone to poverty.

Ultimately, however, virtually no group is immune to the risk of succumbing to poverty.

In this chapter, we place the families discussed earlier in a broader context, examining briefly who the winners and losers are in the battle to avoid poverty. We explore a number of dimensions—race and ethnicity, education, residential location, family structure, and employment status. We also discuss not only those who are poor but those who are extremely poor (defined as having an income below half of the poverty line) and those who are near-poor (an income between 100 and 185 percent of the poverty line). Last, we take a look at the impact that policy can make on poverty, particularly the federal and state Earned Income Tax Credit.

The Demographics of Young Child Poverty

Both the poverty rate for young children and the number of poor young children have declined significantly since 1993, yet they remain well above the levels seen in the past two decades. After a fairly steady fifteen-year increase in the number of young children in poverty, that number has decreased substantially since 1993—by 18 percent—from 6.4 million to 5.2 million (see Figure 11.1). The official poverty threshold in 1997, as defined by the U.S. Bureau of the Census, was $10,473 for a family of two, $12,802 for a family of three, and $16,400 for a family of four.

Although the YCPR declined to 22 percent in 1997 from a high of 26 percent in 1993, it remains far higher than the poverty rate for any other age group. It continues to exceed the rate for older children age six through seventeen, and is more than double the rate for working-age adults (eighteen to sixty-four) and the elderly (sixty-five and above) (see Figure 11.2). It is apparent that the expanded benefits accorded to elderly Americans during the past several decades have improved their lot considerably. By contrast, children have not benefited nearly as much from U.S. policy over the same years.

Many young children, while not poor, live in families with incomes low enough that they are subjected to many of the same health and emotional risks experienced by poor children. Approximately 10 million young children live in low-income families (income less than 185 percent of the poverty threshold).[4]

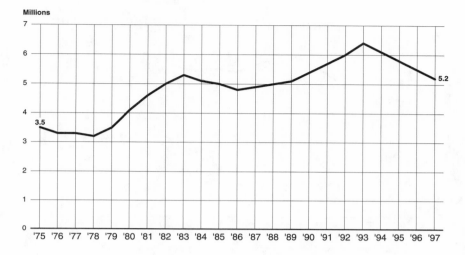

FIGURE   11.1 *Number of Poor Children Under Six, 1975–1997*

In 1997, 42 percent of all children under six were living in poverty or near poverty (income below 185 percent of the poverty line—for example, $23,684 for a family of three). That's 5.2 million young children living in poverty and 4.7 million young children living in near poverty.

When we refer to children in poverty, some might think that these children are hovering just under the poverty line. In fact, nearly half of poor young children live in extreme poverty (in families with a combined family income below 50 percent of the federal poverty line—for example, $6,401 for a family of three). Approximately one in ten young children were extremely poor in 1997, or 2.5 million children. The depth of poverty did not improve from the previous year. Indeed, over the last two decades, the proportion of poor young children who are extremely poor has increased dramatically, from 32 percent in 1975 to 47 percent in 1997.

A critical fact about child poverty is that most poor children have at least one employed parent. Attitudinal research commissioned by the National Center for Children in Poverty has found that there are widespread negative stereotypes about the parents of poor children (for example, that they are lazy, unemployed, or irresponsible). These unfair stereotypes are contradicted both by the family profiles

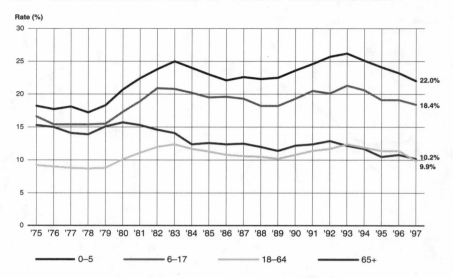

FIGURE 11.2   *Poverty Rates by Age, 1975–1997*

that appear in this book and by the demographic research included in this chapter.

About two-thirds (65 percent) of poor young children live in families in which at least one parent is employed. In 1997, 36 percent of poor children under six lived in families receiving public assistance—down from 53 percent in 1993. Only one out of six poor young children (17 percent) lived in families relying exclusively on public assistance—down by nearly one-half from the level (31 percent) in 1993.

Although it is a fact that most poor young children have at least one working parent, not all young children are at equal risk of experiencing poverty. Poverty rates vary greatly among blacks, Hispanics, and whites, among urban, rural, and suburban residents, among the well-educated and the poorly educated, among single-parent families and two-parent families, and certainly among those of differing employment statuses.

In 1997 white children under six made up the largest racial or ethnic group in poverty. The plurality of the 5.2 million poor children under six in 1997—1.9 million (36 percent)—were non-Hispanic white, while 1.6 million were Hispanic (31 percent), 1.4 million were non-Hispanic black (27 percent), and 0.3 million (6 percent) were members of other racial or ethnic groups.

Poverty rates vary substantially, however, among different racial or ethnic groups. Even though a poor child is more likely to be white than any other racial or ethnic designation, poverty occurs disproportionately among black and Hispanic young children. In recent years, the poverty rates of black and Hispanic young children have converged. By 1997 the poverty rates of the two groups were nearly identical—40 percent among black children under six and 38 percent among Hispanic young children (who can be either black or white). The poverty rate for young white children in 1997 was a mere fraction of the rate among minority young children—13 percent.

We also know that young children living with an unmarried mother are much more likely to be poor than are those living with married parents. In 1997 children under six living with an unmarried mother were more than five times as likely to be poor (56 percent) as were those living with married parents (11 percent). Over half of poor children under six were living only with their mother (57 percent, 3.0 million). About one-third of poor children lived with married parents (33 percent, 1.7 million).

The families profiled in this volume are hindered by a variety of obstacles that limit their earnings potential. We highlight three that have long influenced the economic well-being of families: single parenthood, low educational attainment, and part-time or no employment. Each taken alone raises the likelihood of falling into poverty; taken together, they can deal a crushing blow to the economic viability of a young family.

Young children living in mother-only families are particularly vulnerable to the risk of poverty. Sixteen percent of children under six living with an unmarried mother who worked full-time were poor in 1997. In comparison, 63 percent of young children living with an unmarried mother who worked part-time were poor. The poverty rates of children under six living with unemployed parents were very high, regardless of family structure—74 percent in married two-parent families and 81 percent in families with an unmarried mother. The high rates of poverty among children in single-mother families—even those in which the mother is working full-time—stem primarily from the lack of a second source of income, but also from reduced wages, which are associated with lower educational attainment and gender.

One parent's full-time employment is no guarantee against poverty. One in six children under six (16 percent) living with an unmarried mother who worked full-time were poor in 1997. Among children under six living in married two-parent families in which the father worked full-time and the mother was not employed, the poverty rate in 1997 was 13 percent. For children in both kinds of families, the poverty rate has increased steadily over the past two decades (see Figure 11.3).

The poverty rate for children under six in a married two-parent family was only 6 percent when one or more parents worked full-time. The poverty rate rose to 35 percent among those children under six living in a married two-parent family when at least one parent worked part-time but neither worked full-time.

Young children with at least one well-educated parent are much less likely to be poor, but high school graduation is not enough to ensure against poverty. The poverty rate among children under six whose more-educated parent had more than a high school education was 9 percent, compared with 29 percent among those whose more-educated parent simply graduated from high school and had no further education. The poverty rate was substantially higher—63 percent—among young children who had no parent with a high school degree.

More-educated parents are more likely to be employed full-time and to earn enough to avoid poverty. Individuals with higher levels of education generally have more job opportunities, higher wages, and greater job security than those with lower levels of education. In 1997, among children under six in families whose more-educated parent had more than a high school education, 83 percent lived in a home in which at least one parent held a full-time job. The poverty rate for this group was less than 3 percent. Among children under six whose more-educated parent was a high school graduate and had no further education, 65 percent lived in a home in which at least one parent held a full-time job. The poverty rate for this group was 12 percent.

Among children under six living in a family whose parents did not finish high school, only 39 percent lived in a home where at least

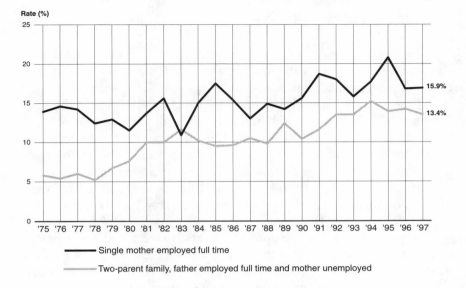

FIGURE 11.3   *Poverty Rates of Children Under Six, in Families with Single Mother Employed Full-time and in Two-Parent Families with Father Employed Full-time and Mother Unemployed, 1975–1997*

one parent worked full-time. The poverty rate for this group was 34 percent.

The Geography of Young Child Poverty

Child poverty cuts across virtually all geographic boundaries. Poverty rates for young children are highest in urban areas. But over the past few years, the poverty rate among children under six in urban areas has declined and approached that among those in rural areas. In 1997 the rate stood at 30 percent among urban young children, a rate that was just a few percentage points above that among rural young children—26 percent. In contrast, the rate among young children in suburban locations was substantially lower, at 16 percent. Of the 5.2 million young children in poverty, a majority—60 percent—lived outside of urban locales. A combined 3.1 million young children lived in either suburban (38 percent, 1.9 million) or rural (23 percent, 1.2 million) areas, while 2.1 million lived in urban areas.

The current disparities across residential location of the young child poverty rate notwithstanding, the YCPR has risen fastest over the long term in suburban areas. Indeed, suburban poverty grew at a much faster pace between the late 1970s (1975–1979) and the mid-1990s (1993–1997)—by 51 percent—than did urban poverty (39 percent). It also outpaced the growth in rural poverty (40 percent).

In several of America's largest cities, the likelihood of being poor is almost twice as high as that in the United States as a whole, or even greater (see Figure 11.4). Young children in Detroit, for example, experienced an exceptionally high poverty rate of 58 percent from 1993 through 1997.

Moreover, in some metropolitan areas, more than half of poor children under six lived in extreme poverty—below 50 percent of the poverty line. In Chicago, for example, 60 percent of poor young children lived in extreme poverty. Fewer than one-third of young children in cities such as Chicago, Dallas, Detroit, Houston, and Los Angeles have escaped poverty or near poverty.

As the era of expanded state responsibility for antipoverty efforts begins, there is significant state-to-state variation in YCPRs. Wages and employment opportunities vary, as do the percentages of young children in poverty. State average YCPRs for the period from 1993 through 1997 ranged from a low of 12 percent in New Hampshire and 13 percent in Alaska, Colorado, and Utah to highs of more than 35 percent in Louisiana, Mississippi, and the District of Columbia (37, 37, and 46 percent, respectively). (See Figure 11.5 and the Appendix for detailed state tables.) The poverty threshold is not adjusted according to local variation in the cost of living. This means that the impact of what we refer to as poverty and near poverty is greater in places such as New York and the District of Columbia, which have both high YCPRs and exceptionally high costs of living.

The relatively low YCPRs in the states that surround Washington, D.C.—Virginia, Maryland, and Delaware—illustrate sharp differences within regions and between urban and largely suburban settings. In the New York tristate region, state YCPRs vary considerably as well. New Jersey's rate is below the national average, Connecticut's rate is similar to the national average, and New York's rate is above the national average.

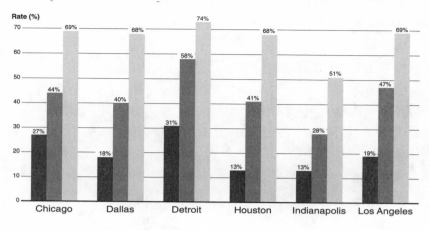

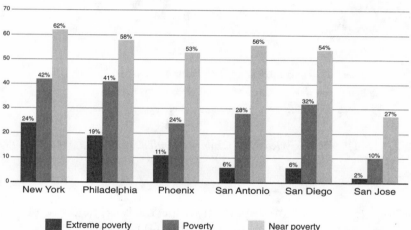

FIGURE 11.4 *Extreme-Poverty, Poverty, and Near-Poverty Rates of Children Under Six, in the Twelve Largest Cities, 1993–1997*
NOTE: Near-poverty rate includes the populations in poverty and in extreme poverty.

The variation of extreme poverty rates among states is even greater. States such as Alaska and Hawaii have extreme-poverty rates below 3 percent. In sharp contrast, over 20 percent of young children in Louisiana and the District of Columbia are extremely poor (22 and 30 percent, respectively) (see Figure 11.6).

In New Hampshire and New Jersey, the proportion of young children who are either poor or near-poor was less than 30 percent in

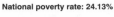

National poverty rate: 24.13%

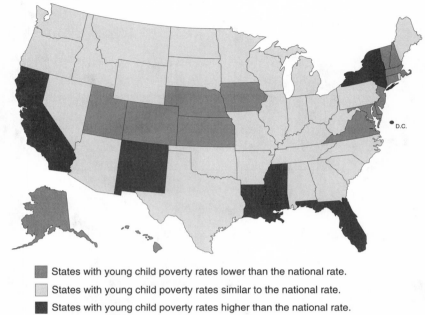

■ States with young child poverty rates lower than the national rate.
□ States with young child poverty rates similar to the national rate.
■ States with young child poverty rates higher than the national rate.

FIGURE 11.5   *Poverty Rates of Children Under Six, by State, 1993–1997*

the mid-1990s (26 and 27 percent, respectively). The corresponding proportions for states such as Louisiana (60 percent) and Mississippi (62 percent), as well as the District of Columbia (67 percent), were approximately twice that level (see Figure 11.7).

Can Policy Work?

One of the most striking features of the debate in America about child poverty is the belief that nothing can be done to solve the problem. This just isn't true. The Earned Income Tax Credit (EITC), which offers dramatic benefits for the working poor population, shows that policy can work.[5]

Using an alternative measure of poverty that allows one to judge the impact of federal, state, and payroll taxes and a range of govern-

National extreme poverty rate: 11.19%

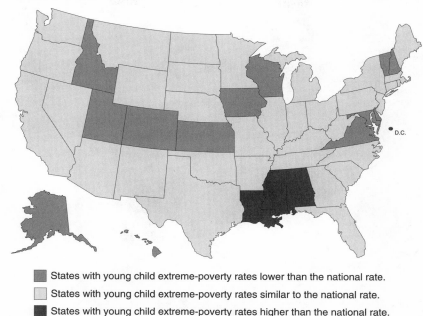

■ States with young child extreme-poverty rates lower than the national rate.
□ States with young child extreme-poverty rates similar to the national rate.
■ States with young child extreme-poverty rates higher than the national rate.

FIGURE 11.6   *Extreme-Poverty Rates of Children Under Six, by State, 1993–1997*

ment programs (such as food stamps, housing subsidies, and school lunch benefits), we find that the Earned Income Tax Credit has been an increasingly effective tool in helping to reduce the incidence of poverty. The effect of this expansion is shown clearly in Figure 11.8, which graphs both the alternative measure alone and the alternative measure excluding the effects of the EITC. In 1997 the alternative young child poverty estimate would have been 24 percent higher in the absence of the EITC. In comparison, the corresponding increase in 1993 would have been only 8 percent.

   The federal EITC was supplemented in 1998 by state EITCs in only ten states—Kansas (a newcomer for 1998), Maryland, Massachusetts, Minnesota, New York, Vermont, Wisconsin, Iowa, Oregon, and Rhode Island. The EITCs are refundable in the first seven states—meaning that the individual receives the full amount of the

National near poverty rate: 44.23%

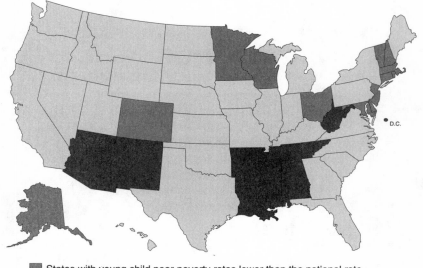

States with young child near-poverty rates lower than the national rate.

States with young child near-poverty rates similar to the national rate.

States with young child near-poverty rates higher than the national rate.

FIGURE 11.7   *Near-Poverty Rates of Children Under Six, by State,*
1993–1997

credit even if that amount exceeds his or her state income tax liability. In the remaining three states, the EITC is nonrefundable—meaning that the individual receives the full credit only if the state income tax liability equals or exceeds the credit amount; otherwise, the taxpayer receives only that part of the credit that will reduce the state income tax liability to zero.

According to our analyses, the effect of state EITCs in the states where it is not refundable is negligible. In the states where it is refundable, as would be expected, the impact of the state EITC programs is much more significant.

As an exercise that illustrates how effective state EITCs would have been had such programs existed nationwide, we suppose that all fifty states and the District of Columbia had in place state EITC

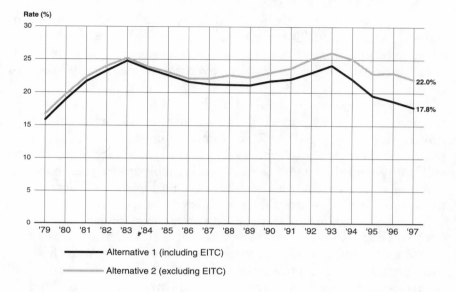

FIGURE 11.8 *Poverty Rates of Children Under Six, by Official and Alternative Measurements, 1979–1997*

programs that provided refundable credits amounting to 25 percent or 50 percent of the federal credit.[6]

Family incomes of well over half a million, or 553,000, children under eighteen would have been pushed over the threshold had the universal 25 percent state EITC program existed. This translates into about 5 percent of poor children.[7] With a 50 percent state EITC program, approximately one million (989,000) young children, or 9 percent of all poor children, would have been raised out of poverty.

Conclusion

The conclusions we draw from the many statistics we cite in this chapter are consistent with the stories told in the profiles comprising much of this book. Certain characteristics are associated with a greater likelihood of falling into poverty than others, but nonetheless, poverty is found among a remarkably wide variety of groups in this country. For example, lack of a high school degree elevates the odds considerably that parents will have to raise their children in poverty. Similarly, children with a single mother are much more likely to be poor than children with married parents. And children in urban areas are at greater risk of poverty than children living elsewhere.

Although poverty is typically thought of as a primarily urban phenomenon, it is nearly as common in rural areas (with suburban poverty growing rapidly). A substantial number of children in a married-parent family in which one parent is working full-time are still poor—and that figure is rising with each passing year. Further, children with a parent who has more than a high school degree are not protected entirely from the possibility of being poor.

Despite these daunting statistics, it is clear that some policies have been successful in reducing poverty. It is also clear that if we as a nation want to make significant progress in this effort, we must first re-examine our preconceptions about poverty's nature and causes and overcome our prejudices toward the poor. Only then can we develop an effective long-term strategy for making widespread child poverty a thing of the past.

12

CONCLUSION

Reading Lives on the Line

What do we think of the families whose stories we've just read? Do we see them as the deserving poor or the undeserving poor? Were we moved or unmoved by their plight? If we were moved, was it to compassion and understanding or to exasperation? Recent research suggests that our moral and emotional reactions to stories about poor people are largely determined by our ideas about the causes of poverty and about its potential solutions. Those who believe that the causes of poverty are beyond the control of the poor tend to feel sympathy toward them, or even solidarity with them, and tend to be moved by their stories. Those who believe that poverty is rooted in the mistakes or inherent character flaws of the poor tend to see poor families as undeserving of help from society and to be moved to irritation or even anger by their stories.

But this is not merely a personal matter—it is also a matter of political significance. The sum total of all of our personal reactions to these stories, after all, constitutes American national opinion about the poor. This national opinion, in turn, shapes both public and private efforts to deal with the seemingly intractable problem of poverty.

In thinking about the stories we've just read, then, it is important to consider carefully what exactly they mean to us, and also to understand how our reactions to such stories affect what we as a nation do about poverty.

In this chapter, we examine more closely the stories we've just read and draw from them broader lessons about the problem of poverty. We pay particular attention to the broader social and economic factors that place many families at risk of falling into poverty and keep many others from rising out of it.

We also look at the ways in which some Americans, motivated by the desire to improve their lives, have fought to overcome these obstacles, and at the ways in which others have joined together to help poor families help themselves. We will see that our shared beliefs in self-help, volunteerism, and the need to build strong communities have moved many of our fellow Americans to make important contributions to the fight against child poverty.

But we will also see that these private efforts are not enough, and that we cannot significantly reduce child poverty unless we take collective action. In doing so, we must craft societal responses to poverty that build on the wisdom of the past without repeating its mistakes. We must develop a new vision of the challenges and opportunities before us; drawing on that vision, we must develop new ways to help vulnerable American families make ends meet. Most important, we must cut through the distorting polarities that characterize our personal and collective thinking about the poor. Once we do, we will unlock our nation's potential for informed and effective action to combat child poverty and to promote the economic security of every American family.

Why Are So Many American Children Poor?

There is no single, easy answer to this question. But we can identify certain factors that play a major role in shaping the contours of the problem of child poverty.

Families at Risk

Several characteristics of the parents and families described in this book placed them and their children at risk for future life difficulties.

Some of the risk factors—teen parenthood, low educational achievement, low-wage work—directly placed the families and children at risk for poverty. Other risk factors—domestic violence, lack of quality child care, other risks to early brain development—are associated with poverty and hampered many of the children's optimal development. Finally, the parents' adult lives were full of challenges that made both work and child-rearing more difficult. Let us take a look, then, at the risk factors for poverty; the risk factors for non-optimal child development; and the risk factors in the lives of the adults in these families whose lives are on the line.

Teen parenthood.   Only three of the ten families whose stories you read—the Keeblers, the Washingtons, and the Scarpatos—were started after the parents had attained adulthood. In seven of the families, children were born to parents who were still in their teenage years. Although teen birth rates are dropping, teen parent-hood makes the education and employment paths out of poverty much more difficult (but not impossible) to travel. For these and other reasons, teen parenthood increases the parents' and children's risk for long-term and extreme poverty.

Low educational achievement.   In half of the ten families, at least one parent received a high school degree. In the other five fam-ilies, neither parent finished high school. As pointed out in Chapter 11, the young child poverty rate in families in which the best-edu-cated parent has not received a high school degree is a staggering 63 percent. The risk for child poverty in a family in which the more ed-ucated parent has a high school degree and no college education is cut in half (to 29 percent), and even some college education in a family brings the risk to children below 10 percent. Clearly, in this information-driven economy, the low educational achievement of parents places their children at serious risk for experiencing long-term and extreme poverty.

Temporary and low-wage work.   What may come as a surprise to many readers is the work effort of parents in poor families. Nearly two-thirds (65 percent) of poor young children have at least one parent who is employed. Among our ten families, only three— the Keeblers, the Scarpatos, and the Washingtons—had no regularly employed parent at the time of their interview. But nearly all the families tell the story of cycling in and out of very temporary, very low-wage work. For instance, Celeste Lyles's work varied with the annual cycle of the Mississippi catfish industry. Carlotta Saylor had to find a summer job because her regular job filled only nine months of the year. Most of the jobs held by parents paid at or just above minimum wage. If a parent works forty hours per week, fifty weeks per year, at the minimum wage, he or she will not be able to lift his or her family out of poverty through earnings alone. The family will need the help of the federal Earned Income Tax Credit (EITC) and other employment-related benefits (child care, health care, and transportation assistance) to lift their income above the poverty line.

Many of the low-wage jobs held by parents in these ten families entail not only unpredictable tenure and low pay but enormous physical and time demands. It is starkly apparent from their stories that for many parents the only way to make more money is to work longer hours; as a result, they are away from their children for even longer periods of the day. The energy of parents is further sapped by the exhaustion and physical danger of some low-wage jobs—caring for violence-prone elderly patients, for example, or killing and cleaning catfish or chicken on an assembly line. What emotional and physical resources are left for taking care of their children, never mind for taking care of themselves and their own development?

*   *   *

These three risk factors—teen parenthood, low educational achievement, and temporary and low-wage work (especially with no benefits or few benefits)—are the "Bermuda Triangle" of family poverty. They define the space where we lose many young persons in their trip from a childhood at the margins of the American public education system to an adulthood at the margins of the American labor force. And in the triangle, they encounter many other associated risks that affect family well-being and their children's development.

Domestic violence.   Only a few of the families seem to have escaped the experience of domestic violence. In some families, the parents were abused as children (the Gonzalezes and the Likios); more often, the children's father or the mother's boyfriend has beaten the mother (the Joneses, the Likios, the Rodriguezes, the Gonzalezes, and the Saylors). Sometimes the young children have been abused (the Keeblers).

Scientific research has begun to help us understand the association between poverty and domestic violence. We now know that severe economic hardship increases both family stress and interpersonal conflict, which in turn lead to harsh, punitive child-rearing. Under conditions of low support and high conflict, everyday disagreements can more easily escalate into violent exchanges.

In addition, although we have always known that a child's direct experience of abuse is harmful to his or her social, emotional, and cognitive development, we have comforted ourselves in the belief that indirect exposure—witnessing or being cared for by an abused parent—is not so harmful. Research has now deprived us of this comfort. Both direct and indirect exposure to violence and abuse profoundly affect young children, including their early brain development, their basic trust in caregivers, the quality of their social relationships with their peers, and their readiness to learn. Thus, the domestic violence associated with poverty places the development of young children at profound risk.

Lack of high-quality child care.   Over half of the families we profiled found that any form of child care other than care by themselves or a relative was too costly. Thus, they reduced their work hours (and slipped behind economically), staggered their shifts, depended on relatives—including their older children—to care for their youngest children, or left their children alone for periods of time. Lack of high-quality child care places these families in double jeopardy—first, by constraining the parents' ability to pursue work vigorously, and second, by failing to provide the children with an enriched learning environment in their early years. Research has clearly demonstrated that good-quality, subsidized child care both increases low-wage parents' employment and earnings and helps their children enter school more ready to learn.

Other risks to early brain development.   In addition to exposure to violence and poor-quality child care, some of the young children in our families experienced other risks to early brain development. For example, in the Saylor family, Orlando was deprived of oxygen owing to preventable birth complications and appears to have suffered some resulting brain damage. Most of the other known risks to early brain development—environmental toxins, malnutrition, maternal depression—are associated with low family income, so Orlando is but one of many poor young children exposed to risks for non-optimal brain development.

Other challenges facing parents.   There are a host of other daily problems faced by the parents in our families. Nearly all the families faced extraordinary housing expenses and significant overcrowding.

When we look at the portion of their monthly budget consumed by rent and compare it to our own, it is hard to imagine paying so much of our monthly income, up to 60 percent, for housing that is so clearly inadequate. And these are the relatively fortunate ones who were not driven for part of their young children's lives into a homeless shelter, as the Scarpatos and Washingtons were.

Additional factors in each of these stories are the health risks and other problems of poverty—such as the Jones family's exposure to pollution and young Andrew's asthma. Moreover, parents' personal experiences with the poverty-related health problems of depression, obesity, diabetes, and heart problems place severe limits on both their employment and their effectiveness as parents.

Finally, many of the families are just a car breakdown away from family breakdown. Convenient and affordable transportation is very hard to come by. An old car in poor condition is often the only thing that makes it possible for children to go to child care or school and for parents to commute long distances to work. If the car goes, the home economy comes unraveled because the major capital investment involved in repairing or replacing a car is way beyond most of the family budgets we saw. And over the last two decades, housing, health care, and transportation costs have risen much faster than have the wages and income supports of low-skilled workers. Getting and keeping a decent roof over your head; caring for and coping with health problems; getting to and from work, the kids' schools, and the grocery store—these are the daily challenges of lives on the line.

Making Ends Meet: The Home Economics of Lives on the Line

Many American families would say it's a struggle to make ends meet, even those with incomes above our national household median of $37,000 per year for a family of four. What parents do not find that their hopes and expectations for their children, and for themselves, seem to grow as the family income grows? The optional vacation becomes a mental health necessity; the private school tuition becomes an educational must. But the struggles of low-income families who live on or near the poverty line are even greater. One look at the monthly budgets of these families shows us that even their very modest regular expenses often exceed their incomes from low-wage work and low-level benefits. It simply does not appear to them (or to us) that it is possible to provide the essentials to their children on their incomes. Something is therefore always being compromised; some corner is always being cut. To find an affordable rent, a family compromises on the safety of the neighborhood and the quality of the school their children attend. To pay the utility bill at the beginning of the month, the kids may have a steady diet of breakfast cereal for the last few days of the month.

Then there is the unpredictability of both income and expenses for these families. When workers are paid by the hour and aren't entitled to sick pay, an unexpected three-day flu cuts their income for the week by 50 to 60 percent. If the car breaks down and needs $500 worth of repairs, they may lose weeks' worth of salary—or they may lose their job because they cannot afford to get the car fixed and there is no public transportation to work, which may be in the suburbs or a town in the next county. For families whose income is very low, there is just that much less room to cope with an unexpected temporary loss of income or a sudden and significant expense.

Moderate- and upper-income families handle such unhappy surprises with the help of benefits (such as paid sick leave), savings, and credit. A low-wage worker who is paid by the hour rarely has paid sick leave. Historically, the welfare system has actually discouraged savings, asking people to spend down their assets before they are eligible for certain public benefits. (Thankfully, this disincentive to save is beginning to be changed by some smart state governments.) And credit, if low-wage workers can even get it, costs them more because their income makes them a greater risk. For these reasons, the unpredictability of income and expenses places low-income families under particularly debilitating stress. Indeed, scientific studies suggest that the stress due to the unpredictability of income and expenses has an especially damaging effect on the quality of parent-child interaction and hence on children's development. So it is not just the amount of their income and the level of their expenses that makes it such a struggle for low-income families to make ends meet—it is also the unpredictability of these factors.

Finally, there is the income "cliff." The cliff is the income threshold at which certain types of vital family supportive benefits (food stamps, subsidized child care, health care, and housing) suddenly end (a true cliff) or phase out (more like a gradual but still uncontrollable drop to the sea). Several families tell the story of losing key benefits when their family income rose to a certain benefits threshold; the couple in Palmerton has postponed marriage because they know they couldn't survive the plunge. Loss of health benefits through Medicaid is especially scary to families with chronically ill or disabled children, as the Keeblers and Saylors make plain. Other families tell of working more hours for nothing when the extra income they earned was immediately needed for a higher copayment level for child care or housing. The benefits cliff is a unique and confusing aspect of the struggle that low-income families face in making ends meet. As good parents, their job is to try to understand the cliff (just as the job of other parents is to try to understand the tax code) in order to provide for their family as well as possible.

Incomes too low to meet even modest expenses, unpredictable income and expenses, and the "cliff"—these are the basics of Home Economics 101 when young families' lives are on or near the line.

Personal and Social Responsibility: Private and Public Responses

The struggle that families face to make ends meet when their incomes hover at or sink below the poverty line is truly an elemental struggle. Throughout the history of our nation, Americans have clearly expressed a strong set of value preferences about how families and society should handle this struggle. First, families should squarely assume their personal responsibility for their condition and do everything possible to lift themselves up by their bootstraps. Then and only then, if they cannot lift themselves—perhaps owing to catastrophic socioeconomic events (the Depression, a major recession) or personal constraints (physical handicap, advanced age)—does society have a responsibility to help them.

Americans have also historically expressed a preference for private-sector (individual, volunteer, and charitable) responses to needy families over public-sector (local, state, or federal government) responses. These value preferences are neither permanent nor absolute: most Americans, for instance, see a clear role for public responses to the challenge of educating the next generation and providing for the public health. But to enhance the economic well-being of families with young children, the majority of Americans ap-

pear to prefer to rely on private efforts, whether voluntary and phil-
anthropic contributions or the self-interested interventions of corpo-
rations.

One of the most interesting features of these lives on the line is
how clearly they demonstrate that the same value preferences operate in the lives of low-income families and communities.

The Commitment of the Poor to Self-help

These ten stories are filled with examples of families striving to help
themselves, sometimes with clearly positive results, sometimes with
mixed results.

Take the Lyles family. Celeste Lyles has identified unmet needs in
her community and sold chicken kabobs at a catfish festival and
made plans to sell dresses designed for the tastes of African American women at local flea markets. By identifying and filling niches in
a local market, Celeste Lyles stands in the great American tradition
of entrepreneurship and has succeeded in supplementing her family's
income, which would otherwise be totally dependent on low wages
and a few public benefits.

The same spirit of independence and practical self-help probably
influenced Celeste Lyles's decision to rely on her eleven-year-old son
to provide child care on a regular basis for her infant son. Here,
however, the benefits are less clear. That's a heavy burden for an
eleven-year-old and a risky situation for an infant. High-quality
preschool and after-school child-care programs are more likely to
foster children's intellectual and emotional development. But for the
Lyles family, in the absence of child-care subsidies, self-help through
sibling care made a vital contribution to the family economy by
enabling Celeste Lyles to save money and giving her the freedom to
work.

Another example is the Keebler family and their purchase of a
house for $27,000. In becoming a homeowner, Nancy Keebler not
only eliminated the financial disincentive to work more that is built
into the copayment schedule of public housing (residents are generally required to pay 30 percent of their incomes for rent) but made it
possible to begin thinking about starting up a small business—in this
case, a family child-care business. Generations of Americans have reduced costs and increased income by combining investments in
home and work (for example, by living above the family store).

In addition to showing families helping themselves, these stories portray the important role played by neighbors, friends, private charity, and professionals (intervening over and above their official roles) in the lives of these families.

Celeste Lyles's best friend teamed up with her to buy and share a car, which was vital to both of their lives but beyond their individual reach. In other families, social workers and medical professionals imaginatively stepped beyond the narrow confines of their professional role to respond to real human needs: Nancy Keebler's caseworker, for instance, facilitated the Keebler family's purchase of a house, and a physician's assistant at the clinic where she receives medical care bought her a car.

Thus, the commitment of the poor to self-help and the nongovernmental private sector's commitment to volunteerism and local charity are vitally important. These commitments, backed by the belief that we should not help those who will not help themselves, strengthen the social contract in America between the haves and the have-nots. They also provide immediate and tangible help by supporting capital investments by the poor in their cars and homes.

But if these stories make us think differently about living life on the line in only one way, it is this: the nature and scope of the needs of low-income families, and the quality and depth of the resources of their own families, friends, and communities, make self-help and private charity insufficient by themselves. In our postindustrial global economy, the job is just too big for poor families and communities to do alone.

Let's step back and think for a moment. We do not raise an army to defend our national interest or educate our next generation through self-help, volunteerism, and charity alone. How can we raise more than one-fifth of the next generation, the 22 percent of young children living in poverty, by asking them, their families, and communities to do it alone?

As these ten stories make clear, the three most important parts of the private sector—the business, civic, and religious communities— are especially hard-pressed in America's poorest communities. Many businesses in the low-wage service sector (for example, child-care facilities and nursing homes) cannot raise wages for low-income workers without raising prices for low- and moderate-income clients. The church in Belzoni, Mississippi, collects money for the poor from the poor and, because it cannot afford its own pastor, has to make do with a circuit-riding preacher. Private strategies are powerful complements to public strategies, but self-help and charity, though a vital part of the mix, cannot possibly substitute for good public policy.

In like fashion, many public policies must be reformed to eliminate crippling disincentives to self-help, volunteerism, and effective private charity. Solutions can and must be found to mitigate the effects of the income "cliff," which causes families precipitously to lose critical benefits (child care, health care) when their earned income passes a certain level.

Our analysis of the risks that families face, of the nature of their struggle to make ends meet, and of American value preferences suggests that America needs a new vision of how public- and private-sector strategies can be developed and creatively combined to help low-income families with young children.

Strategies to Help Young Families Make Ends Meet

What strategies can be used by the public and private sectors to increase family economic security and reduce child poverty? There are four overarching strategies that all families use, but low-income families find it particularly challenging to mount them.

Increase Income

How can the public and private sectors help poor families increase their income? Two important public-sector strategies include increasing the minimum wage and expanding the Earned Income Tax Credit.

For more than thirty years, the federal government has periodically raised the minimum-wage rate that employers are required to pay employees. Some economists and politicians have feared that raises in the minimum wage would increase youth unemployment because employers would be unwilling to hire inexperienced, low-skilled youth at the higher wage rates. But recent studies suggest that the negative effects on employment rates of raising the minimum wage are small or nonexistent. And it goes without saying that a raise from $5.15 an hour to $6.15 an hour significantly increases the take-home pay of workers receiving minimum wage.

Over the last fifteen years, the United States has led the world in experimenting with another strategy to increase the income of low-wage workers, through the tax system rather than through the regulation of wages. The main federal effort is the Earned Income Tax Credit. The purpose of the credit is to supplement the income of low-wage workers with children to help lift their income above the poverty line. As detailed earlier, full-time work at the minimum wage will not permit a worker to lift his or her family above the poverty line. The EITC phases in rapidly for families with incomes below the poverty line, increases to a maximum of $2,312 a year for a family with one child and $3,816 a year for a family with two or more children, then phases out a bit more gradually above the poverty line. The EITC has enjoyed broad bipartisan support because it rewards work and is consistent with the strong American belief that families should work their way out of poverty whenever possible. Studies by such groups as the President's Council of Economic Advisers and the National Center for Children in Poverty at Columbia University strongly suggest that an expansion of the EITC in 1993 was responsible for one-half of the decline in child poverty from 1993 to 1997.

The federal EITC has been so successful that state governments are now beginning to adopt state EITCs. Currently, seven states have created refundable credits worth between 10 and 43 percent of the federal credit. In a simulation study (discussed briefly in Chapter 11), we estimate that if all fifty states created credits worth 50 percent of the federal credit, as many as one million additional children would be lifted out of poverty.

Other public-sector strategies aimed at increasing poor families' incomes include child support assurance and child allowances. Some states have enacted policies that guarantee custodial parents the full value of their child support awards from noncustodial parents even if the noncustodial parent does not pay. In these instances, the state government becomes the custodial parent's partner by ensuring that the children do not suffer because the absent parent fails to make payments. Some countries have adopted a flat child allowance, usually calculated as a percentage of national median income, to recognize the parent's economic sacrifice in raising the next generation and to enhance the ability of child-rearing families to make ends meet. Research clearly indicates that countries with child allowances have much lower child poverty rates.

Up to this point, we have emphasized a range of public-sector strategies to help poor families increase their income. But the private sector can and should play an important role as well. Businesses, both small and large, can commit to creating jobs that pay a livable wage. Or if the market forces operating in their industry would make that effort very difficult or impossible, businesses could become especially effective advocates for policies, like the EITC, that turn poverty wages into livable wages. In either case, the private sector can forge effective partnerships with government to create and extend strategies that make work pay.

Reduce Costs

As the stories in *Lives on the Line* illustrate, meeting the costs of the basic needs of a modern American family usually exceeds the incomes of poor families. Indeed, many of the public-sector efforts on behalf of low-income families are aimed at helping them with the prohibitive costs of such basic needs as food, child care, health care, and housing. These programs can have other positive benefits. Research has documented that programs like food stamps and the WIC (Women, Infants, and Children) nutrition program reduce both child hunger and malnutrition. Research has also clearly demonstrated that child-care subsidies can increase both the employment and earnings of low-skilled workers. And programs like the Gautreaux experiment in Chicago prove that housing assistance that permits low-income families to move to middle-income neighborhoods can have positive effects on parents' employment and children's school achievement.

The private sector can also play an important role in helping low-income families with the costs of basic needs. Perhaps the most important thing that employers could do would be to design and implement benefits packages to help low-wage workers support their families. Child care, sick pay, and health-care benefits lead the list. And again, if market forces make private-sector provision of benefits difficult, businesses can become advocates for public provision of benefits, as several major employers of low-wage workers have done in states like Florida. Business involvement is not motivated by altruism but by the self-interest of reducing absenteeism and increasing productivity.

Another role the private sector could play is in sponsoring the research and development necessary to design new ways to organize and finance benefits for low-wage workers.

Increase Human Capital

A third way to help low-income families make ends meet is a longer-term strategy. In an information economy, education has become a more important predictor of long-range family economic success than ever before. Hence, it is vital that the public and private sectors both invest intensively and creatively in the development of human capital—the set of skills, abilities, and dispositions that increase people's effectiveness as future workers and future parents. If sufficient investments in the human capital of the parents in our ten families had been made during their childhood and adolescent years, their ability to make ends meet and to lift their children out of poverty would be greatly enhanced today. So, too, with their children. Now is the time to invest in their children's long-term future.

There is much good news on this front. Over the last decade, and in most states, the public and private sectors have entered into new partnerships to generate new investments in early childhood care and education, school reform, and after-school and youth development programs that work. But even as these new partnerships are being formed, we learn how far we have to go. Take one example. Thirty years after the creation of Head Start, the goal of creating a system of high-quality early childhood education programs that serve all eligible children still has not been achieved.

Increase Opportunities

A fourth and final strategy that the public and private sectors can employ to help low-income families is to help create new economic opportunities for them. America has been and remains a land of opportunity. Over the last several decades, our economy has been a virtual job creation machine and thus has been able to absorb rapidly millions of new entrants (especially women and legal immigrants) into the workforce. Despite the generation of millions of new jobs, child poverty has risen. Why?

One important reason is that many of the jobs are in the service sector and do not pay a living wage. Strategies like expanding the EITC and guaranteeing benefits (like child care and health care) to all working families will help address this problem.

But another set of problems centers on the combined effects of racism, continued residential segregation, and the migration of jobs and the middle class out of central cities. As researchers like William Julius Wilson and Douglas Massey have documented, work is disappearing in many inner-city neighborhoods; because those neighborhoods remain highly racially segregated, the absence of work has a disproportionate influence on families of color. Numerous policy proposals have been made to address the challenges facing inner-city families. The politics surrounding these proposals is intense and centers on the right balance between market forces and public investments in generating new economic opportunities in inner-city poor neighborhoods. Of the four major strategies to help families make ends meet, the real politics of increasing opportunities, especially in inner cities, is especially contentious.

Toward a New Vision

America has faced the challenge of helping young families before. In the nineteenth century, when the challenge was to integrate many new citizens into our economy and society and the primary resource was ample land, we created the Homesteading Act to help stake families to our future as a nation. In the mid-twentieth century, when the challenge was to provide for the soldiers and mothers who had interrupted their young lives to serve their country in World War II and the resources included both a system of higher education and a building industry poised for rapid expansion, we created the GI Bill to help give families a stake in our nation's future.

Now, on the cusp of the twenty-first century, the challenge is to find a place in our restructured information-age economy for the large numbers of low-skilled workers and single parents who find it very difficult to compete for non-poverty-wage jobs. What are our unique resources? And how do we create a new American solution to address the struggles of young families to make ends meet?

In both the nineteenth and twentieth centuries, America crafted public policies that helped parents to earn a living in a rapidly changing (agricultural or industrial) economy and to build or buy a home they could call their own.

How do we help young persons succeed in making a decent living in our economy today? How do we help them build or buy a home? Can we create a twenty-first-century equivalent to the Homesteading Act or the GI Bill that will enjoy broad public support and transform the life chances of generations of young American families?

We urge you—the citizens, opinion leaders, and policymakers of this country—to engage these questions as we begin a new century. The health and well-being of future generations depend on our answers and on our follow-through in implementing a new vision.

EPILOGUE

This epilogue revisits the ten families in *Lives on the Line* two years after they first opened their lives to help readers understand what it's like to raise a family below the poverty line—or just above—in the midst of an economic boom.

Two years is a long time in the life of any family. Couples become engaged, babies enter the world, marriages fall apart, wages go up, and sometimes wages go down. But two years is not a long enough period in the context of an entire lifetime to reach a definitive conclusion about the direction of the trajectory. At a moment's notice, progress in one area (for instance, a promotion at work) can be wiped out by a calamity in another (an unforeseen illness, an automobile accident, an unplanned pregnancy, a broken furnace).

Before the paperback edition of this book went to press, we visited again with the ten families whose profiles appeared in the original hardback edition, which was published in the fall of 1999. (We talked only with a friend of the Scarpato family of Westchester County, New York, since the parents' whereabouts aren't known.) As before, family members were surprisingly frank about their lives. They talked openly of strains in their personal relationships, of mounting debts, of pride in a new home, of concerns about a child's rocky passage through puberty, of joy in celebrating a child's high school graduation, of xenophobia and racism. And some of them talked about the impact on their families of reading about their lives in the first edition of this book. "Some good things have come out of it," says Carlotta Saylor, a single mother in Louisville. "I'm going to take my GED pretest next week, which will tell me how much work I need to do to actually get it. Reading your book made me decide to do it, because it was like looking at my life through somebody else's eyes. I read it and saw that most of my life I had been giving up and not doing something because I was afraid."

Both the promise and peril of what is known as "welfare reform" are quite evident in what's happened to some of these families in the last few years. Government-provided benefits, such as Medicaid coverage, food stamps, and housing subsidies, continue to be very important to the day-to-day survival of a few of these families. For others the loss of those benefits, whether because of time limitations or increased income, has been traumatic. For most of the families, the Earned Income Tax Credit (EITC), usually distributed to them in a lump sum each spring, continues to be an important source of funds for major purchases, including, in one family's case, the down payment for a home.

If there's any generalization to be made from our two-year backward glance at these families' lives, it's this: it's too soon to write happy endings for their stories. Moving out of poverty is a complex process that depends not just on a healthy national and local economy and humane public policies but on personal resourcefulness, hard work, access to opportunity, and, in many cases, luck.

What follows are updates on the lives of the ten profiled families, as of April 2000.

Chapter 1: Palmerton, Pennsylvania

Megan Jones and Ron Morgan are finally getting married. After postponing their wedding twice, they've set a new date—September 9, 2000—and this time they say they're really going to go through with it. They're planning a wedding in the church in Neffs that five generations of Megan's family have attended, followed by a casual reception at a local grange hall.

What's more, they've bought a home together—a brand-new, three-bedroom modular home that cost about $41,000. They moved in with their children in May 1999. For the down payment they used Megan's 1998 income tax refund, which included an Earned Income Tax Credit of nearly $3,000, plus four weeks of extra pay that Ron received in lieu of taking vacation in 1998.

Still working at the nursing home, Megan is now making top scale—$10.45 an hour—or a total of almost $21,000 in 1999. Ron is making $10.50 an hour in his construction job, for a total of about $27,000. (In the summer he works a lot of overtime.) Now that they've combined their incomes, they're squarely in the middle class.

But it sure doesn't seem that way. "With me and Ron both paying child support, and my new car payment, and the house expenses, things are a little tight," Megan says. "In the summer, when Ron works fifty or sixty hours a week, we do okay. But now he's down to thirty hours because it's winter and construction is slow. We both just got paid on Friday, and after paying our bills, we have $10 cash and $2 and some cents in our checking account."

Megan is paying child support now because her oldest son's father, Todd, initiated a custody fight two years ago, and their child, Andrew, ultimately went to live with him. Megan pays Todd child support—$119 every two weeks—way more than Todd ever paid her. Andrew is supposed to visit Megan and his brothers regularly. But Megan reluctantly put a halt to the visits in December 1999 after Andrew choked Justin so hard he left finger marks on his neck. "I can't have Justin afraid of being in his own home when his brother comes to visit," Megan says. "I've asked his father to get him some counseling, and maybe after that. . . . " Her voice trails off as a sob catches in her throat.

Losing custody of Andrew just about broke Megan's heart. It also thrust her more deeply into debt, since the court battle cost her almost $4,000 in attorney's fees. Because she paid that bill by refinancing her car, it will take her two years longer—and $50 more a month—to pay it off.

Ron and Megan were able to buy the modular home by pooling their resources and incomes and virtually eliminating their child care expenses. Instead of paying a child care center to care for the two boys, which would have cost them $1,060 a month after losing their state subsidy, they're paying Ron's disabled mother $120 a month to baby-sit. That's about all they can afford after paying $600 a month for their 9.9 percent mortgage and lot rental, Megan says.

Megan is glad to have the boys in the care of someone who loves them. But it's by no means an ideal arrangement, she says. "She plunks them in front of the TV all day," Megan says. "In the morning they watch *Sesame Street* and the Disney Channel. But at one o'clock the soaps come on, and she watches them the rest of the day. I wish I'd been able to afford to keep them in day care for the social experience. But this is the best I can do for now."

The boys are healthy, but Megan has had lots of health problems in the last two years. She continues to suffer from cervical dysplasia, a precancerous condition, and is preparing herself psychologically for the hysterectomy that her gynecologist tells her is inevitable. In the middle of the custody fight, she developed high blood pressure and a rapid heartbeat. She now takes blood pressure medication but can't seem to get her blood pressure under control. In December 1999, she broke a toe, which forced her to miss three weeks of work, for which she received no sick pay.

Megan also suffers from bouts of depression. She'd like to go for counseling but can't afford it. "I'm trying to learn to take things day by day," Megan says. "My doctor said I better start doing that or I'll end up dead. He told me stress is the number-one killer."

Megan and Ron derive great pleasure from their new home, which is in a modular home subdivision outside Palmerton, quite near her mother and stepfather. "We're close to a field where the bears come down in the spring, and wild turkeys," she says. "We're down a ways from the road, so if the kids are outside I don't have to worry much. Once spring comes we want to put a swing set on layaway for the kids. It'll keep them busy in the back."

Ron still has his hopes set on some day acquiring some land. "He'd like to refinance in ten years, buy a piece of property, and move our house there," Megan says. "I don't want to do that. We've got a twenty-five-year mortgage already, and I'd like to live long enough to pay it off."

Chapter 2: Oakland, California

Between August 1998 and August 1999, Magda Rodriguez spent a lot of time crying.

Frustrated by constant shift changes at work and the resulting difficulty in finding a steady baby-sitter for her two sons, Magda had reluctantly sent them back to Mexico to live with her parents for a year. "Sometimes I needed the baby-sitter in the morning, and sometimes in the afternoon, and sometimes at night, so it was very difficult," she says. "But when they were gone, I was so sad. I was crying every day for my boys."

When the boys returned to Oakland just before the start of the 1999–2000 school year, Magda introduced them to their new brother, Hector. She had unexpectedly become pregnant by Tony, her boyfriend of two years, and the couple had moved in together.

Today Magda and Tony and the three boys live in a three-room house in East Oakland, which Magda says is a big improvement over the one-room apartment where she and the boys lived before.

In some ways the year in Mexico was good for her sons, Magda says. "They liked to see their father," she says. Because they had been so young when they left Mexico, so they were very curious.

Magda is also glad that they had the chance to get to know her parents and some of her siblings better.

Magda sent money to pay the boys' tuition at a private school so they didn't fall too far behind during their year away from the States. However, their English suffered from lack of use, and the current academic year in Oakland has been tough for both of them, even Manuel, now eleven, who had previously been an A student. It doesn't help that he's in the throes of puberty.

"This year I have some problems with him," Magda says. "I think it was because of the change—the different schools, the different places. He is nervous. He was in trouble with some kids at school, fighting and disturbing somebody. But now we're going to see a therapist, and things are getting better."

Both Manuel and nine-year-old Jorge have had trouble adjusting to Tony's full-time presence in their lives, as well as to the demands of a baby. "They are very jealous," Magda says. "They say I love Hector more than them. I tell them I love them all the same, but they don't believe me."

Magda's wages are up to $10.97 an hour now. With Tony earning about $600 a week from a construction job, she's thinking of trying to cut back her hours, or even taking a leave of absence, so she can spend more time with her children. "Tony says it's okay," Magda says. "But it's one thing to say it's okay and another thing when I do it."

Part of her reluctance to give up her job to become a full-time mother is that Magda is not sure that the relationship with Tony is totally solid. Tony moved out for a month during 1999. "He's a good guy, but this is the first time he lives with somebody," she says. "We didn't plan the baby, so it was hard for him and hard for me too. He's not hurting me, or talking to me bad words, like my husband did. But we have to work on our relationship."

Now that she's been in the United States for eight years, Magda is starting to understand more about the nuances of life here. She's become more and more disturbed by what she regards as the country's antipathy toward immigrants. "It's hard coming from Mexico," she says. "There are many people who don't like us here. I have problems with that almost every day on the street, and my boys at school. In Oakland there are people from many places and with many skin colors. But I think people from Mexico are treated the worst."

Magda continues to believe that she did the right thing by bringing her children to the States, because their prospects for the future are so much brighter here than they were in the Mexican village where they were born. But she worries about the impact on them of discrimination.

"I don't feel like people here treat us as equals," she says. "I feel that they think Latino people mean trouble. I tell my boys that if they try to do good work at school, maybe they can have a better life after they grow up. But I worry that people will still treat them like trouble."

Chapter 3: Randolph County, Illinois

By many of the indicators against which the success of welfare reform is being measured, Nancy Keebler is a success story. In October 1998, she went to work as an aide in a nursing home, making $6.40 an hour. She's received regular raises and now earns $7.95 an hour, the maximum possible. Her income has disqualified her family from receiving either cash assistance or food stamps from the state of Illinois.

But independence from the welfare system has come at a terrible price. When her transitional Medicaid benefits ended a year after she left the welfare system, Nancy was left without health insurance for herself. As a result, she's had to stop taking the twice-daily insulin shots that used to keep her blood sugar levels below the danger level most of the time. "I just can't afford the insulin on what I make," she says. "Every penny I get is going out for bills and food."

Nancy also can no longer afford to buy prescription inhalers to ward off her asthma attacks. These days, when she has an attack, she takes a quick hit from her daughter's inhaler, for which Medicaid continues to pay. "I only use it on the days when it's really bad," Nancy says apologetically.

Because of the income from her job, Nancy also has to worry about jeopardizing Benji's eligibility for $401 in monthly Supplemental Security Income (SSI), the need-based federal disability program. "If I get three full paychecks in a month, they cut his SSI," she says. "They've told me I can earn up to $1,300 a month without it being affected, but last month I went over a little, and they cut the SSI to just over $200. Every month it changes, which means money I count on to pay bills ain't there."

Drawing a regular paycheck has enabled Nancy to solve one of her problems—transportation. In October 1998, after years of frustration from depending on a series of unreliable junkers, Nancy splurged on a new Chrysler Neon. Making both the house payment and the $285 car payment each month has proven tough, and Nancy has fallen behind on her house payments. "I guess it was stupid to go buy that car," she says ruefully, "but I was so tired of spending all that money fixing up old cars."

The Keebler children are doing as well as can be expected, although Nancy's erratic work schedule is hard on them. She works variable shifts, some day shifts and some evening shifts. When she works the day shift, she has to wake Benji at 4:30 A.M. to dress him, because it's too difficult for Alice, just thirteen, to do by herself. Alice takes care of her brother until the school bus picks them both up at 7:45 A.M. Nancy returns home in the afternoon just before the bus drops him off.

When Nancy has to work the night shift, which runs from 4:00 to 10:00 P.M., it's Alice again who takes care of Benji. "I always have supper fixed so all she has to do is microwave something," Nancy says. "She feeds him, does her homework, and they watch TV or play. We've had our problems with this arrangement. She sometimes wants to go and be with her friends. After all, she's thirteen. But she just can't."

Alice's earlier psychological problems appear to be in abeyance. "She's getting along at school, and now she has lots of friends," Nancy says. "I don't know what's happened to make her better—just growing up maybe. She seems to be happy with herself." However, Alice's weight continues to mount. At her last doctor's visit she weighed 256 pounds.

Benji, now seven, outgrew his leg braces a few months ago. Because of her work schedule, Nancy hasn't been able to get him to St. Louis to have new ones fitted, so right now he's not walking much. Academically, Nancy says, "he's making no progress. He's about the same." He splits his school day between kindergarten and preschool.

Nancy sounds weary when she talks about her life. "I take it one day at a time," she says. Behind her calm demeanor, she's angry at the impact that welfare reform has had on her family. "I think the way they've done it is wrong," she says. "They tell people they'll be better off if they go to work. Well, that ain't entirely true. The minute I went to work they cut my food stamps. Then the cash grant went. And a year later the medical card. I don't think it's right, but I don't know what the solution is."

Chapter 4: Honolulu, Hawaii

Ed McMahon still hasn't knocked at the Likios' front door. But Jeanette Likio is making more money, Bobby Likio is finally employed, and the couple's two youngest sons are contributing to the household income as well. Life is by no means rosy. But in many ways they now have some breathing room.

"I'm up to about $28,000 a year now, and Bobby's making about $600 a month," Jeanette says. "Our cupboards are still bare, and Bobby stills goes fishing for food. But now with the boys working, if there's nothing to eat, one of them will go out and buy food. Before, when it was only my income we had coming in, if I didn't have money, we didn't eat."

In the last two years Jeanette's responsibilities at work have increased. Her title is still the same–family development specialist—but she now works for two Early Head Start programs, one at the public housing project in Honolulu where she has worked for years, and a new one in a poor neighborhood on Oahu's North Shore. Some of the salary increases she has received because of her added responsibilities go to keeping her 1989 Ford running so she can get to the North Shore, which has little public transportation.

Bobby started working in 1999 as a part-time security guard. The work is erratic, so his income isn't dependable. Moreover, he works off the books, so he has to settle for less than $5 an hour. But it's important to his self-esteem and the family's perception of him that he's finally contributing to the household income.

Jeanette's oldest son, Keanu, twenty-two, seems to have turned a corner in his life. He too is working as a part-time security guard, and he's also close to obtaining a GED. "I'm so proud of him," Jeanette says. "He's really trying. He's more into going to school and taking care of his family. Before he never cared about anything, just being with his friends and staying out all night long." The mother of his four children, who had been dependent on welfare for a long time, is working full-time as a parking lot attendant.

Twenty-year-old Kalani dropped out of Hawaii Pacific University after one year because he was having trouble with English and math. He enrolled at a local community college to brush up on those subjects and has applied to several schools on the mainland for admission in the fall of 2000. For the time being he's working in Waikiki as a tout for a photography company that takes pictures of tourists. "He has goals in his life, and I support him in them as much as I can," Jeanette says. "I don't like him spending his money on the family because I want him to save it for college."

Eighteen-year-old Kawailani graduated from high school in June 1999. "He was so popular," Jeanette says. "The class chose him to lead them in song at commencement. Everybody called him 'The Man' and 'The Great One.'"

Kawailani had intended to start at Honolulu Community College in the fall of 1999. But a month before school started he was struck with appendicitis. "He's so tough," Jeanette says. "He can usually handle just about anything. But this time he was curled up on the sofa moaning, 'Mom, it hurts.' I knew it was serious." The emergency room doctor wasn't sure it was appendicitis and sent him home. The next day another doctor admitted him to a hospital, and he was operated on that night.

"The kids still don't have health insurance, so now we have medical bills up the ying-yang—$8,000 for the hospital, plus the surgeon's and the anesthesiologist's bills, and the X-rays," Jeanette says. "I think it's about $20,000 altogether. Every paycheck I'm paying $50, and that's only for the surgeon and anesthesiologist. I haven't even attempted to work out something with the hospital or the X-ray guys."

After he recovered, Kawailani took a $6-an-hour job in the warehouse at Sears Ala Moana Center so he could help pay off his medical bills, which, because he's legally an adult now, jeopardize his own credit record as well as his mother's. He plans to enroll in community college in the fall of 2000 to study computer applications. He also hopes to be able to play football and baseball and maybe earn a scholarship to a four-year school.

At sixteen, Keola is a sophomore in high school, "still dancing and swaying her hips," Jeanette laughs. "We call her 'Miss Aloha.' She's still playing ball—volleyball and softball. She's doing better in school than last year. At least she can play the whole season. Last year she had to sit out during the playoffs because of her grades."

Elena, now thirteen, is growing up. "She's doing real well in school," Jeanette says. "She's always coming home and telling me about this award and this and that. She's still playing softball, so we're happy." Because of her bout with rheumatic fever a few years ago, she still has to receive monthly injections of antibiotics, but otherwise her health is fine.

There's another person living in the Likio household now—Jeanette's fifteen-year-old nephew, Donnie. Jeanette took him in after becoming concerned that his mother (one of her sisters) was neglecting him. "I feel so bad for him," Jeanette says. "But if he can handle all my rules, I think he's going to make it. The year before he came to me, he was skipping school and had to be held back. He was honor roll the two semesters he's been living with me."

Chapter 5: Louisville, Kentucky

The Saylor family is one step closer to having a kitchen table to gather around for family dinners. In February 1999, they moved into a two-story, four-bedroom house in Louisville that, unlike their old apartment, has a kitchen big enough to accommodate a table for six.

"It has a big kitchen, and a big fenced-in backyard, and a front yard," Carlotta says proudly. "It's a very quiet neighborhood. I can sit out on my front porch and just enjoy myself."

The Saylors were able to move out of the violence-wracked public housing project where they had lived for nine years because their name finally got to the top of the waiting list for a Section 8 certificate, which can be used to subsidize the rent in privately owned houses or apartments. They pay $373 a month for the house, not much more than they did for their old apartment, which was not nearly as nice. And through a self-sufficiency program sponsored by the Louisville Housing Authority, 5 percent of their rent is being set aside in an escrow fund for use as a down payment on the purchase of a house.

Carlotta's five boys all seem to be more or less on track. Freddy graduated from high school in June 1998, at the age of twenty-one. "It was a very proud day," Carlotta says. "We all went to see him get his diploma." He's had a series of low-paying jobs since then and plans to enroll in the fall of 2000 in a technical school to study computer programming. "He just has to line up the grants," Carlotta says.

Nineteen-year-old Stephen expects to graduate from high school in June 2000. Then he wants to enroll in the baking and pastry arts program at Sullivan College in Louisville. How did a kid whose high school passion was wrestling get interested in becoming a pastry chef? "He likes to put things together for the family," Carlotta says. "He likes to make fancy things."

Orlando, now seventeen, managed to avoid repeating ninth grade. Now in eleventh grade, "he's still struggling, but he hasn't gave up," his mother says. "The school is doing much better helping him and pushing him a little more. He finally got a teacher who understands him. She says he needs special help, but he needs to stand on his own too. She's giving him more responsibility than he's used to having. It's more difficult for him, but he's getting used to it. I know he's limited, but I can't let him quit on himself, and I'm not going to quit on him." Two years ago Orlando began receiving SSI benefits, which adds $142 a month to the family budget.

Twelve-year-old Martin is struggling with puberty. "He got into middle school, and for some reason he's shutting down academically," his mother complains. "He says it's too hard, he can't do it. If I stay on him, he'll pick it up a little bit. But as soon as I let down my guard, he falls back."

At ten, Kevin seems to be modeling his school performance on Martin's. "He don't want to be there," Carlotta says. "'I'm ready to drop out' is his statement. I just look at him and say, 'You gonna go until you graduate.' Then he says, 'Yes, ma'am,' and off he goes. It's a constant struggle getting the homework done, and sometimes even getting him to bring it home."

Carlotta experienced a major personal and financial setback in August 1998 when she suffered a heart attack while she was walking to work at the community center. "I went back home and laid down across the bed," she says. "I knew it was something serious, and I told my boys, 'Somebody's got to take me to the hospital.'"

It turned out that two of her arteries were blocked, and she had to undergo a balloon angioplasty procedure to clear them. "I was in the hospital for fourteen days, the whole time in the cardiac ICU," Carlotta says. "They also found out I had diabetes. I didn't have health insurance, so now I owe a whole lot on top of what I already owed before. I'm going to have to start paying them something every month."

Carlotta had to stay home from work for two and a half months. For most of that time she wasn't paid. "My family helped me out," she says, "and we managed to make it. We got food stamps for a while, and Freddy was working."

Carlotta's doctors have prescribed two different medications to treat her various conditions, each of which costs more than $100 a month—more than she can afford. "The other hospital talked the drug companies into giving them to me for free for a while," she says. "Now I'm on my last free prescription, so we have to start the process again."

The heart attack had some positive effects. "My heart attack was a warning that I needed to slow down and put my priorities together and try not to let life stress me out," Carlotta says. Importantly, she has stopped smoking and is watching what she eats. "I had to give up hamburgers, sausage, red meat in general," she says. "The dietitian told me I could have two strips of bacon every week. What I do is take these two strips and cut them in half. That way it looks like I have four."

Carlotta still daydreams about someday gathering her family together around a kitchen table for a big Sunday dinner in their own house, just like her grandmother used to do when she was a little girl. "I still can't afford a table," she says. "When we moved in here, I had to buy living room furniture and some beds for the boys. Maybe this time next year I'll have a kitchen table. I have to take things a step at a time."

Chapter 6: Basalt, Colorado

By many measures, the Gonzalez family of Basalt, Colorado, is better off than it was two years ago.

Juan, now thirty, is still cooking for the same upscale restaurant and getting paid a little more. Although she has changed jobs and is making a little less, Maria's new work environment is much less stressful than her old one, leaving her more energy to expend on her three children at the end of her workday.

And for the first time ever the whole family has health insurance. "Even though I'm making less money an hour, the health insurance makes up for it," Maria says. "I don't have to worry so much about paying medical bills."

But the best news of all is the family's new home. The construction of a housing development forced them to move from their rental trailer in a bucolic setting outside Basalt in 1999. They bought a brand-new $35,000 trailer home, which they've parked in a mobile home court a few miles down the road. "Our new home is wonderful," Maria says. "Getting it was a dream come true. We prayed a lot, and God blessed us."

Maria is thrilled to be building equity every time she writes a check for the mortgage. "Renting is like throwing money out the window," she says. "Buying, you know you're going to get money back." Even though their monthly payments are less than their rent had been, the couple is still renting one of their three bedrooms to boarders to help make ends meet.

Maria reports that the couple's three children are doing well. But uncertainty over Juan's and Maria's immigration status still clouds the family's future. A few months ago Maria took a day off from work and went to Denver to try to determine the status of her application for a change in immigration status. Four years before she had paid a lawyer $2,600 to file papers for her. As she had feared ever since she found out that the attorney's phone had been disconnected, the INS has no record of her application.

"I can't believe that man went off and took my money," she says. "I'm praying for a miracle."

Chapter 7: Westchester County, New York

The Scarpato family has fallen apart.

In August 1999, Louis Scarpato was arrested for beating up his wife, Elise. When he was released, Elise ran away. Louis failed a drug test for cocaine use, so Westchester County authorities placed the four children in foster care. "When they took them away, the girls cried a lot, but the boys went quietly," says Annie Caldecott, the teacher who had taken the Scarpato children under her wing.

Over the next year both Elise and Louis went through separate residential drug rehabilitation programs and visited periodically with their children. County authorities were making plans to return the two girls to Elise, with the condition that she agree not to return to Louis. But early in 2000 she moved back in with him. "The sad truth is that she is completely in love with Louis," Annie says. "She is stuck in an awful relationship with him that has led her into poverty and abuse and extreme family dysfunction, but she doesn't seem to be able to leave."

Annie visits the four Scarpato children, who are in two different foster placements, as often as county child welfare authorities allow her to. The girls, eleven-year-old Jessica and six-year-old Maggie, live in a neighboring town with a nice foster mother. "They are doing well in school and being well cared for," Annie says. "Next week Jessica is having a birthday party at Kid Aerobics, and she is very excited about that. I don't know if she has ever had a real birthday party before."

The twin boys, now eight, were placed initially with a single foster father in Yonkers. "But he was getting old, and he couldn't handle the demands of caring for the extra challenging needs of Jeremy," Annie says. "He still wets his bed." So the boys were transferred to Children's Village, in Dobbs Ferry, the largest residential treatment center for children in the United States. It costs the state about $100 a day for each of them, not counting psychiatric treatment or medical care. "It's supposed to be a place of last resort, for boys who are desperately needy and troubled and emotionally disturbed," Annie says.

Annie recently took Star Wars toys to Louis Jr. and Jeremy as presents for their eighth birthday. "They loved them and had so much fun playing with them," she says. "I tried to get permission to take them to my family's house for the holidays, but there was a lot of red tape, and ultimately they would not allow it. I hope they get placed in a good home soon, so that I can resume the kind of relationship I used to have with them."

For a while Annie considered applying for a foster care license so the boys could live with her. Eventually she decided that Jeremy's problems would be too much for her to handle at the same time she was working full-time as a kindergarten teacher. Instead, she's made a promise to herself "to be in touch with the kids for a long, long time, and be, to them, the person who is good and constant in their lives. Someone who they can count on to always show them kindness. Someone who doesn't go away. Someone who can't be taken away. Someone who cares about them."

Chapter 8: Suburban St. Louis

Despite a series of moves, Ron Peterson is still trying his best to give his two daughters a normal life. He has been working steadily for two years, secured a spot for his four-year-old in a Head Start program this summer, and, since he's become a single father, even learned how to braid hair.

Meanwhile, Laura Peterson, his estranged wife, seems to have set aside the aspirations she once had for herself. Since she left Ron and the girls in the summer of 1998, she's had two more children by two different men.

Ron has been caring for the couple's two girls, Erica, now six, and Claire, now four, since Laura left him in August 1998. At first they lived with one of Ron's sisters and her family. Then they lived briefly in a house of their own, and later, for a while, with a woman to whom Ron had become engaged.

When Ron's fiancée decided to move to Georgetown, Colorado, in the winter of 2000 to be closer to her father, Ron and the girls went with her, and he found an $18-an-hour job in construction right away. But after a month there, with the temperature frequently below zero and the local roads often covered with snow, she announced abruptly that she didn't like either Colorado or Ron and went back to Missouri. "I think she wanted to play mom for a while and found out she couldn't handle it," Ron says.

With no good reason to remain in Colorado, Ron and the girls followed a week later. His 1991 pickup truck broke down a couple of hundred miles from home. It was only because of the kindness of a truck driver who saw them stranded at a truck stop that they were able to finish the final leg of the trip.

For the last two weeks Ron and the girls have been staying with Laura's brother and his wife in their apartment in north St. Louis County. "If it wasn't for them, I don't know what I would have done," he says. But his in-laws' apartment is small, and they'll soon have to find another place. He hopes that a half-brother who lives alone in a house nearby will let him and the girls move in. "He's looking for someone to move in and help pay bills," Ron says optimistically.

As soon as he got back to St. Louis, Ron enrolled Erica in the first grade in the elementary school near his in-laws' apartment, where she'll be able to remain in school if his half-brother lets them move in. Finding a job turned out to be easy. "I got a roofing job the day after we got back—at $10 an hour—and I've been working every day since, with lots of overtime," he says.

One of Ron's priorities in the next few months is to file for divorce. He couldn't while Laura was pregnant, since Missouri courts won't permit a couple to divorce while the wife is pregnant, even if the husband isn't the father of the child. "Now that she's done having babies I can go ahead and file," he says. "All we want from each other is an uncontested divorce. She keeps what she has, I keep what I have. I don't know how we'll handle the debts—the foreclosure and everything else."

Ron's goals in life remain pretty much as they were two years ago: "Start paying my bills off and living happily ever after."

Laura doesn't have a phone and couldn't be reached for comment. But she regularly calls her daughters, so Ron knows what she's up to. Ron said she too had bounced from place to place since the couple split up in the summer of 1998. Last week she and her boyfriend, who fathered the second child she has had since she left Ron, moved into a trailer in Branson, Missouri, with their newborn, Alexander, and her one-year-old daughter. "She seems to be happy," Ron says.

Chapter 9: Belzoni, Mississippi

Celeste Lyles doesn't even have to stop and think about her answer when asked whether her family's circumstances are better or worse than they were two years ago. "Things are worse," she says with conviction. "Ooooh, it's bad. I just pray and pray. I say to God, 'I know this is just a test.'

"I don't want to be unappreciative of what I do have, but if it gets too much worse, I don't know what we'll do. Last Christmas I wasn't able to get my children anything because I wasn't working, and my oldest son wasn't working either. I prayed on it and fasted on it, but God didn't come through. My children said it was the worst Christmas of their lives."

Celeste's financial health is dependent on how American cooks feel about catfish. Although her wages have gone up $.30 an hour in two years—to $6.50 an hour, after twelve years on the job—her hours are not dependable because of fluctuations in the demand for catfish. "Right now I'm on a three-day schedule, maybe twenty-eight hours a week," she says. "My take-home this week was $132 after deductions."

Ominously, management is talking about a planned three- to four-month layoff a few months from now. "We're on pins and needles at work," Celeste says. "There's a rumor that they might even close us down altogether."

As a result of her diminished weekly income, it now takes nearly two of her weekly paychecks to pay her rent, which has gone up to $303 a month. "If I pay the rent this week, that throws me behind on my lights and gas bill," she says. The family still receives food stamps, but the amount varies with Celeste's income, so they're never quite sure how much they're going to get. "Last month I got $47," she says. "This month I got $172. Next month I'm getting cut to $143, because I made about $20 more."

Despite the family's financial problems, the children seem to be coping. Curtis, now twenty-four, received an associate's degree in criminal justice as well as certification as an electrical technician. He couldn't find work in either field, so after graduating he went to work for $8 an hour at a feed company, a job that ended when winter came. He got married in December 1999, but is now living with his mother while his wife completes basic training. He's planning to join her wherever she's stationed and to seek work in the criminal justice field.

At the beginning of her junior year at the nearby state university, Latoya, twenty-one, moved on-campus, with her mother's blessing. "She's in lots of activities at school, and she wanted to join a sorority," Celeste says. "You never know how that can help in the future." Latoya comes home on weekends to spend time with her daughter, five-year-old Jonquil.

Nelson Mandela had to repeat the eighth grade, as Celeste had feared. "But he's doing good now," Celeste says. "He's got his priorities straightened out, and he's made a lot of improvement. And he grew. He's finally taller than his younger sister."

Brittany, twelve going on sixteen, is still a star at school. "She's awesome, nothing but As," Celeste says proudly. "She has five new trophies for academics. And she's all legs. Believe me, I keep a tight leash on her."

Celeste and her best friend, Theresa, are still thinking about starting a women's apparel business together. "We're still dreaming," Celeste says. But a year ago Theresa was laid off from the job she had held for twenty-two years, and she hasn't been able to find another one. "She's been applying in at least five different counties," Celeste says. "The only thing I can think is holding her back is her age: forty-five. Her unemployment ran out, and she's basically surviving on prayers."

The two women no longer travel over to the riverboat casinos on weekends. "With what?" Celeste asks. "If I did, I've have to stand at the door with a tin can and beg for money to play."

Chapter 10: Grand Rapids, Michigan

Sylvia Washington is finished with welfare. For the last two years she has been working full-time, at first in an office job, and more recently in a factory. In a few weeks she's going to start an on-the-job nurse's aide training program. While working full-time as a home health aide, she'll also be earning nursing credentials—first as a certified nurse's aide, then as a licensed practical nurse, and eventually, she hopes, as a registered nurse.

Sylvia dropped out of the YWCA's Project FIT (Families in Transition) program in late 1998. "Part of their requirement was that I had to be able to meet with their counselors a couple times a month, and after I went to work full-time I couldn't do that anymore, so I had to leave the program," she explains. The problem was that the counselors were available only from about 8:30 A.M. to 5:00 P.M.—the same hours that Washington worked.

By dropping out of the program she lost her housing and child-care subsidies. But Sylvia says the program's negatives outweighed the pluses. "There was a lot about the program I didn't care for," she says. "There were a lot of strings attached. I think it was really meant more for young mothers who needed to learn how to put structure into their lives."

Sylvia found a rental house in a nicer neighborhood. Her market-rate rent is $550 a month—a lot more than the $96 a month she paid when she was in Project FIT. But she recently learned that she was getting a Section 8 certificate, another rental subsidy for low-income families, so her out-of-pocket costs for housing are likely to go down.

For the last year Sylvia has worked on the overnight shift at an auto-parts factory, making about $9 an hour, or a total of $21,000, in 1999. She's had enough of it.

"I hate factory work," she says. "There's a lot of wear and tear on your body. All of the people around me at work have to wear wrist braces because of carpal tunnel syndrome. And there are a lot of fumes from the oil we use. When I blow my nose after I get home, the stuff that comes out is black with soot. Inhaling that stuff for eight hours a day can't be good for you. Besides, I've concluded I like working with people more than I like working with machines."

Sylvia's oldest daughter, Letisha, graduated from high school in June 1999. She decided to take a year off before entering college, so she's been working as an assistant manager at a dry-cleaning store, making about $7 an hour and saving up to buy a used car. In the fall of 2000, she'll enter Grand Valley State University. She plans to continue to live at home.

Laura is a junior in high school. Sylvia thinks that Laura, with her interest in computers, is more likely to go to vocational school than to college.

Both girls have been a great help to their mother since she returned to work, Sylvia says. They share responsibility for Tyrone while Sylvia works from 11 P.M. to 7:00 A.M., and again while she sleeps during the day. Some of the pressure will be relieved when Tyrone, now three, begins a half-day Head Start program in September 2000.

The calamities that Sylvia experienced a few years back—her health problems, the eviction, the car accident, and the period of homelessness—are now just memories. "I did what I had to do," she says of that time in her life. "I've had ups and downs in the last two years, but I can't complain. We're surviving."

POVERTY RATES OF
CHILDREN UNDER SIX,
BY STATE, 1993–1997

	Poverty Rate (%)	Number of Children		Confidence Interval (90%)	
		In Poverty	Total	Lower	Upper
United States	24.13	5,792,446	24,005,164	23.40	24.86
States with young child poverty rate lower than the national rate					
Alaska	12.69	7,655	60,321	8.39	16.99
Colorado	13.16	41,854	318,042	8.22	18.10
Connecticut	17.64	50,494	286,246	11.50	23.78
Delaware	13.97	8,281	59,278	8.35	19.59
Hawaii	16.55	17,489	105,673	10.90	22.20
Iowa	16.50	42,616	258,278	11.30	21.70
Kansas	17.92	44,567	248,699	12.72	23.12
Maryland	17.78	82,551	464,289	12.18	23.38
Massachusetts	18.57	91,038	490,242	14.66	22.48
Nebraska	14.66	23,823	162,505	9.92	19.40
New Hampshire	11.89	13,273	111,632	6.84	16.94
New Jersey	14.20	100,370	706,829	11.18	17.22
Utah	13.38	31,541	235,732	9.49	17.27
Vermont	14.61	7,685	52,601	9.05	20.17
Virginia	14.66	79,349	541,261	9.82	19.50
States with young child poverty rate similar to the national rate					
Alabama	30.67	107,146	349,351	23.97	37.37
Arizona	26.71	123,075	460,782	21.27	32.15

(continues)

	Poverty Rate (%)	Number of Children		Confidence Interval (90%)	
		In Poverty	Total	Lower	Upper
Arkansas	28.25	63,682	225,422	22.05	34.45
Georgia	19.86	129,506	652,095	14.77	24.95
Idaho	27.98	31,352	112,053	22.19	33.77
Illinois	23.66	255,474	1,079,771	20.28	27.04
Indiana	19.29	96,731	501,458	13.62	24.96
Kentucky	28.30	93,102	328,984	21.85	34.75
Maine	21.37	20,125	94,175	14.58	28.16
Michigan	23.46	211,086	899,769	19.98	26.94
Minnesota	19.01	80,775	424,907	13.56	24.46
Missouri	18.49	79,644	430,739	12.57	24.41
Montana	25.47	18,810	73,853	19.38	31.56
Nevada	19.22	27,494	143,048	13.61	24.83
North Carolina	22.01	124,071	563,704	17.88	26.14
North Dakota	19.39	10,232	52,771	13.63	25.15
Ohio	21.29	211,172	991,884	17.92	24.66
Oklahoma	26.56	74,012	278,660	20.40	32.72
Oregon	22.46	61,290	272,887	16.17	28.75
Pennsylvania	22.16	217,048	979,458	18.76	25.56
Rhode Island	19.89	15,593	78,397	13.19	26.59
South Carolina	29.91	94,724	316,696	23.29	36.53
South Dakota	22.94	13,875	60,483	17.10	28.78
Tennessee	26.71	123,396	461,983	20.45	32.97
Texas	27.80	545,444	1,962,027	24.84	30.76
Washington	21.02	101,514	482,941	15.14	26.90
West Virginia	31.91	34,841	109,185	24.17	39.65
Wisconsin	18.93	90,662	478,933	13.68	24.18
Wyoming	26.14	10,706	40,958	19.38	32.90

States with young child poverty rate higher than the national rate

	Poverty Rate (%)	In Poverty	Total	Lower	Upper
California	28.33	964,784	3,405,519	26.02	30.64
DC	45.78	24,144	52,739	38.05	53.51
Florida	29.86	357,362	1,196,793	26.45	33.27
Louisiana	36.94	133,875	362,411	30.05	43.83
Mississippi	36.88	82,695	224,227	30.03	43.73
New Mexico	33.14	58,001	175,017	27.17	39.11
New York	29.33	463,254	1,579,455	26.52	32.14

EXTREME-POVERTY RATES OF CHILDREN UNDER SIX, BY STATE, 1993–1997

	Extreme-Poverty Rate (%)	Number of Children		Confidence Interval (90%)	
		Extreme Poverty	Total	Lower	Upper
United States	11.19	2,685,050	24,005,164	10.65	11.72

States with young child extreme-poverty rate lower than the national rate

Alaska	2.91	1,757	60,321	0.66	5.17
Colorado	5.50	17,495	318,042	2.33	8.67
Delaware	4.38	2,593	59,278	2.32	6.43
Hawaii	2.53	2,672	105,673	0.11	4.94
Idaho	6.45	7,233	112,053	2.33	10.58
Iowa	5.07	13,085	258,278	1.99	8.14
Kansas	5.59	13,894	248,699	2.22	8.95
Maryland	7.91	36,736	464,289	5.70	10.13
New Hampshire	4.82	5,381	111,632	2.06	7.58
Utah	6.12	14,435	235,732	3.39	8.86
Vermont	4.97	2,616	52,601	2.30	7.65
Virginia	6.53	35,344	541,261	3.02	10.04
Wisconsin	4.64	22,234	478,933	2.97	6.32

States with young child extreme-poverty rate similar to the national rate

Arizona	13.49	62,168	460,782	11.23	15.75
Arkansas	12.92	29,113	225,422	8.03	17.80

(continues)

	Extreme-Poverty Rate (%)	Number of Children		Confidence Interval (90%)	
		Extreme Poverty	Total	Lower	Upper
California	10.25	348,916	3,405,519	5.21	15.28
Connecticut	7.84	22,451	286,246	3.92	11.77
Florida	16.17	193,553	1,196,793	10.42	21.92
Georgia	10.61	69,203	652,095	6.23	15.00
Illinois	13.11	141,593	1,079,771	7.98	18.25
Indiana	8.31	41,688	501,458	4.79	11.84
Kentucky	14.43	47,473	328,984	11.39	17.47
Maine	9.19	8,658	94,175	5.00	13.39
Massachusetts	8.07	39,584	490,242	4.32	11.83
Michigan	10.95	98,500	899,769	6.92	14.98
Minnesota	8.13	34,524	424,907	4.20	12.05
Missouri	8.58	36,936	430,739	4.78	12.37
Montana	10.59	7,818	73,853	8/06	13.11
Nebraska	7.31	11,887	162,505	3.00	11.63
Nevada	7.05	10,083	143,048	3.02	11.07
New Jersey	9.11	64,364	706,829	4.64	13.57
New Mexico	14.58	25,522	175,017	9.59	19.57
New York	15.67	247,469	1,579,455	9.81	21.52
North Carolina	9.76	55,029	563,704	5.62	13.91
North Dakota	7.21	3,803	52,771	3.51	10.91
Ohio	12.16	120,635	991,884	9.73	14.59
Oklahoma	13.11	36,537	278,660	8.40	17.82
Oregon	11.53	31,476	272,887	6.92	16.14
Pennsylvania	10.59	103,748	979,458	5.60	15.58
Rhode Island	10.09	7,913	78,397	8.55	11.64
South Carolina	15.51	49,111	316,696	10.66	20.35
South Dakota	11.61	7,024	60,483	7.04	16.19
Tennessee	14.04	64,874	461,983	9.63	18.45
Texas	11.82	231,994	1,962,027	6.95	16.69
Washington	7.95	38,378	482,941	4.24	11.65
West Virginia	16.68	18,209	109,185	10.99	22.36
Wyoming	9.33	3,820	40,958	5.12	13.53

States with young child extreme-poverty rate higher than the national rate

Alabama	16.28	56,882	349.351	14.00	18.56
DC	29.85	15,744	52,739	23.50	36.21
Louisiana	22.11	80,123	362,411	18.69	25.52
Mississippi	19.07	42,765	224,227	15.16	22.98

APPENDIX C

NEAR-POVERTY RATES OF CHILDREN UNDER SIX, BY STATE, 1993–1997

	Near-Poverty Rate (%)	Number of Children		Confidence Interval (90%)	
		Near Poverty	Total	Lower	Upper
United States	44.23	10,616,788	24,005,164	43.38	45.07
States with young child near-poverty rate lower than the national rate					
Alaska	33.82	20,400	60,321	27.48	40.16
Colorado	32.40	103,056	318,042	25.90	38.90
Connecticut	32.53	93,122	286,246	25.69	39.37
Delaware	38.10	22,586	59,278	33.22	42.99
Maryland	32.69	151,757	464,289	28.83	36.54
Massachusetts	31.98	156,799	490,242	25.56	38.41
Minnesota	34.00	144,482	424,907	27.20	40.81
New Hampshire	26.36	29,431	111,632	20.68	32.05
New Jersey	26.68	188,583	706,829	19.81	33.55
Ohio	37.27	369,693	991,884	33.67	40.87
Rhode Island	39.58	31,028	78,397	37.07	42.08
Vermont	34.00	17,882	52,601	28.17	39.82
Wisconsin	32.62	156,224	478,933	28.89	36.35
States with young child near-poverty rate similar to the national rate					
California	49.96	1,701,452	3,405,519	41.66	58.26
Florida	50.68	606,573	1,196,793	42.88	58.49
Georgia	45.60	297,379	652,095	38.51	52.70

(continues)

	Near-Poverty Rate (%)	Number of Children		Confidence Interval (90%)	
		In Poverty	Total	Lower	Upper
Hawaii	37.72	39,855	105,673	30.26	45.17
Idaho	52.79	59,147	112,053	44.41	61.16
Illinois	42.81	462,246	1,079,771	35.28	50.34
Indiana	38.01	190,581	501,458	31.81	44.20
Iowa	41.17	106,329	258,278	34.27	48.06
Kansas	41.23	102,531	248,699	34.02	48.43
Kentucky	48.42	159,300	328,984	44.10	52.74
Maine	44.48	41,885	94,175	37.26	51.69
Michigan	39.91	359,110	899,769	33.59	46.23
Missouri	41.74	179,797	430,739	35.06	48.42
Montana	48.41	35,751	73,853	44.31	52.50
Nebraska	36.37	59,105	162,505	28.40	44.34
Nevada	38.51	55,093	143,048	30.86	46.17
New York	45.76	722,797	1,579,455	37.74	53.79
North Carolina	44.67	251,813	563,704	37.73	51.62
North Dakota	40.70	21,480	52,771	33.68	47.73
Oklahoma	50.92	141,898	278,660	43.94	57.90
Oregon	46.38	126,569	272,887	39.18	53.58
Pennsylvania	38.00	372,232	979,458	30.13	45.88
South Carolina	51.20	162,148	316,696	44.51	57.89
South Dakota	45.00	27,220	60,483	37.90	52.10
Texas	51.72	1,014,784	1,962,027	44.18	59.26
Utah	38.72	91,269	235,732	33.16	44.28
Virginia	40.80	220,856	541,261	33.83	47.78
Washington	37.25	179,913	482,941	30.63	43.87
Wyoming	48.48	19,855	40,958	41.25	55.71

States with young child near-poverty rate higher than the national rate

Alabama	52.11	182,051	349,351	49.03	55.20
Arizona	53.28	245,515	460,782	49.99	56.58
Arkansas	56.93	128,329	225,422	49.72	64.14
DC	65.38	34,482	52,739	58.78	71.99
Louisiana	56.54	204,894	362,411	52.46	60.62
Mississippi	58.34	130,810	224,227	53.43	63.25
New Mexico	54.96	96,183	175,017	47.92	61.99
Tennessee	51.88	239,658	461,983	45.54	58.22
West Virginia	55.73	60,849	109,185	48.16	63.30

NOTE: Near-poverty rate includes all children in families under 185 percent of the poverty line, that is, the near-poverty rate is the sum of the poverty and extreme-poverty rates plus those between 100 percent and 185 percent of the poverty line.

NOTES

Introduction

1. Greg J. Duncan and Jeanne Brooks-Gunn, eds., *Consequences of Growing up Poor* (New York: Russell Sage Foundation, 1997).

2. Lorraine V. Klerman, with M. B. Parker, *Alive and Well?: A Review of Health Policies and Programs for Poor Young Children* (New York: National Center for Children in Poverty, Columbia University School of Public Health, 1990).

3. Lorraine V. Klerman, "The Association Between Adolescent Parenting and Childhood Poverty," in *Children in Poverty: Child Development and Public Policy,* edited by Aletha C. Huston (New York: Cambridge University Press, 1991), pp. 79–104.

4. S. Korenman, J. E. Miller, and J. E. Sjaastad, "Long-term Poverty and Child Development in the United States," *Children and Youth Services Review* 17, nos. 1–2 (1995): 127–151.

Chapter 5

1. E. Lewitt and L. Baker, "Child Indicators: Health Insurance Coverage," *The Future of Children* 5, no. 3 (Winter 1995): 192–204.

Chapter 10

1. Jeanne Brooks-Gunn and Greg J. Duncan, "The Effects of Poverty on Children," *The Future of Children* 7, no. 2 (Summer-Fall 1997): 55–71; Mary E. Corcoran and Ajay Chaudry, "The Dynamics of Childhood Poverty," ibid.: 40–54.

Chapter 11

1. Throughout this chapter, "young children" refers to children under the age of six.

2. All statistics are derived from analyses of the March Current Population Survey, published annually by the U.S. Bureau of the Census.

3. Analyses conducted by Timothy Smeeding and Lee Rainwater for the National Center for Children in Poverty (1996).

4. We use the 185 percent level because many children in families with incomes between 100 and 185 percent of the federal poverty line are eligible for a number of government assistance programs, such as Medicaid, the school lunch and school breakfast programs, and WIC (Women, Infants, and Children), the special supplemental nutrition program.

5. The federal EITC was created in 1975 to aid working poor families by alleviating the burden imposed by Social Security and Medicare payroll taxes and to enhance incentives to work. For the tax year 1998, the maximum credit was $2,312 for families with one child and $3,816 for families with two or more children.

6. Nine states have no state income tax and would therefore need to support working families outside of a state income tax system.

7. According to our alternative measure, there were 11.0 million poor children in 1997.

ABOUT THE AUTHORS

Martha Shirk is a freelance journalist and writer in Palo Alto, California, who reported for the *St. Louis Post-Dispatch* for twenty-three years. She is considered one of the pioneers of in-depth reporting for newspapers on children's and family issues. She has won numerous awards for her reporting on child abuse, juvenile justice, child poverty, and child support issues.

Neil G. Bennett is director of demographic research and analysis at the National Center for Children in Poverty at Columbia University's Joseph L. Mailman School of Public Health, and professor of public affairs at the Baruch School of Public Affairs at the City University of New York. In addition to his work on child poverty, he has conducted much research in the areas of social and mathematical demography, such as marriage, cohabitation, divorce, nonmarital childbearing, mortality, and demographic forecasting. He was previously on the sociology faculty at Yale University and the University of Michigan and formerly a Scholar-in-Residence at the Russell Sage Foundation.

J. Lawrence Aber is director of the National Center for Children in Poverty, codirector of the Institute on Child and Family Policy, and associate professor at Columbia University's Joseph L. Mailman School of Public Health. During his tenure on the psychology faculty at Barnard College, he also directed the Barnard Center for Toddler Development and codirected the Project on Children and War. His basic research interests focus on the social, emotional, behavioral, and cognitive development of children and youth at risk due to family and neighborhood poverty, parental psychopathology, and exposure to violence, abuse, and neglect. His applied research focuses on process and outcome evaluations of innovative programs and policies for children and families at risk, including welfare-to-work programs, comprehensive service programs, and violence prevention programs.

INDEX